IMAGES
of America

PLEASURE ISLAND

"May I personally welcome you to our Pleasure Island Organization . . ."

Our goal is a simple one. We want every person who visits Pleasure Island to experience a day of Pleasure and Fulfillment.

The creation of Pleasure Island has required years of planning, plus the combined efforts of artists, designers, engineers, craftsmen, economic specialists and men of finance. Now we are ready to dedicate this entertainment center to our guests from all fifty of the United States and the Four Corners of the World.

No effort has been spared to create for future guests a family recreation center which re-creates the proud history of our New England heritage. And now you have been "signed on" as part of the crew which will operate Pleasure Island. This guide is to help you "learn the ropes" of this new enterprise.

Make no mistake about it. It is the PEOPLE who work at Pleasure Island . . . "Pleasure Islanders" we call ourselves . . . who will build our reputation for friendly New England hospitality. Your pleasant smile—your pleasant appearance—your pleasant attitude—are the things which will make for the guests pleasant days at Pleasure Island.

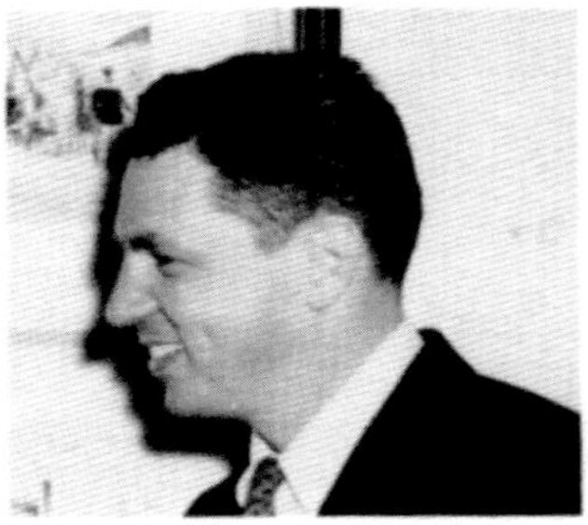

It is an exacting type of work—sometimes a bit hectic. But when the guest says that heartfelt "thank you," you will know you are doing your job. And what is a more pleasant bit of Boston graciousness than for us to say . . . "It's Been Our Pleasure!"

W. S. Hawkes

WILLIAM S. HAWKES

President

Van A. France, Pleasure Island's training director (hired away from Disneyland by Marco Engineering) wrote the training booklet for Pleasure Island's employees. Above is the introduction. (Courtesy of Friends of Pleasure Island archives.)

On the cover: The Moby Dick Hunt was high-tech for 1959. Guests were transported by boat in search of the great white whale Moby Dick. This attraction met Pleasure Island's recreational and educational standards. Guests encountered a charging rhinoceros, cannibals, and a huge whale rising from the water's surface. Sound effects, narration, and a school of porpoises rounded out the voyage back safely to Clipper Cove. (Courtesy of Patrick Farino.)

IMAGES
of America

PLEASURE ISLAND

Robert McLaughlin

ARCADIA
PUBLISHING

ISBN 978-0-7385-6460-9

Published by Arcadia Publishing
Charleston, South Carolina

Printed in the United States of America

Library of Congress Control Number: 2008939172

For all general information contact Arcadia Publishing at:
Telephone 843-853-2070
Fax 843-853-0044
E-mail sales@arcadiapublishing.com
For customer service and orders:
Toll-Free 1-888-313-2665

Visit us on the Internet at www.arcadiapublishing.com

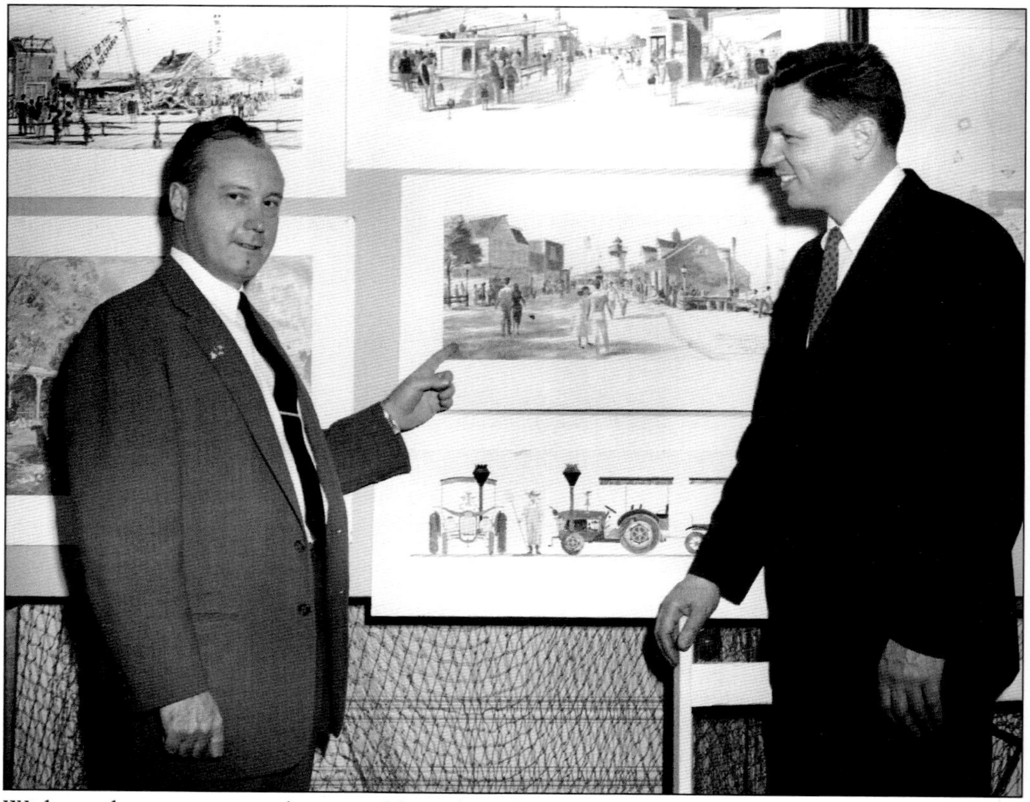

Without these two men, there would not have been a Pleasure Island: the late Robert Linnell (left) from Cabot, Cabot and Forbes and the late William S. Hawkes, publisher of *Child Life* magazine. (Courtesy of Friends of Pleasure Island archives.)

Contents

ACKNOWLEDGMENTS

I am indebted to William S. (Bill) and Jean Hawkes for the generous donation of photographs and other materials to the Friends of Pleasure Island (FOPI). Their collection made this book possible. Sadly, Bill passed away in 2007. I would like to thank everyone who has contributed to Pleasure Island's collective history. First, to my wife, Terry, and our granddaughter Danielle, thank you for translating this dyslexic writer's text into its final form. I am grateful to my editor, Erin Rocha, who has led me through this project with complete professionalism. A number of images from slides and negatives were digitalized by Kris Thomas. Cofounder and former board member Kory Hellmer created the excellent Web site for FOPI.

Dr. Todd Pierce from California Polytechnic State University has completed a yet-untitled book that is coming out soon about Disneyland and includes information about Pleasure Island. I was fortunate to accompany Pierce on some of his interviews. I conducted many interviews in the early 21st century with Jim Hill, an expert on all things Disney. The *Wakefield Daily Item* and the Lucius Beebe Library do an excellent job of maintaining microfilm records. I am grateful for the safe storage of the Hawkes collection to FOPI at the Savings Bank in Wakefield. Local train historian Richard W. Symmes gave me guidance on this book's train chapter. Patrick McKnight, historian for Steamtown National Historic Site, contributed information about the Boston and Maine Railroad No. 3713. Carousel historian and collector Michelle Carpenter contributed information on the carousel's history. Thank you to all the former park employees who allowed me to conduct on-camera interviews as part of the FOPI oral history project, including Ed Atwater, Sam Donato, Joseph Doyle, Bob Harmon, Al Krever, Sy Milano, Dave Mitchell, Ken Saunders, and Herb Sauve. Patrick Farino, Buddy Bourdon, Russ Adams, Laurence Lowry, Fay Foto Service, and others deserve a special thank-you for their talents as professional photographers. Since 2000, former park employees and people with an interest, like me, have been involved with FOPI, including Raymond DiPirro, Mary K. Galvin, Sid Hodson, Larry Cultera, Priscilla DiDonato Hendrick, and the late Bill Valentine. Most of all, I would like to thank my four children, Kerry, Jamie, Tracy, and Micah, for putting up with their dad's hobby (Pleasure Island) for the last nine years—I hope you enjoy the book.

INTRODUCTION

On July 17, 1955, a completely new type of amusement park opened. It was called a theme park, and that park was Walt Disney's Disneyland in Anaheim, California. The concept was themed entertainment in a clean, controlled environment and was unlike any amusement park in America and even beyond.

This is where the Pleasure Island story begins. About the same time Disneyland opened, William S. (Bill) Hawkes of Gloucester, the publisher of *Child Life* magazine, decided to build a Storyland-type park to be named Child Life World. He hired a local artist to draw concept renderings and started to research existing parks and attractions in the New England area and as far away as the West Coast.

Meanwhile, in 1953, Walt and Roy Disney hired Stanford Research Institute to do a study to pick the location for Disneyland. The head of the team for this assignment was a young man from Texas, C. V. Wood. This study not only decided the location to build Disneyland but also projected how many guests would come and how much they would spend. The study relied on travel and population trends, past weather cycles, and many other factors. The Disney brothers were so impressed with this study they hired Wood and made him the first vice president of Disneyland.

Wood was involved in many aspects of getting Disneyland off the drawing board and to completion. Within two years from the start of the Stanford study, Disneyland was open, and the theme park business was born. Wood was the first general manager at the brand-new Disneyland for what turned out to be just months. Wood left Disneyland to start up his own company called Marco Engineering.

Disneyland was basically a large movie set and was designed by many of the most talented people from the movie industry. Marco Engineering hired away several Disney employees, including set designers, special effects personnel, artists, and other talents. With postwar income increasing, America's love affair with the automobile continuing, and road system upgrades in the 1950s, investors started to take a closer look at the Disneyland theme park model.

Marco Engineering had just what investors were looking for—the talent and playbook to design Disneyland-type parks anywhere they were willing to build them. Marco Engineering got involved in several existing park upgrades, but its first stand-alone theme park was built in Golden, Colorado, just west of Denver. Construction there started in 1957. The partially finished park opened during the summers from 1958 through 1960. However, lawsuits and other factors contributed to the end of Magic Mountain.

In 1956, Hawkes was introduced to Wood, and Child Life World started to evolve into what would be Pleasure Island.

Under the leadership of Gerald Blakeley Jr., Cabot, Cabot and Forbes developed several industrial parks along the newly constructed circumferential highway more commonly known as Route 128. The section of Route 128 from Route 9 in Wellesley to Lynnfield opened on August 23, 1951, with a cavalcade led by Gov. Paul Dever. Blakeley had researched the Massachusetts 1948 master plan for Route 128, and Cabot, Cabot and Forbes started buying up farmland and pig farms at major intersections along the new route even before Route 128 was built. Land along the new highway accelerated in value overnight, including in Wakefield.

As early as 1953, Wakefield's planning board set the stage for the eventual rezoning of the northeast section of the town from the north edge of Route 128 to the Lynnfield line. By 1956, Cabot, Cabot and Forbes had assembled more than 300 acres for a proposed industrial park. On August 10, 1956, Wakefield's town meeting voted 772 to 31 in favor of rezoning this site from residential to industrial. Out of the more than 300 acres, only 140 were of solid ground, above water, and suitable for development.

With zoning in place and Marco Engineering on board, Hawkes struck a deal with Cabot, Cabot and Forbes to break off the northernmost section of Wakefield in the rear portion of its site. On October 28, 1958, Pleasure Island was launched at a press party starting at 4:00 p.m. at the Hotel Somerset in Boston.

Site work commenced while Marco Engineering's art directors Wade Rubottom and Richard Kelsey (hired away from Disney) drew up plans and park layouts. It should be noted that according to the Cabot, Cabot and Forbes preconstruction information booklet for Pleasure Island, "Gabriel Scognamillo, a member of the society of motion picture art directors and designer of 'Tomorrowland' at Disneyland, designed Pleasure Island." In a *New York Times* obituary on December 4, 1992, another veteran art director, Randall Duell, is listed as codesigner of Pleasure Island in Boston and Freedomland in the Bronx.

A massive construction project began in the fall of 1958 in the marshlands off Route 128. While site work continued on through the winter and into 1959, design work from Marco Engineering ramped up for the building of Pleasure Island in late winter and into the spring.

The first phase of building construction to take place included the Diamond Lil Saloon, the Chisholm Trail, the print shop, the sheriff's office, and a hotel exhibit. Just like at Disneyland and Magic Mountain, the first buildings housed the shop to construct the woodwork for the rest of the park. The Diamond Lil Saloon was the shop.

While Pleasure Island was being built in Wakefield, major components were designed and assembled all over the country. The whaleboats were built at a boatyard in Maine, and the Jenney cars were manufactured in Mountain View, California, along with the track and cars for both of the dark rides. Moby Dick was built in Culver City, California. Just like Disneyland did when it opened in 1955, Pleasure Island underwrote its construction costs by incorporating industrial advertising. Exhibitors paid a fee plus rent to operate inside the park. Disneyland's and Pleasure Island's saloons were both sponsored by Pepsi-Cola and were brokered by Wood. Jenney Oil sponsored the Jenney cars. Several companies were involved in this type of advertising.

It is amazing to look at images and records that exist just how Hawkes, Marco Engineering, and Cabot, Cabot and Forbes pulled off announcing Pleasure Island on October 28, 1958, and then opened the park on June 22, 1959.

One

Concept to Construction

According to press releases by Howard Fitzpatrick of the Pleasure Island public relations division, the following are some fun facts: "Pleasure Island is a big city by any standards, with a mile of water pipe, 100,000 yards of paving, 100 acres of property, 3,000 trees, a mile long approach road, 10,000 feet of railroad track, and more than 7,000 feet of fence surrounds it." According to this author, that was not quite enough fence, as any number of former guests opted to skip the front gate and simply walk into the park. Also included in the press releases are the following facts:

> Four feet of frost was blasted to lay the foundations. Aberthaw Construction Co. joined by a dozen sub contractors, moved men and machinery into the swampland. Thousands of tons of earth were excavated and relocated, and miles of swampland were dredged to create the inland sea. Carpenters, electricians, plumbers, roofers, and every other tradesman converged to install power lines, sewer pipes, buildings, etc. More than 1,000 yards of white sand were spread along the beaches.

Because this was a summer-only operation, the buildings were not heated. That made it really interesting for employees and guests in the mid-1960s when the Christmas lights were on display and some of the rides were in operation. Despite the environment and horrible weather conditions, Pleasure Island was built on time, with a few exceptions, but it was certainly not under budget.

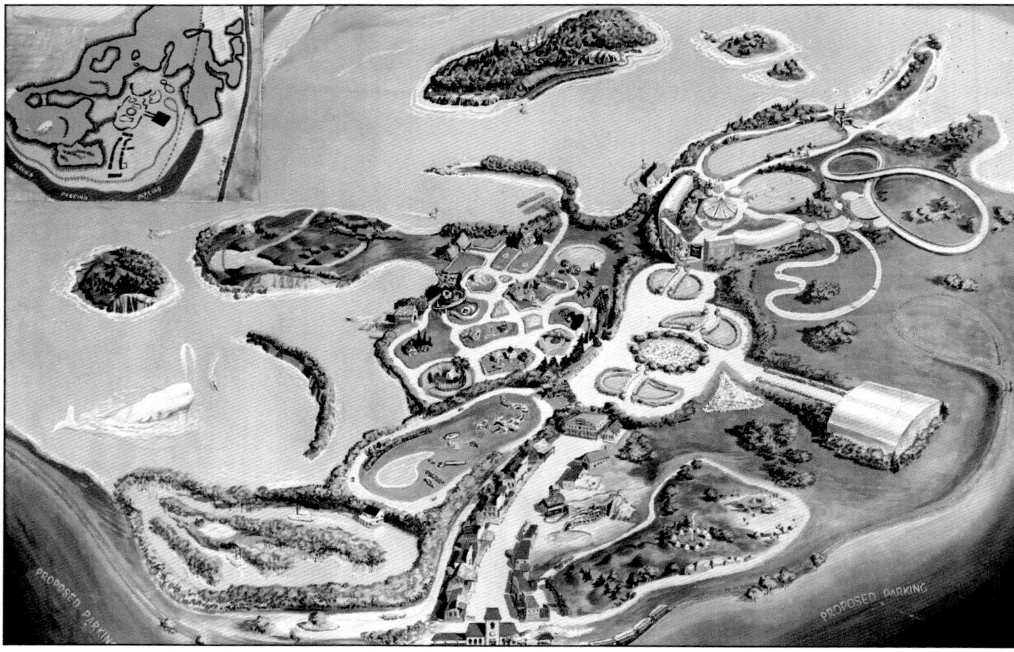

Both of these images are early concept drawings done by Sol Levenson (1910–2006), who was hired by William S. (Bill) Hawkes to create renderings for Child Life World. Some elements from Levenson's work were incorporated into the Marco Engineering plans for Pleasure Island. According to Web pages by John Goff about Levenson, he was widely considered a genius. During his career, Levenson taught painting in Mexico and Colombia, won multiple Fulbright fellowships, and wrote a book on the history of drawing. He was considered perhaps the last surviving artist from the Depression-era Works Progress Administration public employment program. (Courtesy of FOPI archives.)

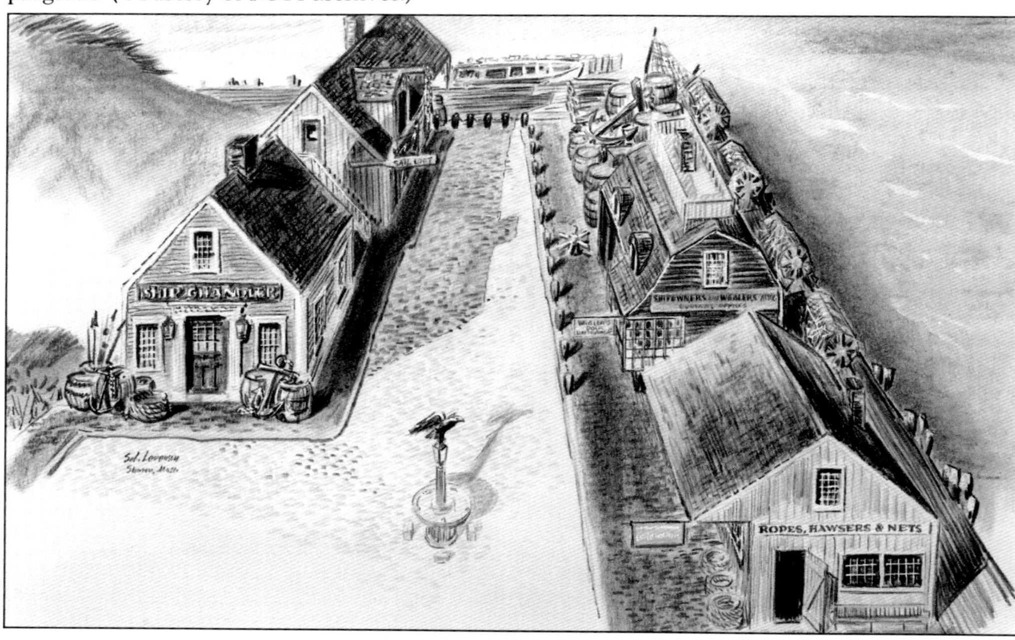

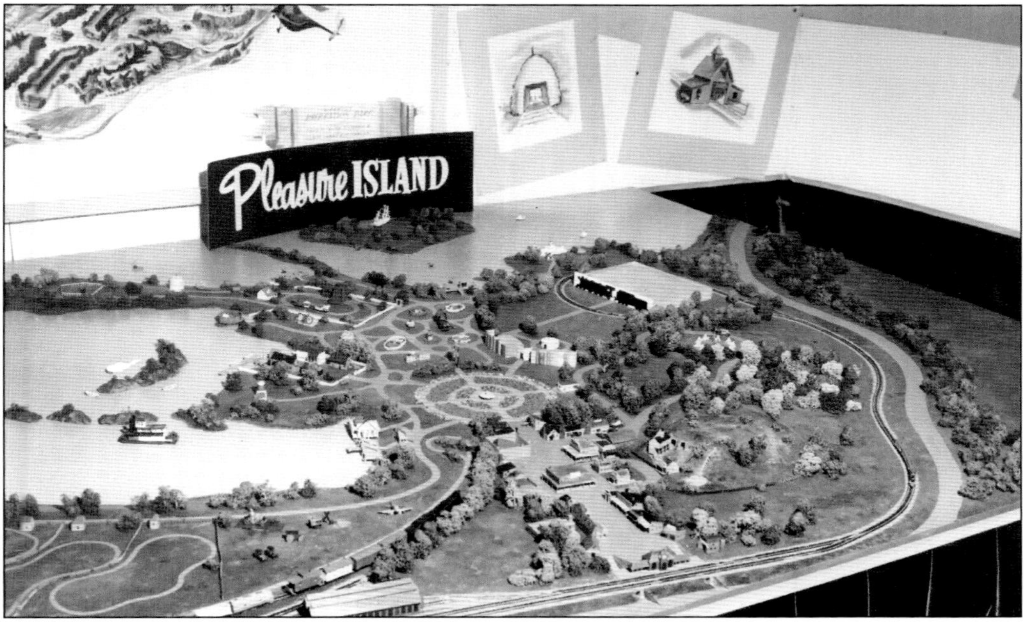

This early scale model of Pleasure Island during the conceptual stage was presented at the press party held in Boston on October 28, 1958. Interestingly, this model, outside of a train and whale, has no resemblance to what was actually built. (Courtesy of FOPI archives.)

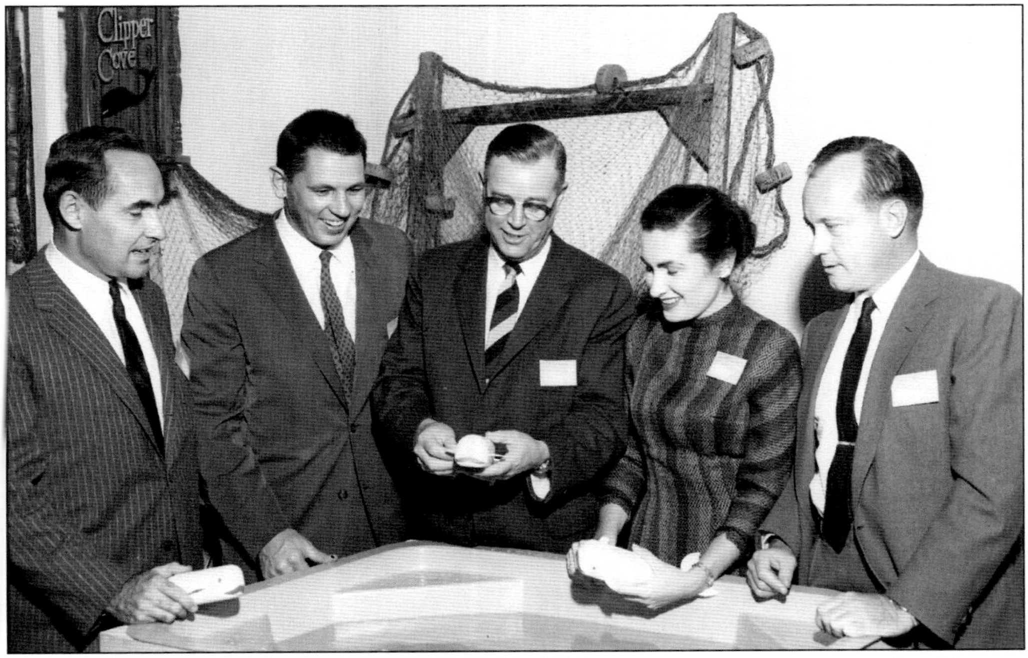

This photograph was taken at the October 28, 1958, press party to announce that Pleasure Island was coming to Wakefield. From left to right are Gerald Blakeley Jr., president of Cabot, Cabot and Forbes; Bill Hawkes, president of Pleasure Island; Ambrose Burton, president of Aberthaw Construction; Irene Murphy, Cabot, Cabot and Forbes secretary; and Robert Linnell, vice president of Cabot, Cabot and Forbes. (Courtesy of FOPI archives.)

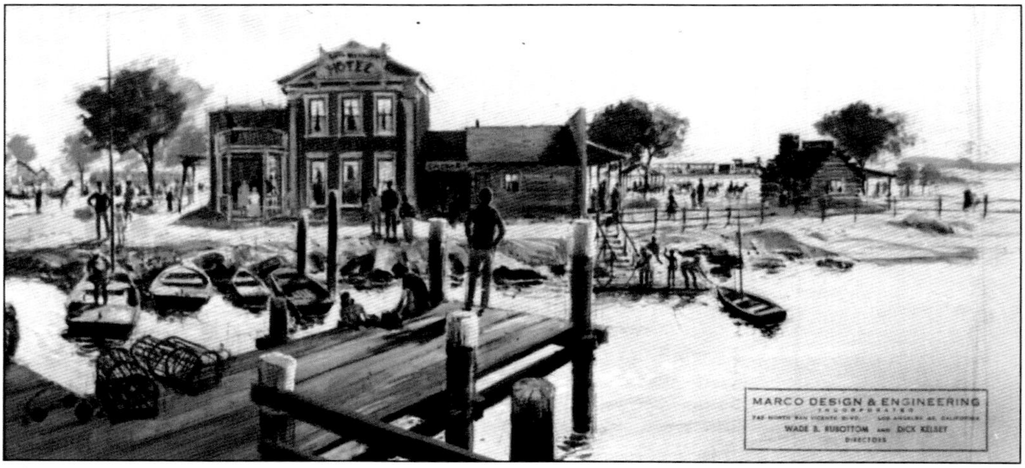

This rendering by Marco Engineering artists is looking toward what was to be the western section. Wade Rubottom, a movie artist who also worked on Disneyland, and Richard Kelsey, an Academy Award–winning artist who was with Disney Studios for 12 years, were art directors for the Pleasure Island project. (Courtesy of FOPI archives.)

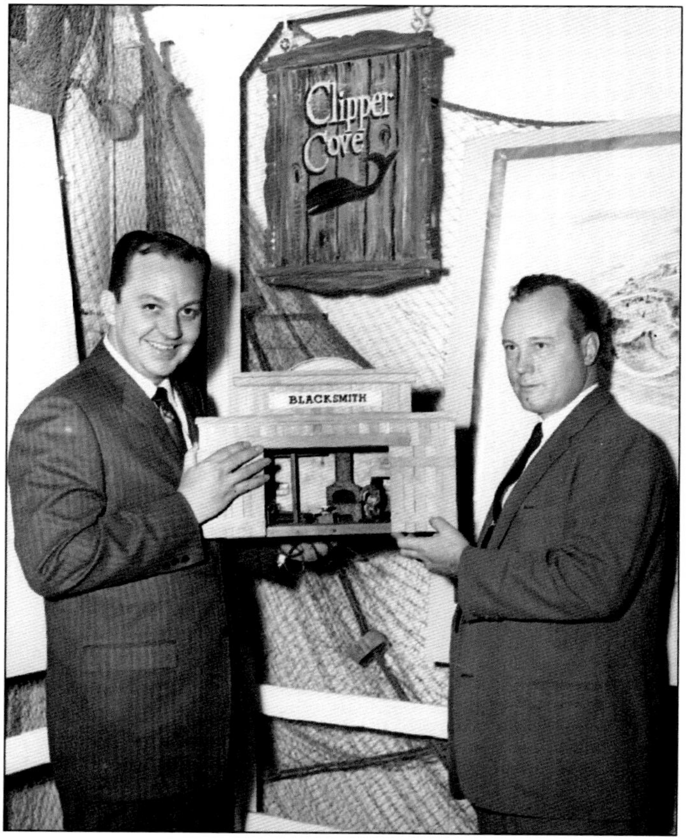

Here are C. V. Wood (left) and Robert Linnell at the October 28, 1958, press party, announcing that Pleasure Island was coming to Wakefield. Wood, owner of Marco Engineering, designed Pleasure Island, trained personnel, and so on. Linnell was vice president of Cabot, Cabot and Forbes and was on the board of directors of Pleasure Island. (Courtesy of FOPI archives.)

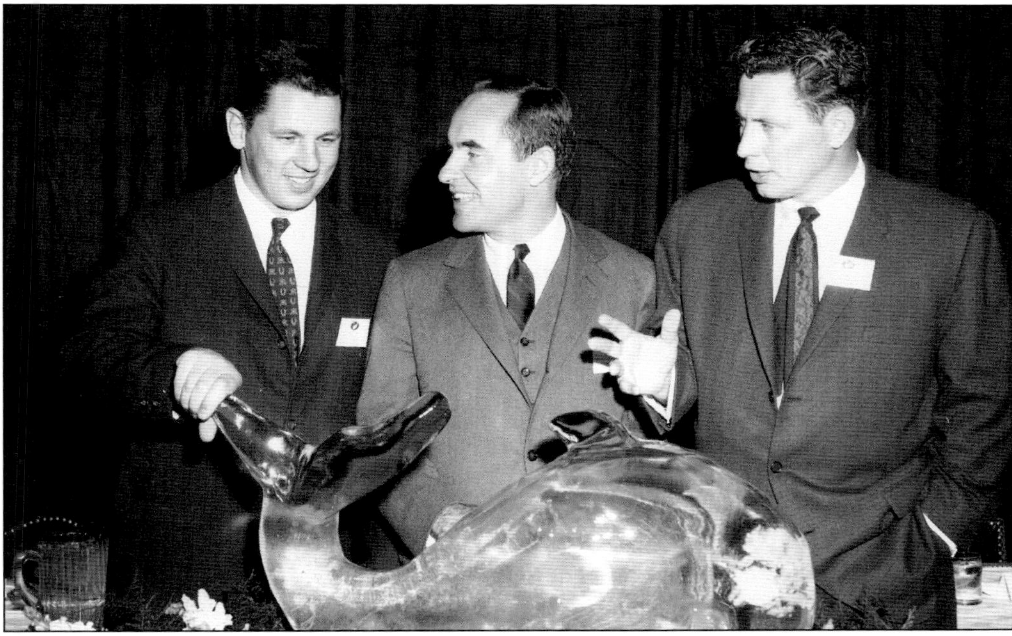

A luncheon for the press took place at the Parker House in Boston on April 8, 1959. Bill Hawkes (left), Gerald Blakeley Jr. (center), and Lloyd D. Settle (right) outlined Pleasure Island's June 1959 opening along with the economic impact and projected attendance of 1.2 million guests for the first season. Brought in by Marco Engineering, Settle was the top management consultant to Pleasure Island. He also served as executive administrator of the park's marketing, public relations, and show activities. He held former executive positions at Disneyland and Pacific Ocean Park. (Courtesy of Magna Film Productions.)

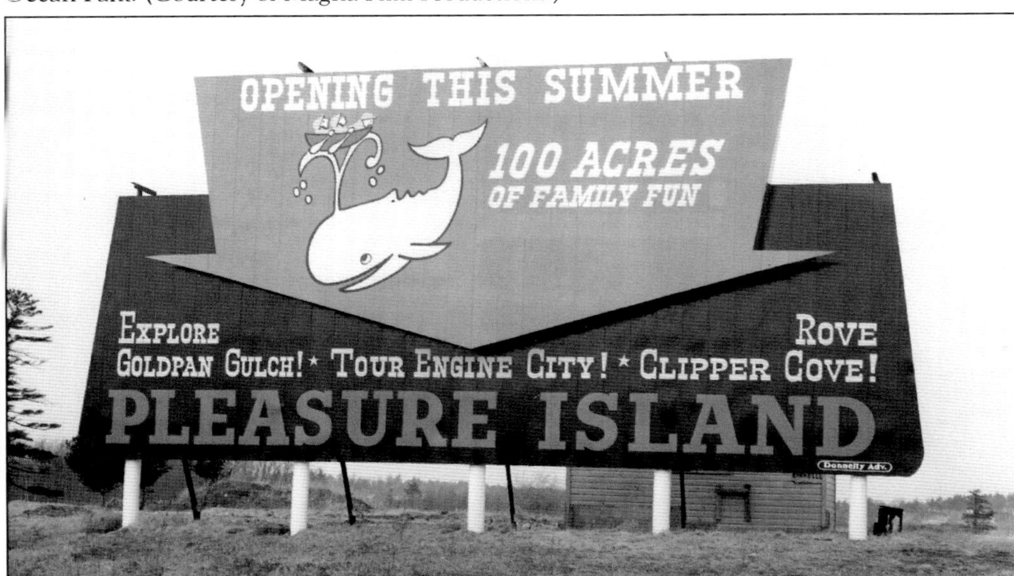

With Moby Dick as Pleasure Island's official logo, this billboard was located along Route 128 in Wakefield. This particular location was eventually home to several industrial buildings developed by Cabot, Cabot and Forbes. (Courtesy of Bourdon Studios.)

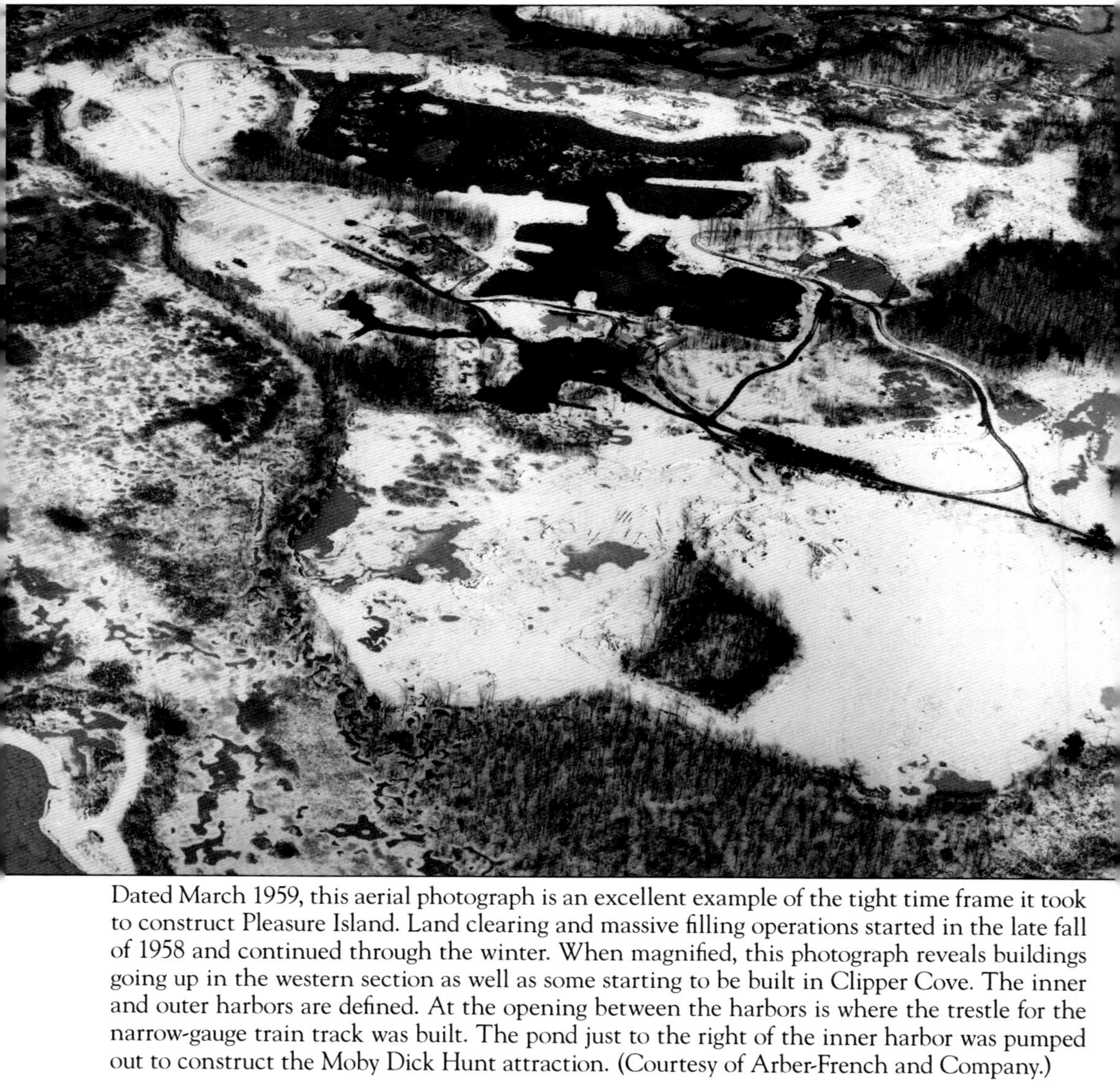

Dated March 1959, this aerial photograph is an excellent example of the tight time frame it took to construct Pleasure Island. Land clearing and massive filling operations started in the late fall of 1958 and continued through the winter. When magnified, this photograph reveals buildings going up in the western section as well as some starting to be built in Clipper Cove. The inner and outer harbors are defined. At the opening between the harbors is where the trestle for the narrow-gauge train track was built. The pond just to the right of the inner harbor was pumped out to construct the Moby Dick Hunt attraction. (Courtesy of Arber-French and Company.)

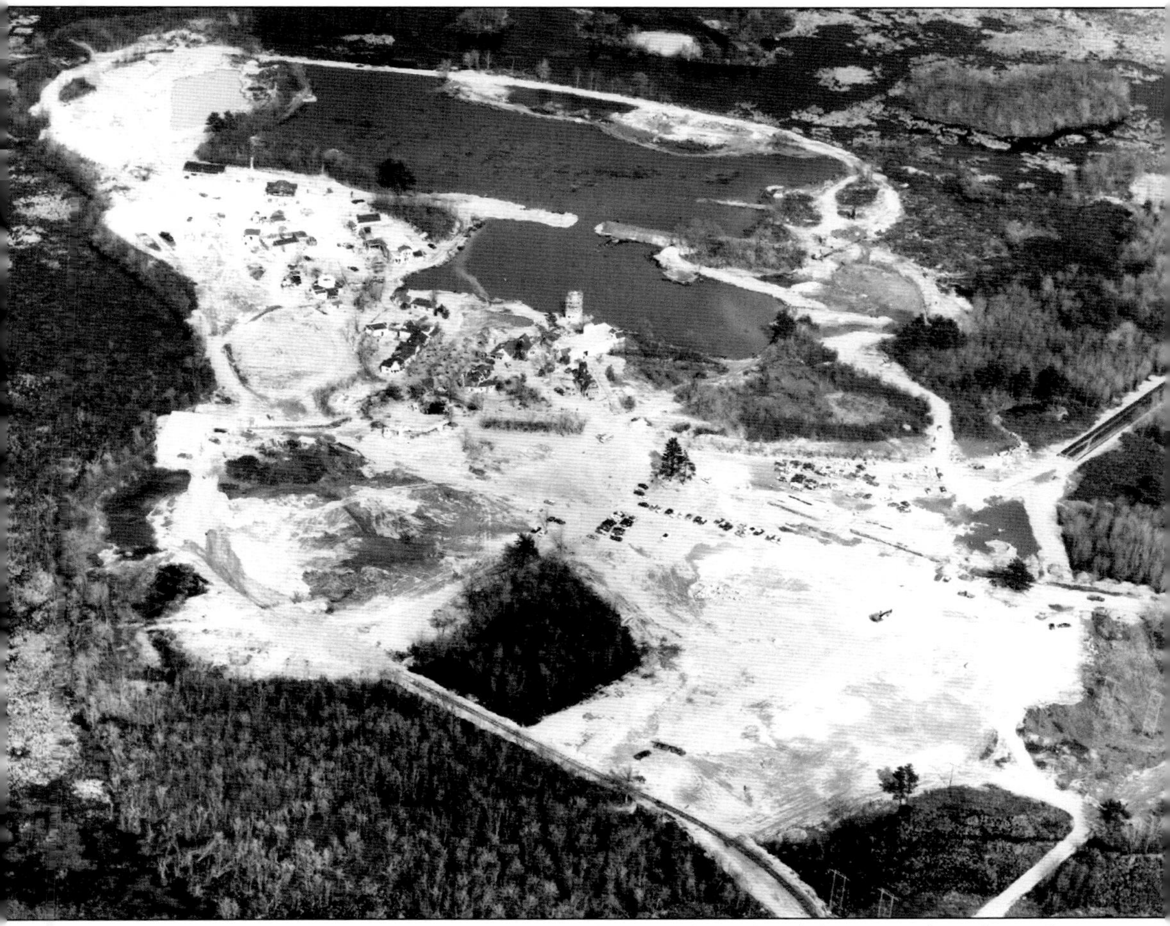

Dated May 1959, this aerial photograph shows just how much work is left to complete the park. The center right of the image shows the access road leading toward the 3,000-car parking lot area. At Clipper Cove, the lighthouse is being built. At the right of the inner harbor is where the Moby Dick Hunt attraction is under construction. At this point, the layout track bed for the narrow-gauge train is in place, including the relocated station from the Greenwood section of Wakefield. At the bottom of the image is the Boston and Maine Railroad standard-gauge spur track heading toward what will be Engine City. (Courtesy of Arber-French and Company.)

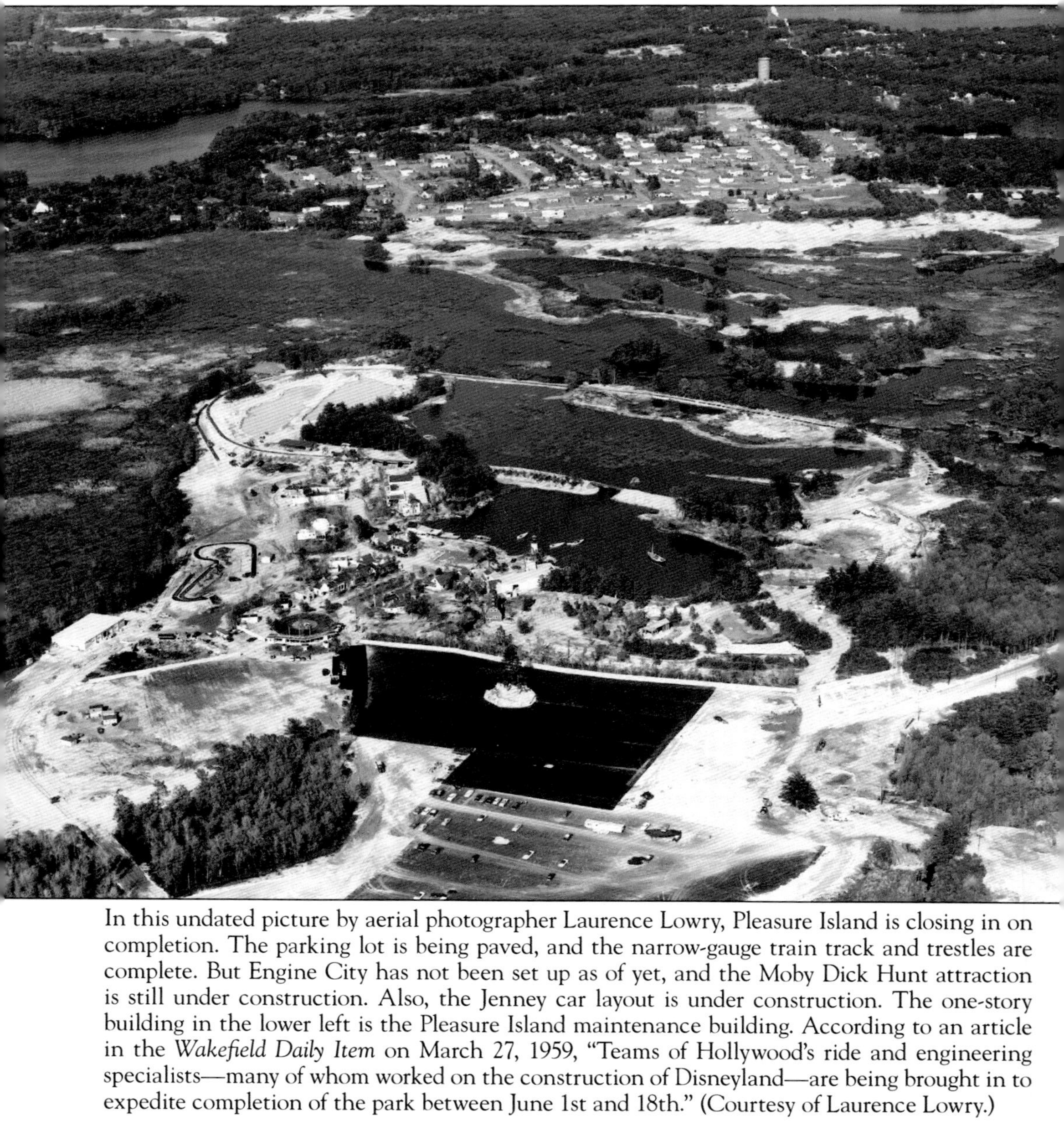

In this undated picture by aerial photographer Laurence Lowry, Pleasure Island is closing in on completion. The parking lot is being paved, and the narrow-gauge train track and trestles are complete. But Engine City has not been set up as of yet, and the Moby Dick Hunt attraction is still under construction. Also, the Jenney car layout is under construction. The one-story building in the lower left is the Pleasure Island maintenance building. According to an article in the *Wakefield Daily Item* on March 27, 1959, "Teams of Hollywood's ride and engineering specialists—many of whom worked on the construction of Disneyland—are being brought in to expedite completion of the park between June 1st and 18th." (Courtesy of Laurence Lowry.)

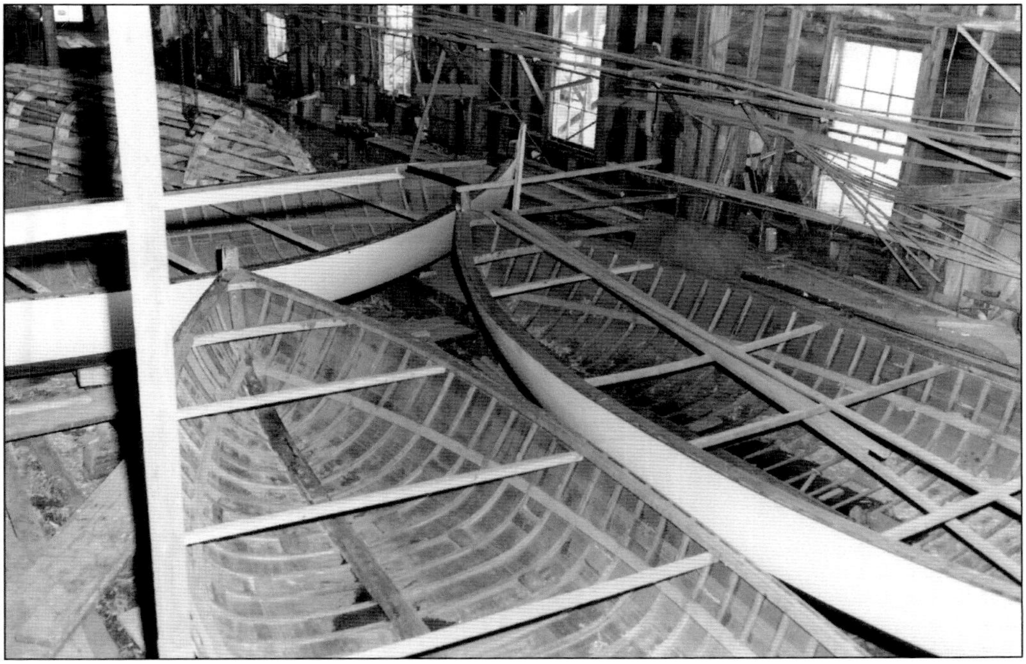

These photographs from March 1959 show a fleet of six authentic whaleboats for the Moby Dick Hunt attraction being built by shipwrights at the Newbert and Wallace boatyard in Thomaston, Maine. They were 30 feet long, weighed 3,500 pounds, and accommodated 30 passengers. According to Pleasure Island's public relations division, "The fleet of six 19th century whaleboats was to be the first launched in at least a half century." Instead of oars, 25-horsepower engines supplied the go power. (Courtesy of FOPI archives.)

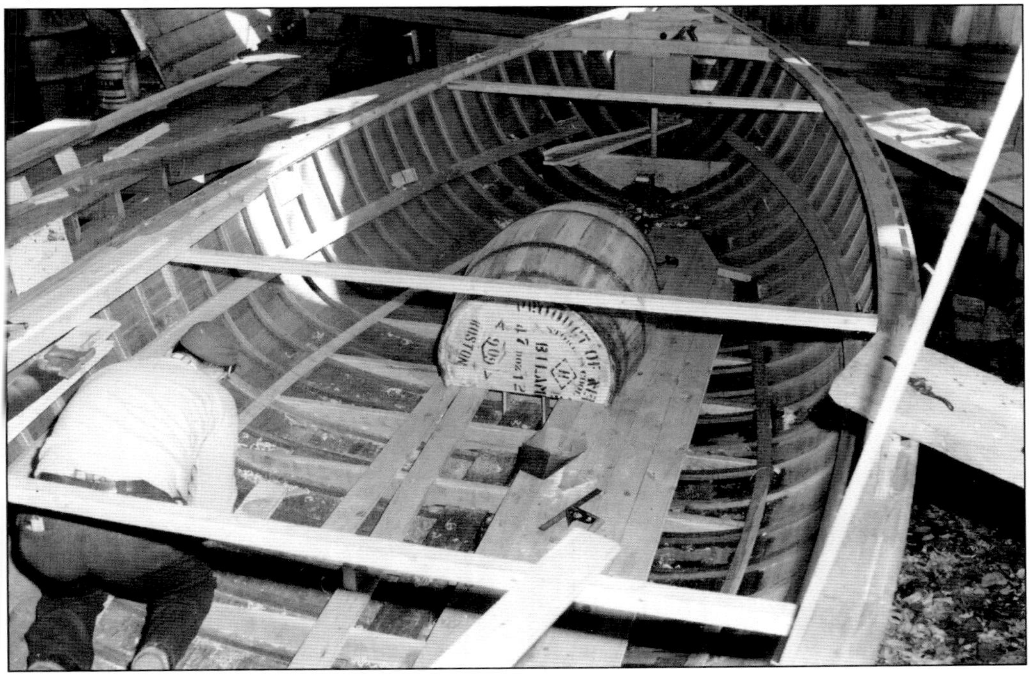

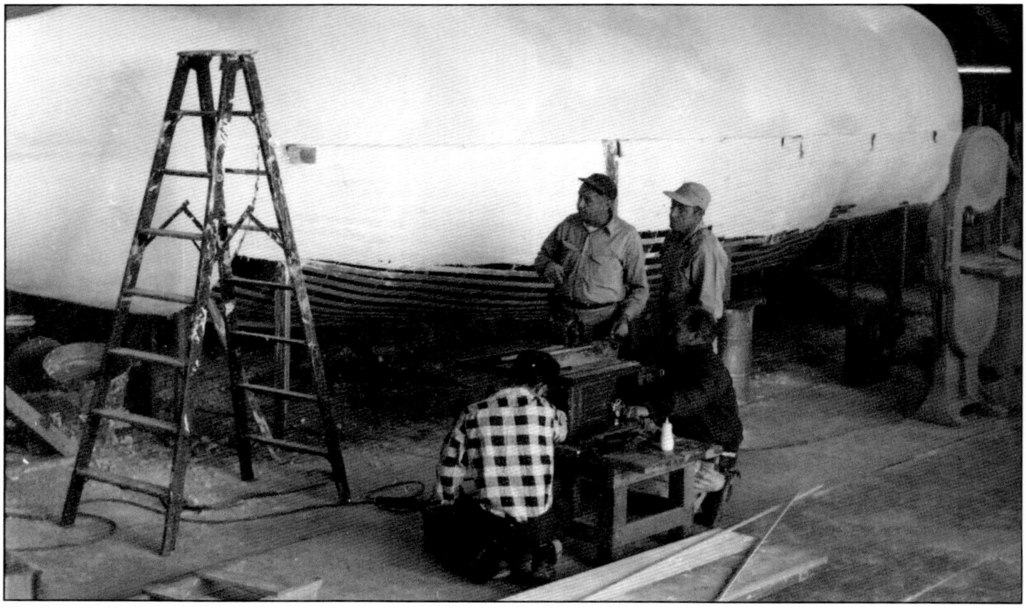

Both of these photographs dated March 1959 were taken at an unidentified location in the Los Angeles area. Glen Robinson, who headed his own special effects studio from Culver City, California, was hired to build and install the components for the Moby Dick Hunt attraction and to supply and set up props and gags for both of Pleasure Island's dark rides. With just photographs and no plans, it appears that Moby Dick gets molded in fiberglass over a wood frame. Moby was then cut into sections off the wood frame and shipped for assembly in Wakefield. Some of the larger props for the dark rides and the Moby Dick Hunt attraction were probably built by movie people in the Los Angeles area. (Courtesy of FOPI archives.)

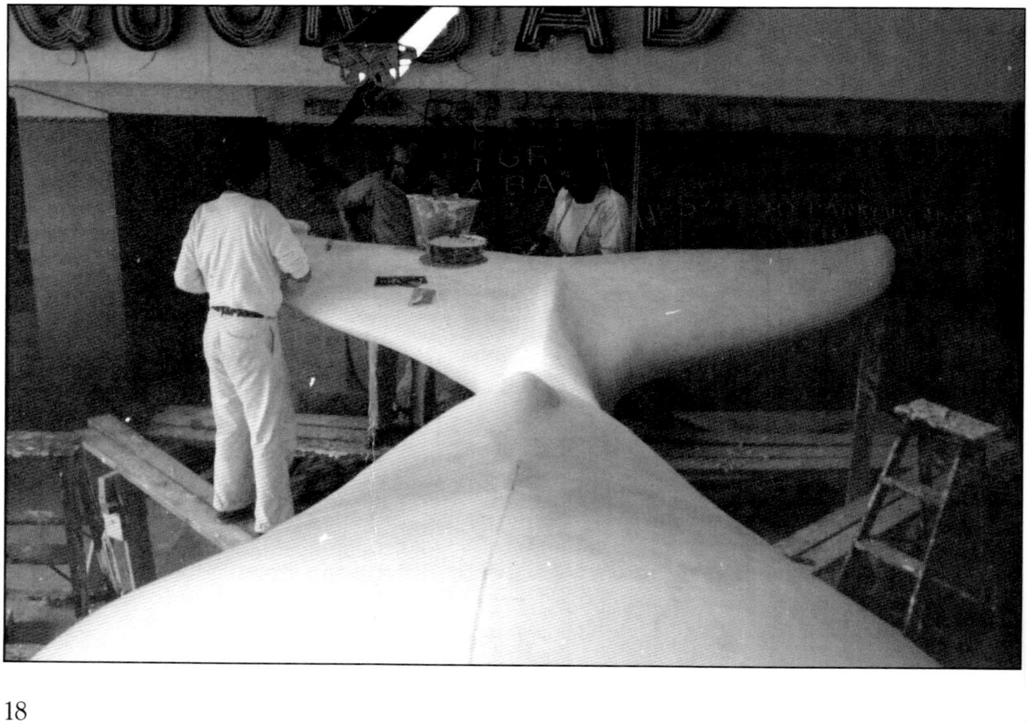

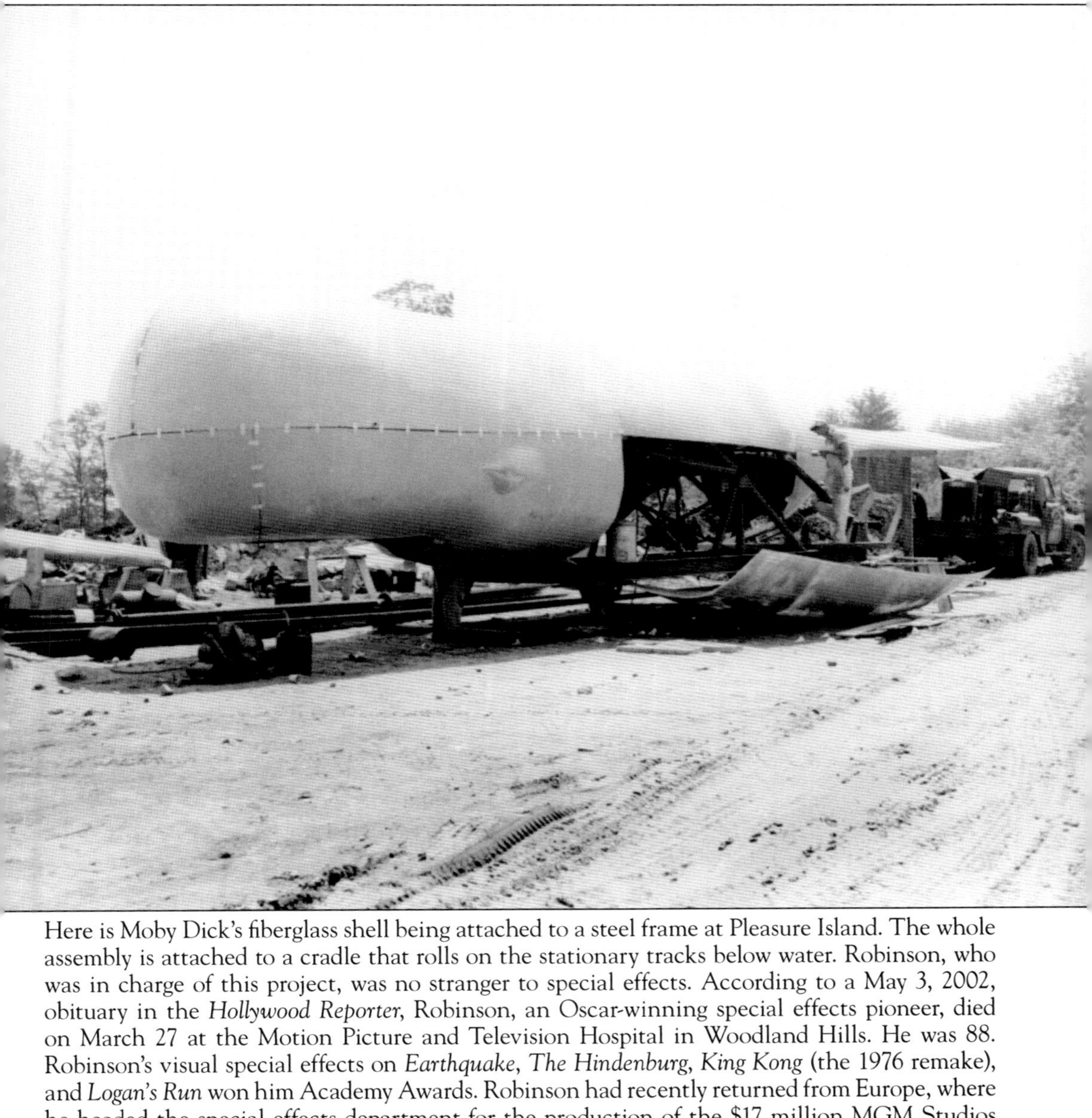

Here is Moby Dick's fiberglass shell being attached to a steel frame at Pleasure Island. The whole assembly is attached to a cradle that rolls on the stationary tracks below water. Robinson, who was in charge of this project, was no stranger to special effects. According to a May 3, 2002, obituary in the *Hollywood Reporter*, Robinson, an Oscar-winning special effects pioneer, died on March 27 at the Motion Picture and Television Hospital in Woodland Hills. He was 88. Robinson's visual special effects on *Earthquake*, *The Hindenburg*, *King Kong* (the 1976 remake), and *Logan's Run* won him Academy Awards. Robinson had recently returned from Europe, where he headed the special effects department for the production of the $17 million MGM Studios epic *Ben-Hur*. According to a *Boston Globe* article from July 6, 1959, Dick Parker, who helped Cecil B. DeMille film *The Ten Commandments*, also worked on this attraction. (Courtesy of Fay Foto Service.)

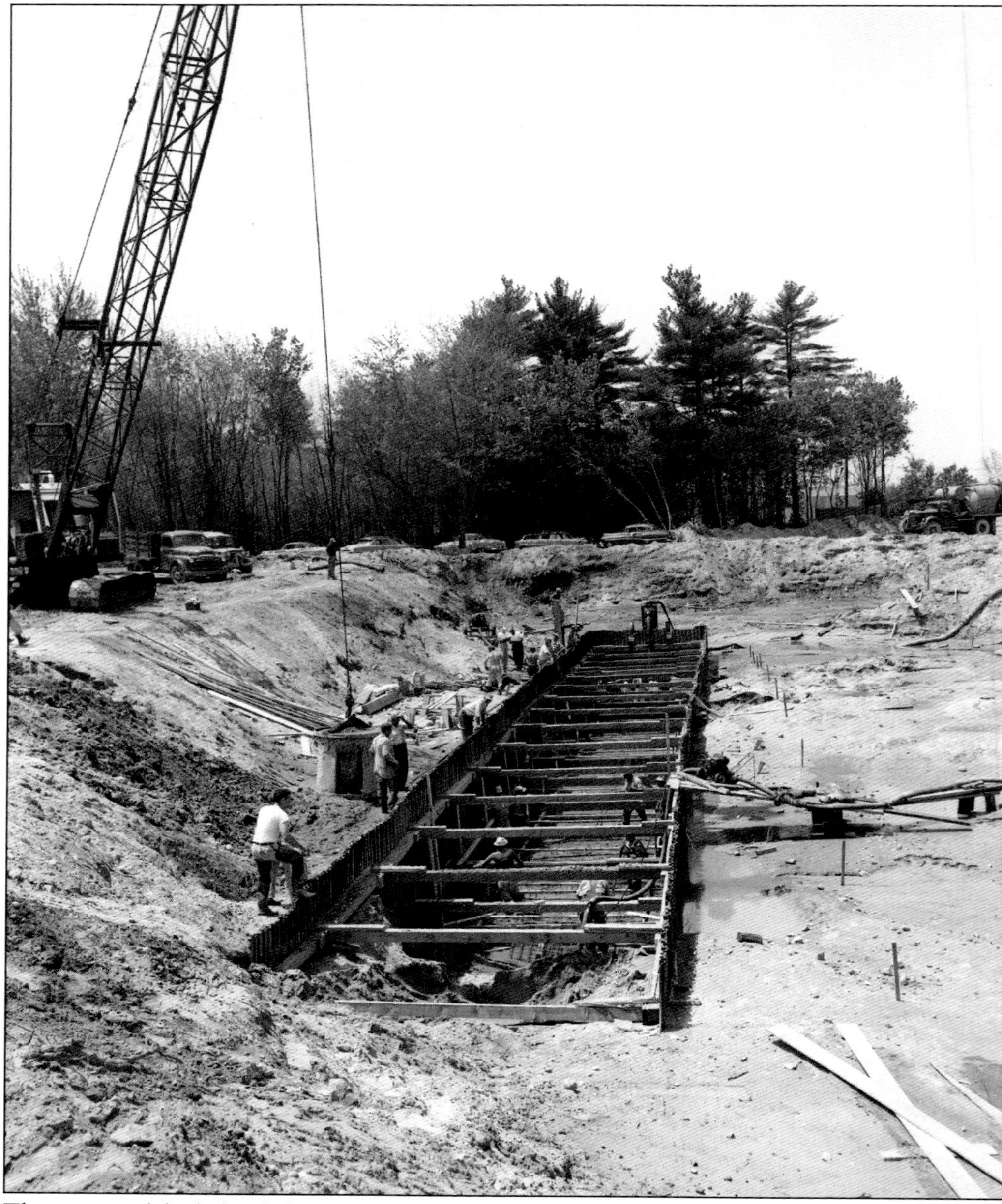

This is part of the behind the scenes, or in this case below water scenes, for the great Moby Dick Hunt attraction. This natural pond had to be pumped out before construction could begin. In this photograph, work is being done to support the track system for Moby. A great story was written by Paul Benzaquin from the *Boston Globe* and reprinted in the *Wakefield Daily Item* dated July 17, 1959. Benzaquin had an in-depth interview with special effects lead Glen Robinson. This is an excerpt from the story: "Just off the port bow a stream of water and steam began to shoot up some 15 feet. Suddenly the great head of Captain Ahab's nemesis—Moby Dick himself—broke water. More and more and still more of the awful bulk swam up, until at last the entire 45 foot body was on top of the water." Moby Dick reportedly weighed three tons. (Courtesy of Fay Foto Service.)

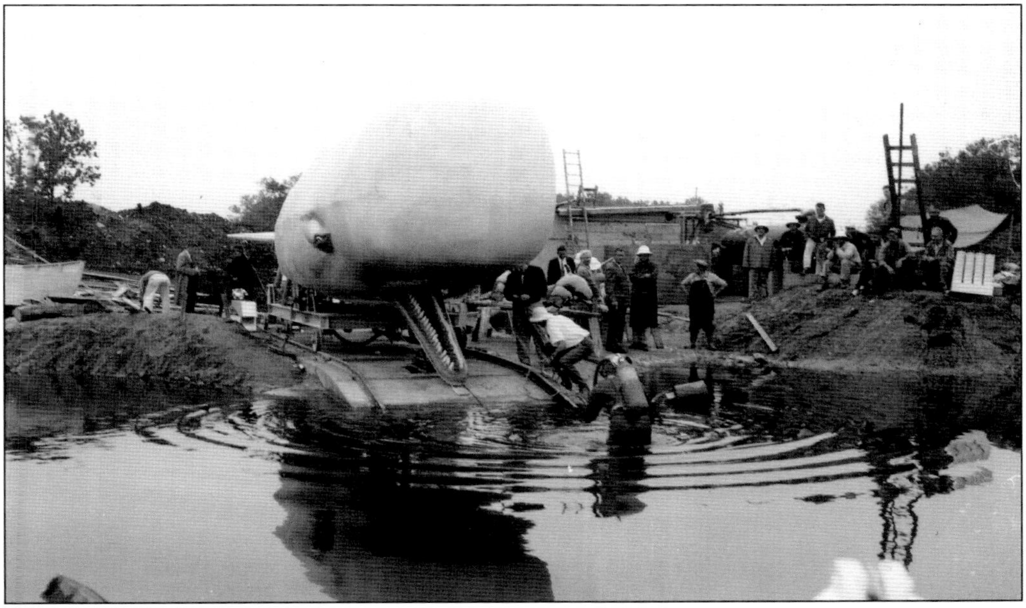

Bill McGrath, an electrician who worked on the Moby Dick Hunt attraction while Pleasure Island was being built, gave a firsthand account of Moby Dick's problems. He said everything worked great until they put the water in. Because of buoyancy problems, Moby Dick floated off the tracks. Moby Dick did not work again until July 5, two weeks after Pleasure Island opened, and continued to have problems for the life of the park. (Courtesy of Bourdon Studios.)

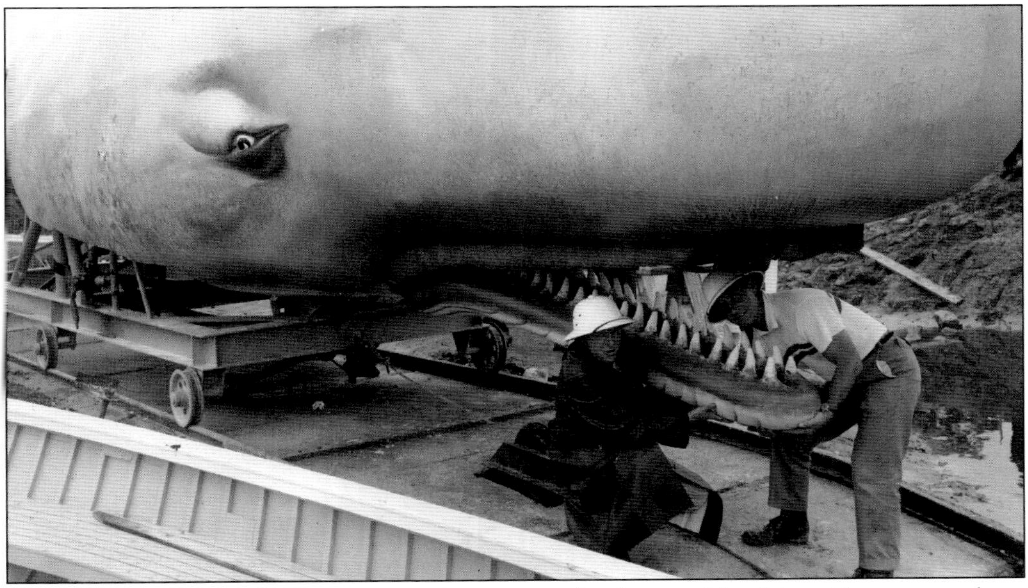

Construction personnel were instructed to wear safari hats to blend in with cast members, according to Bill McGrath. This photograph is dated June 26, 1959, just a few days after Pleasure Island's official opening. After the *Boston Globe* posted a photograph of Moby Dick on July 6, according to a follow-up story, "Whale lovers phoned, wrote and wired that the Wakefield Moby Dick doesn't spout right. It was back to land for the relocation of Moby's blowhole." (Courtesy of Bourdon Studios.)

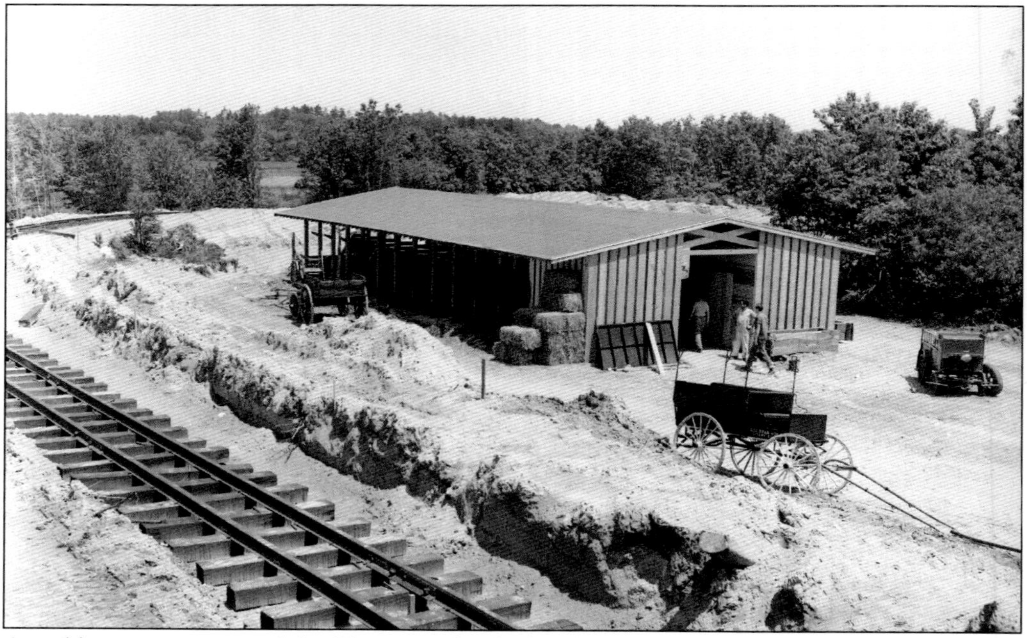

A stable was constructed for Pleasure Island's four-legged friends. According to Sy Milano, former sheriff of Pleasure Island, it housed the sheriff's horse, the horses for the stagecoach, miscellaneous wagons, and the burros. The narrow-gauge track is in place yet incomplete at this point of construction. (Courtesy of Fay Foto Service.)

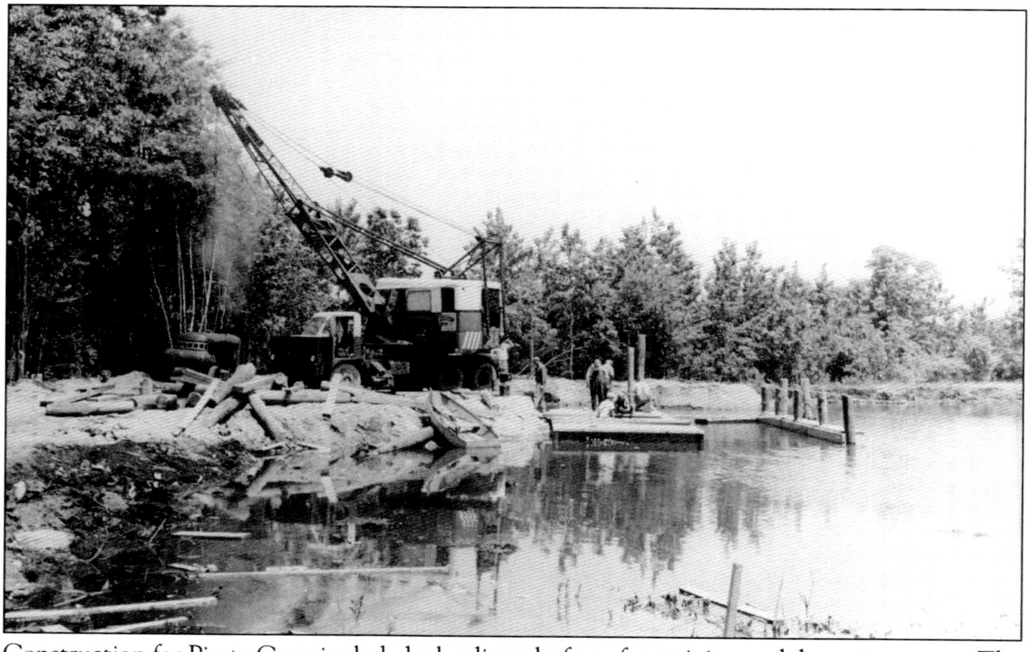

Construction for Pirate Cove included a loading platform for arriving and departing guests. The illusion was that Pirate Cove was an island, but, in fact, it was not. Effects like this are what made Pleasure Island so special. There were many subcontractors involved in building Pleasure Island, including pile drivers for the docks and building supports. (Courtesy of FOPI archives.)

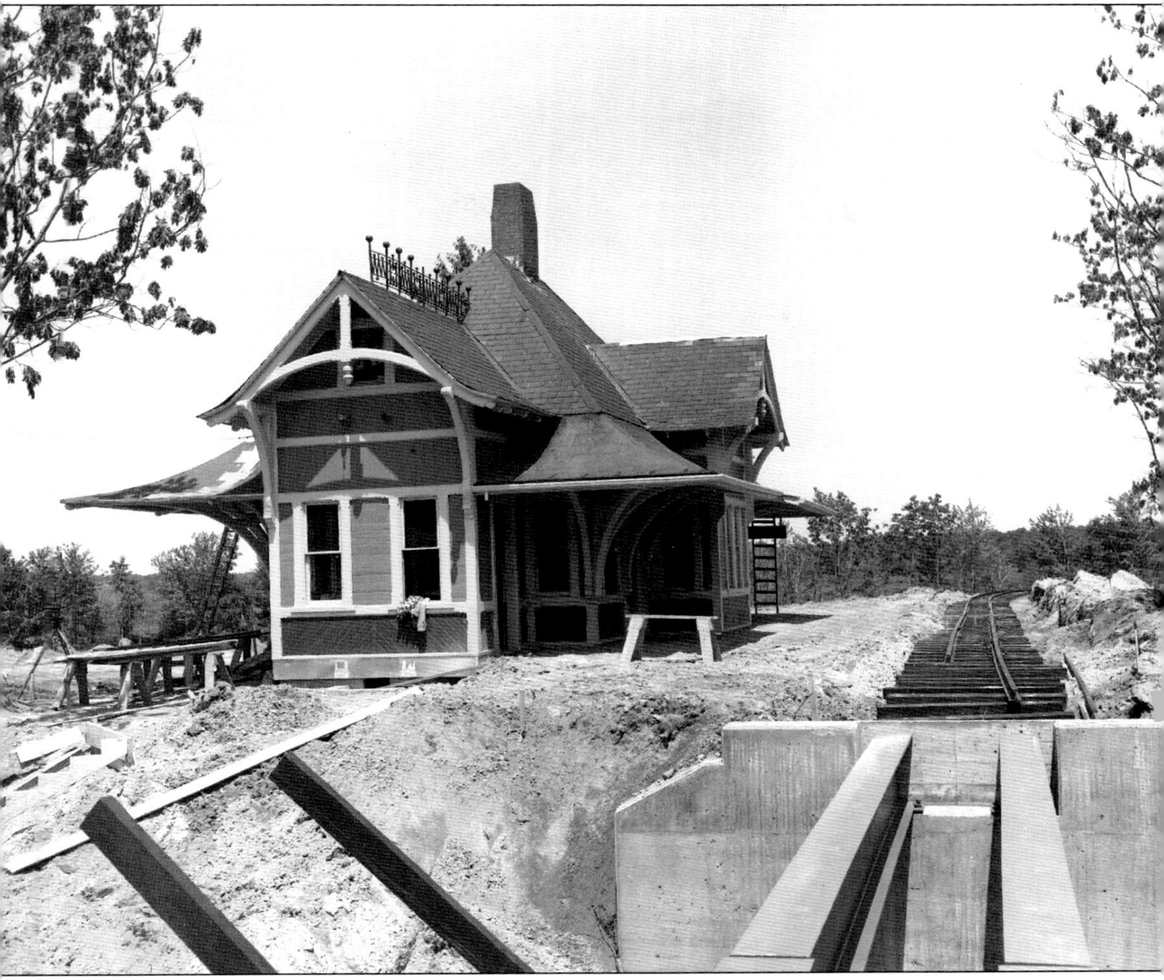

The Greenwood station is in place and is being restored as Goldpan Gulch, the centerpiece of the Pleasure Island and Western Railroad. The bridge and track are still under construction, as is the staircase, shown in the lower left of the photograph, which leads down to the rest of the western section. A story from the *Wakefield Daily Item* dated March 27, 1959, stated, "Over a million cubic yards of dirt already have been excavated at the park site." The grade here was elevated so the stagecoaches and guests would have access under the tracks. Also, the Burro Trail went under the tracks at this location. (Courtesy of Fay Foto Service.)

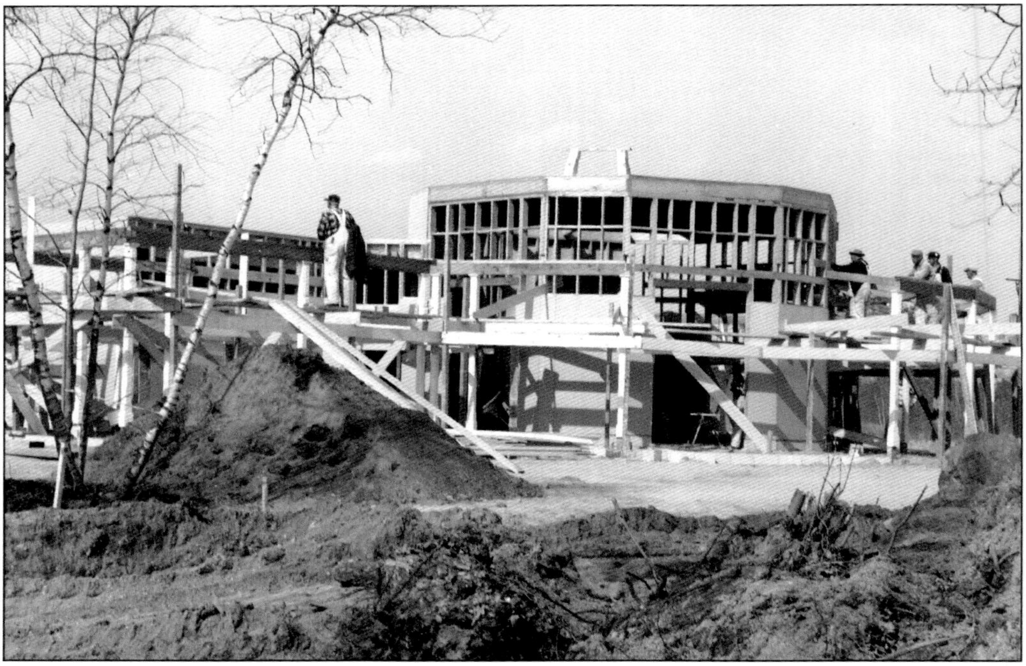

H. P. Hood and Sons was a major investor at Pleasure Island. This is Hood's Ice Cream Parlor under construction. It was located next to the Slanty Shanty. Most buildings were of wood construction, and because of wetlands, there were no basements. (Courtesy of Bourdon Studios.)

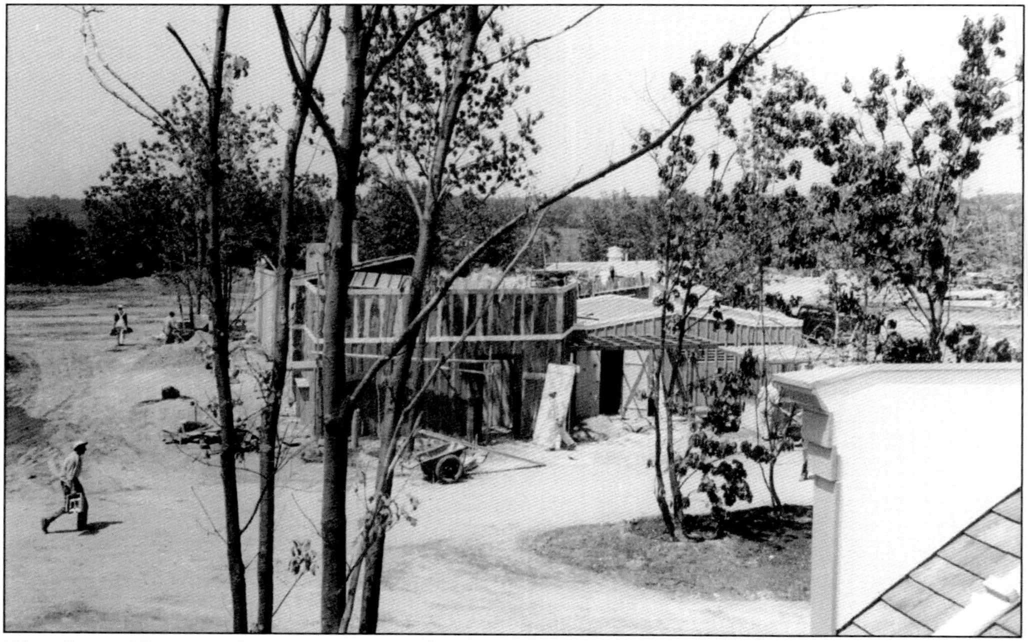

The Slanty Shanty is being constructed across from the Diamond Lil Saloon. This photograph was taken from the roof of the print shop. To the rear is present-day Reedy Meadow. It is reported that workers building the Slanty Shanty were actually getting seasick. It was a walk-through attraction unlike any other. (Courtesy of Fay Foto Service.)

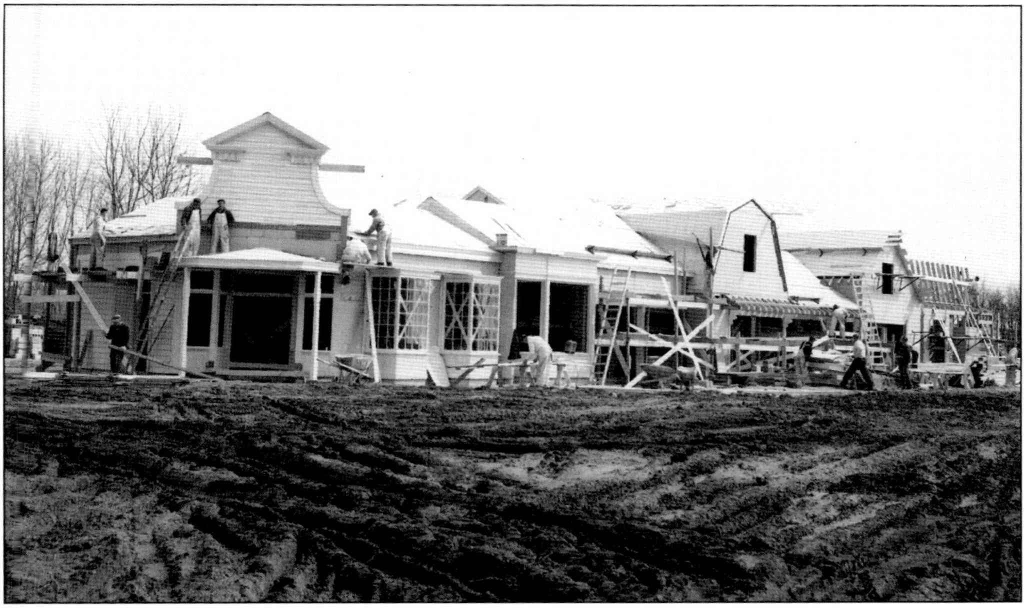

This photograph shows the working condition of construction in a wetland with above-average rainfall. Records from the Wakefield annual report books indicate that for June 1959, when the rush was on to complete Pleasure Island, 8.72 inches of rain fell versus 2.42 inches in June 1958 and only 1.7 inches in 1960. (Courtesy of Bourdon Studios.)

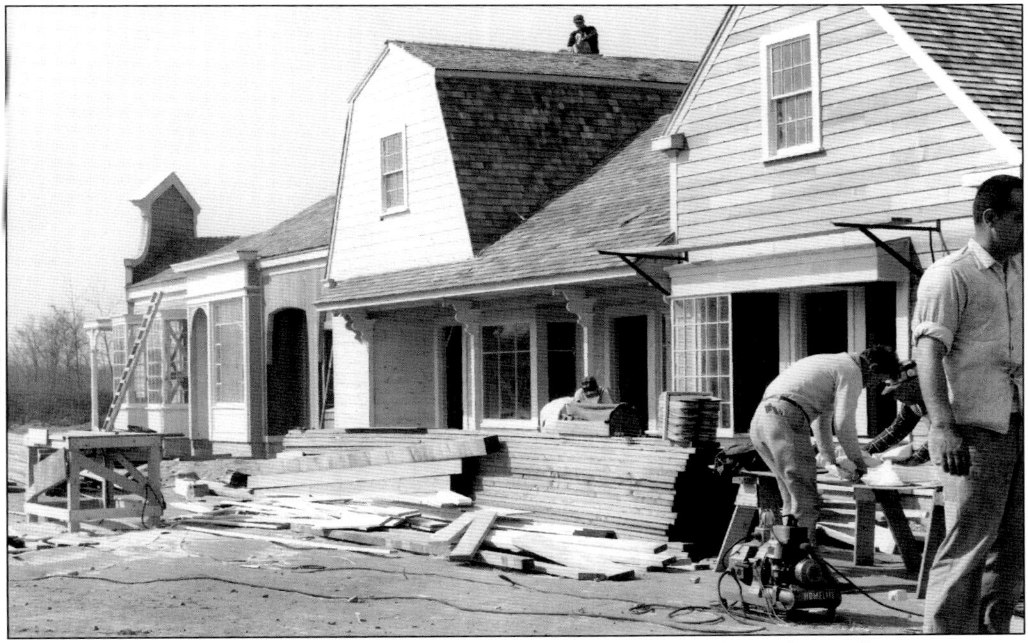

This is a progress photograph of the same group of shops shown above. Space does not permit pointing out shop by shop except that like a strip mall or shopping center, tenants change over time, and Pleasure Island was no exception. Keep in mind that these buildings were designed by former Disneyland artists who created a New England village with a Disney touch. (Courtesy of Bourdon Studios.)

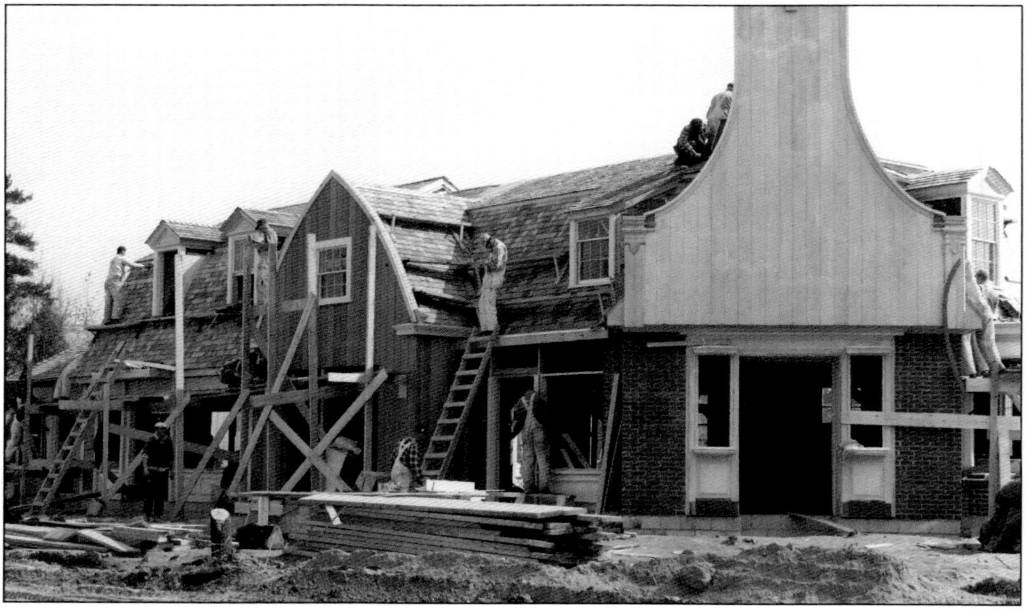

As reported in the *Wakefield Daily Item* on April 28, 1959, Theodore Ogden, assistant general manager of Pleasure Island, spoke to the Wakefield Chamber of Commerce. When questioned about the progress of construction, Ogden replied, "Some people wondered, a few weeks ago, how we could make the June opening date, because they saw little signs of construction. What they didn't realize is that building was going on in the shops, so that the units could be quickly constructed when the foundations were ready." (Courtesy of Bourdon Studios.)

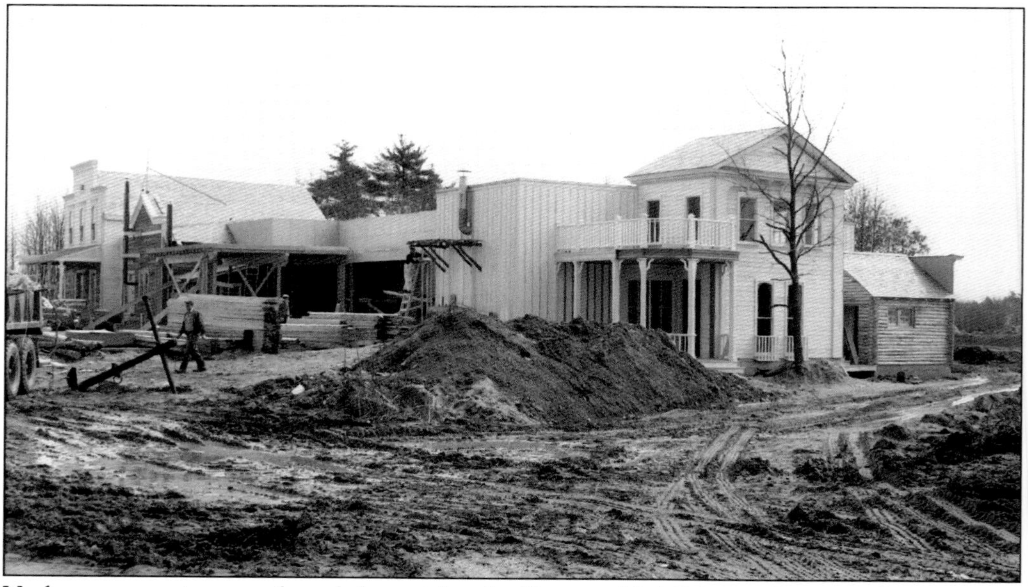

Under construction are, from left to right, the Diamond Lil Saloon, the print shop, and the Chisholm Trail dark ride. The building on the right corner was called the Charter House, with a lobby of an old western hotel on the first floor and a modern hotel room exhibit on the second floor. It was sponsored by the Hotel Corporation of America. The log cabin to the rear was a jail and sheriff's office. (Courtesy of Bourdon Studios.)

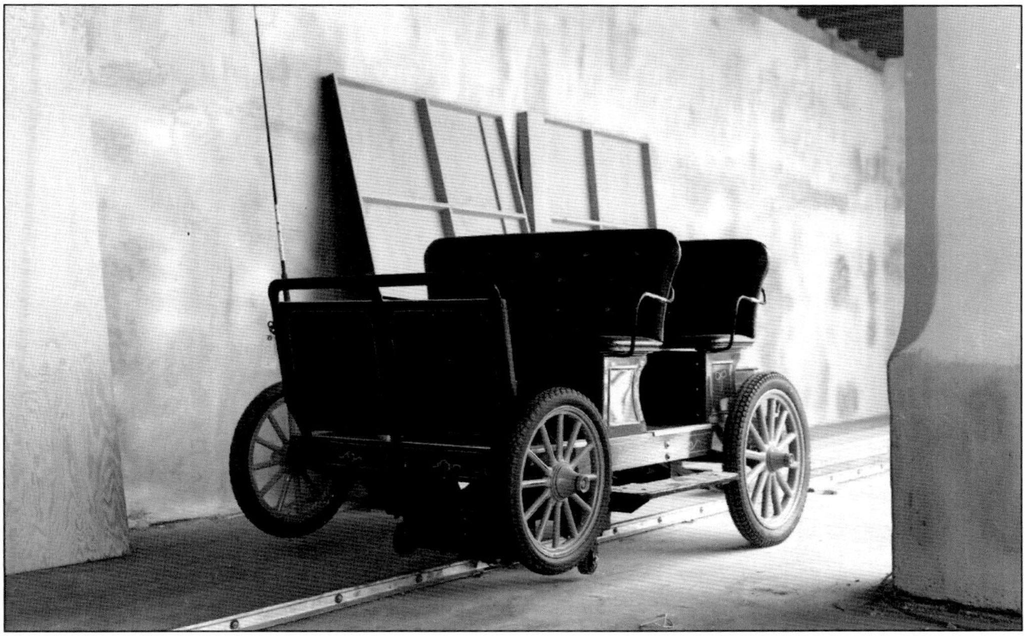

The track and cars for both dark rides at Pleasure Island and the Jenney cars came from the Arrow Development in Mountain View, California. The photograph above shows a simulated buckboard that took guests on a tour of the Wild West. Arrow also made components for the attractions at Disneyland, including the Teacups. (Courtesy of Fay Foto Service.)

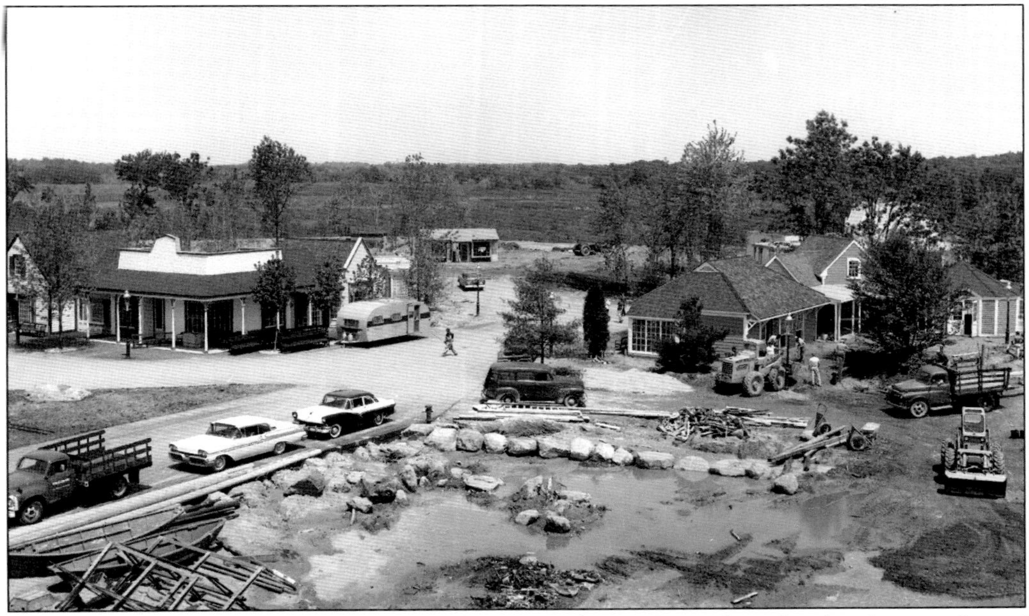

This photograph was taken from the lighthouse at Clipper Cove. Straight ahead is a replica of an early Jenney Oil gasoline station at the Jenney car attraction, which is under construction. According to a *Wakefield Daily Item* story dated June 9, 1959, "Ambrose Burton, in charge of construction, described Pleasure Island's construction as unusual, none of the buildings was standardized, each has a character strictly its own." (Courtesy of Fay Foto Service.)

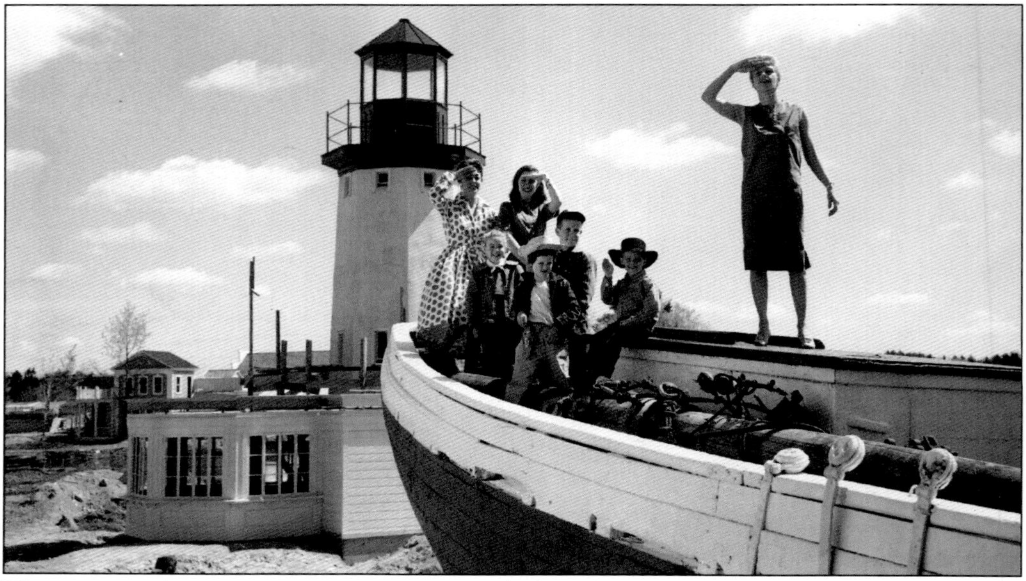

This is one of many preopening promotional shots by the Pleasure Island public relations division. The schooner is a prop for Clipper Cove. According to a story from the *Wakefield Daily Item* dated May 6, 1959, "The 53 foot, 20 ton two-masted Newfoundland swordfish schooner made its final voyage, over the road from Portland, Maine. The 80 year old vessel had sailed with the Grand Banks Fishing Fleet before the turn of the century and was wrecked off the coast of Cuba." (Courtesy of Bourdon Studios.)

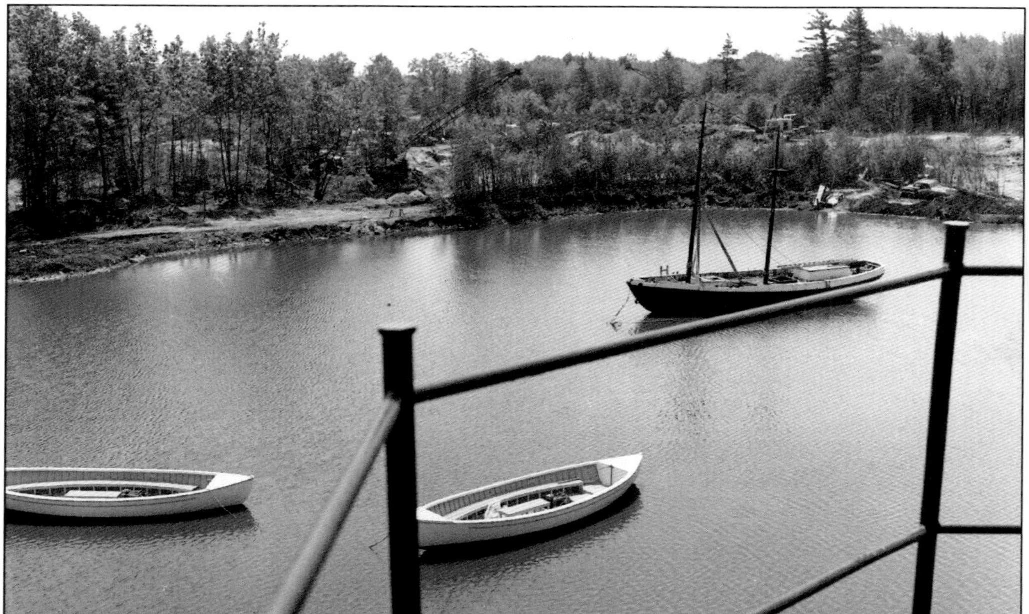

This photograph was taken from the lighthouse. The schooner is at anchor as are two of the whaleboats. The cranes are busy on the Moby Dick Hunt underwater track system. When completed, earth was removed on either side of the lagoon to create the island for additional special effects. (Courtesy of Fay Foto Service.)

Two

Pleasure Island Trains

On October 28, 1958, Pleasure Island held a press conference at 4:00 p.m. in Boston to introduce plans for a new recreation center. At 8:00 p.m. the same day, Atlantic Refining Company was at a hearing in front of the Wakefield Board of Selectmen. According to a *Wakefield Daily Item* article, "Atlantic had entered into an agreement with the Boston and Maine Railroad for the purchase of the Greenwood Depot, where it will construct a modern two bay filling station, the present depot on Main Street which has been closed to the public for months will be razed."

As they say, the rest is history. Who knows how the deal was struck, but on January 13, 1959, the board of selectmen voted at its meeting for a permit to be granted for moving the Greenwood railroad station building to Pleasure Island. The approved route for this activity went north along Main Street from its present location to Route 128, east along Route 128 to Lyons Lane, and west along Lyons Lane into the Wakefield Industrial Center.

What was not planned for was a memorandum Bill Hawkes wrote on January 30, 1959. "We have received the ticket from Sergeant O'Malley for illegally parking one railroad depot on the Rotary Club's winter picnic grounds. Was the mover carrying insurance which covers this, or must I write a change order to transfer funds from the steam train ride? William S. Hawkes." The biggest question is what is a winter picnic ground? The original design for the Pleasure Island trains was twofold. One was to have a steam-powered, narrow-gauge excursion train, and the other was an attraction named Engine City, which would be a stationary, hands-on, climb-aboard exhibit of standard-gauge locomotives and cars.

F. Nelson Blount was a major player at Pleasure Island. He was on the board of directors, supplied and operated the excursion train, and also set up Engine City.

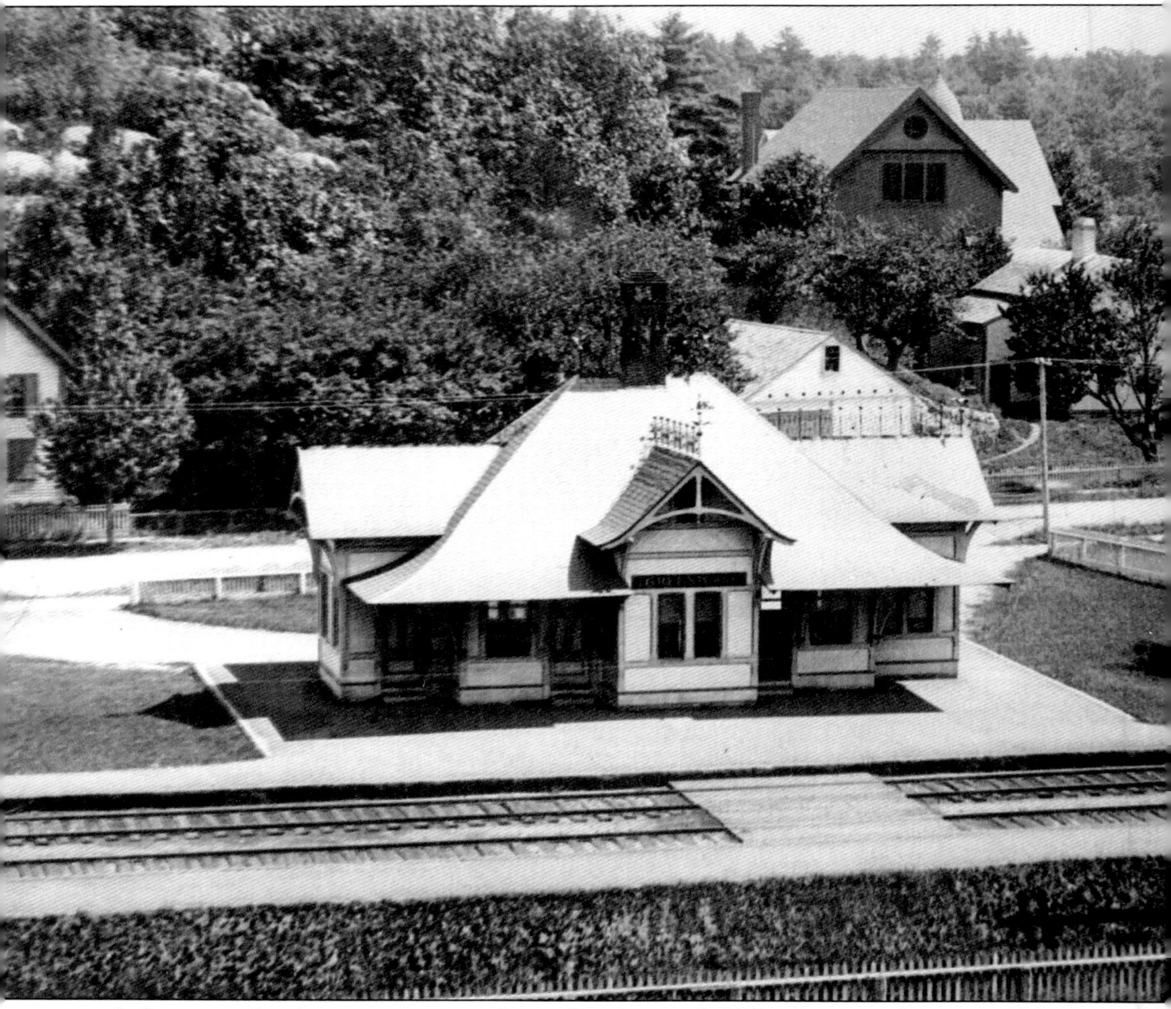

Information for this caption comes from a brochure titled *The Greenwood Station 1885–1971 by the Savings Bank of Wakefield.* The station was dedicated on July 6, 1885. For an unusual reason, the Greenwood railroad station was one of the best known in the country. In the days when railway station agents wore uniforms with brass buttons, the official button bore the picture of the Greenwood station. There were thousands of such agents, four just in Wakefield's Greenwood. A unique feature of the station was that it was reportedly the only station in the commuting area of any double-tracked railroad in the United States that was located on the side of the outbound tracks. (Courtesy of FOPI archives.)

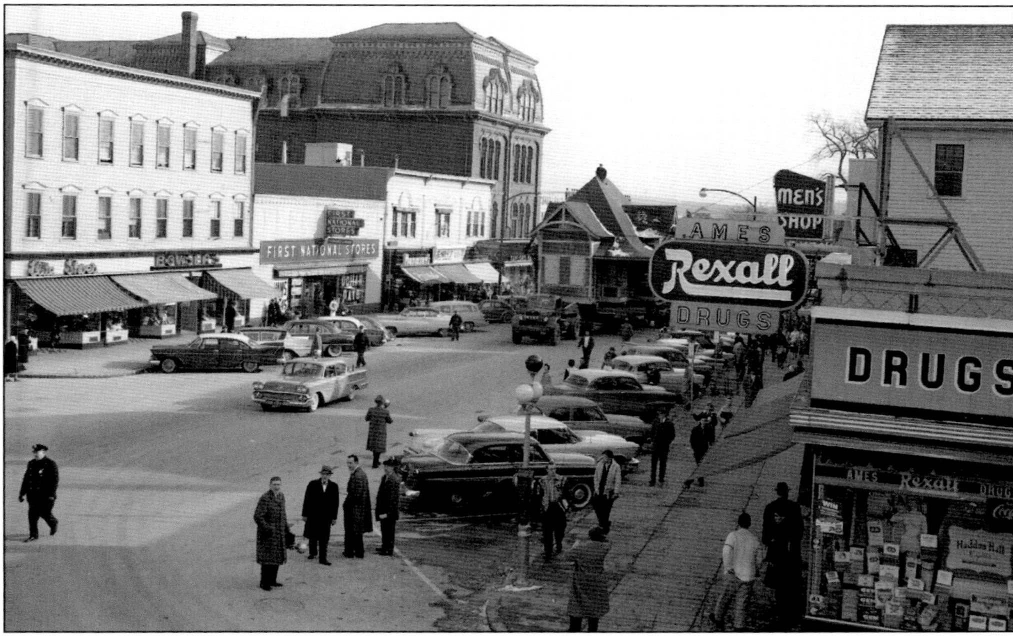

With former lineman James Scott from the Wakefield Municipal Light Department riding topside, the Greenwood station makes its way through downtown Wakefield. With information from the Boston and Maine Railroad Historical Society, here is a time line of the station's trip to Pleasure Island: On Tuesday, January 27, 1959, the station was moved off its foundation. On Wednesday, it was placed on a flatbed. On Thursday, the trip started from Greenwood through downtown Wakefield to the north end of Lake Quannapowitt. On Friday, it was moved along Route 128. On Sunday, February 1, 1959, the station arrived at Pleasure Island. One can only imagine that Sergeant O'Malley had something to do with getting a parked train station off the side of Route 128 on a weekend. (Courtesy of Bourdon Studios.)

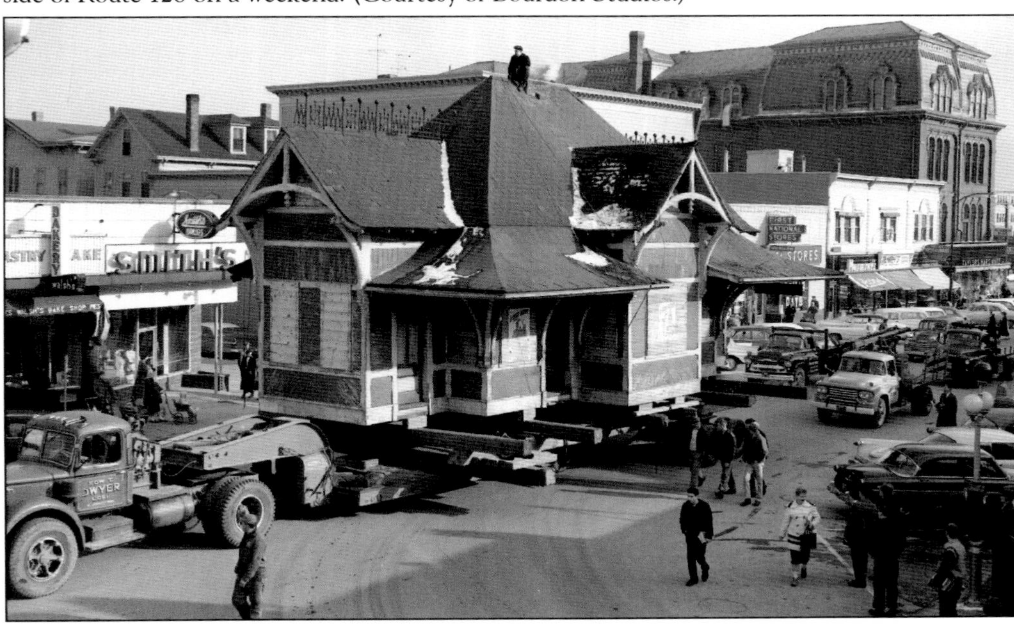

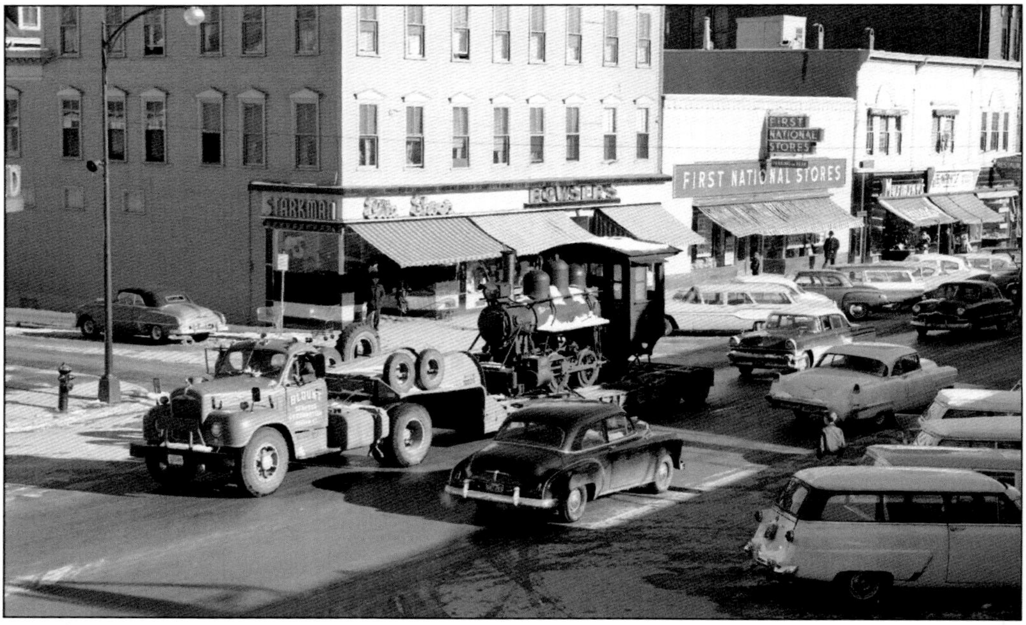

Less than a month after the Greenwood station cruised through downtown Wakefield, engine No. 6 was just behind, heading to Pleasure Island on Main Street on February 15, 1959. This was the first train engine brought to Pleasure Island for the Engine City attraction. A story from the *Wakefield Daily Item* dated February 26, 1959, explains the engine's past history: "The locomotive is a Davenport 2-6-0 narrow gauge engine and used as recently as last summer to haul sugar cane from the fields at Reserve, Louisiana. The designation 2-6-0 means that the engine has two pilot wheels and six drive wheels. Experts guess that the engine was built around the turn of the century." (Courtesy of Bourdon Studios.)

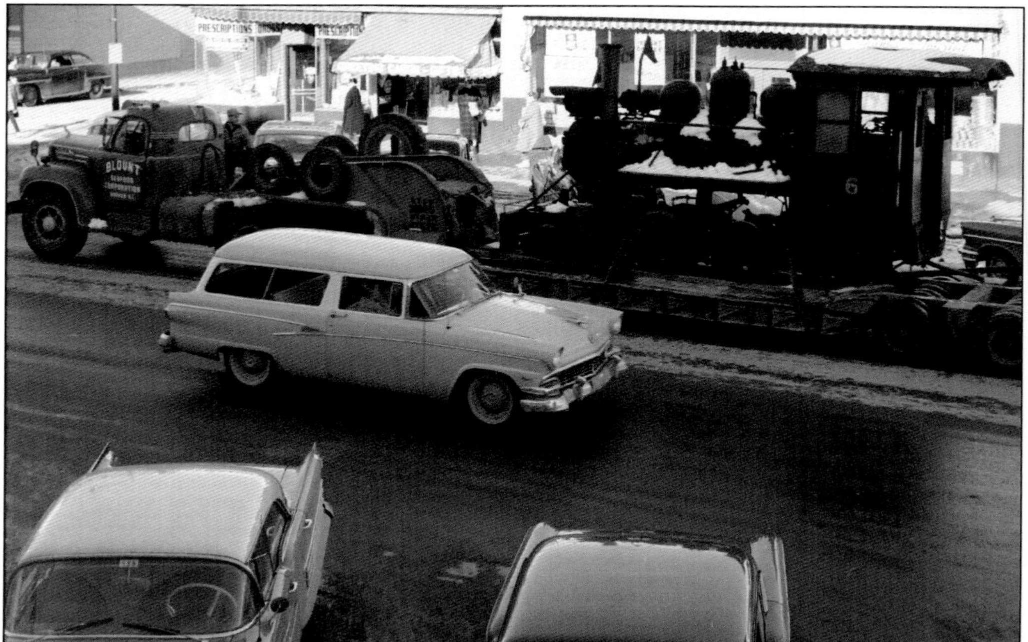

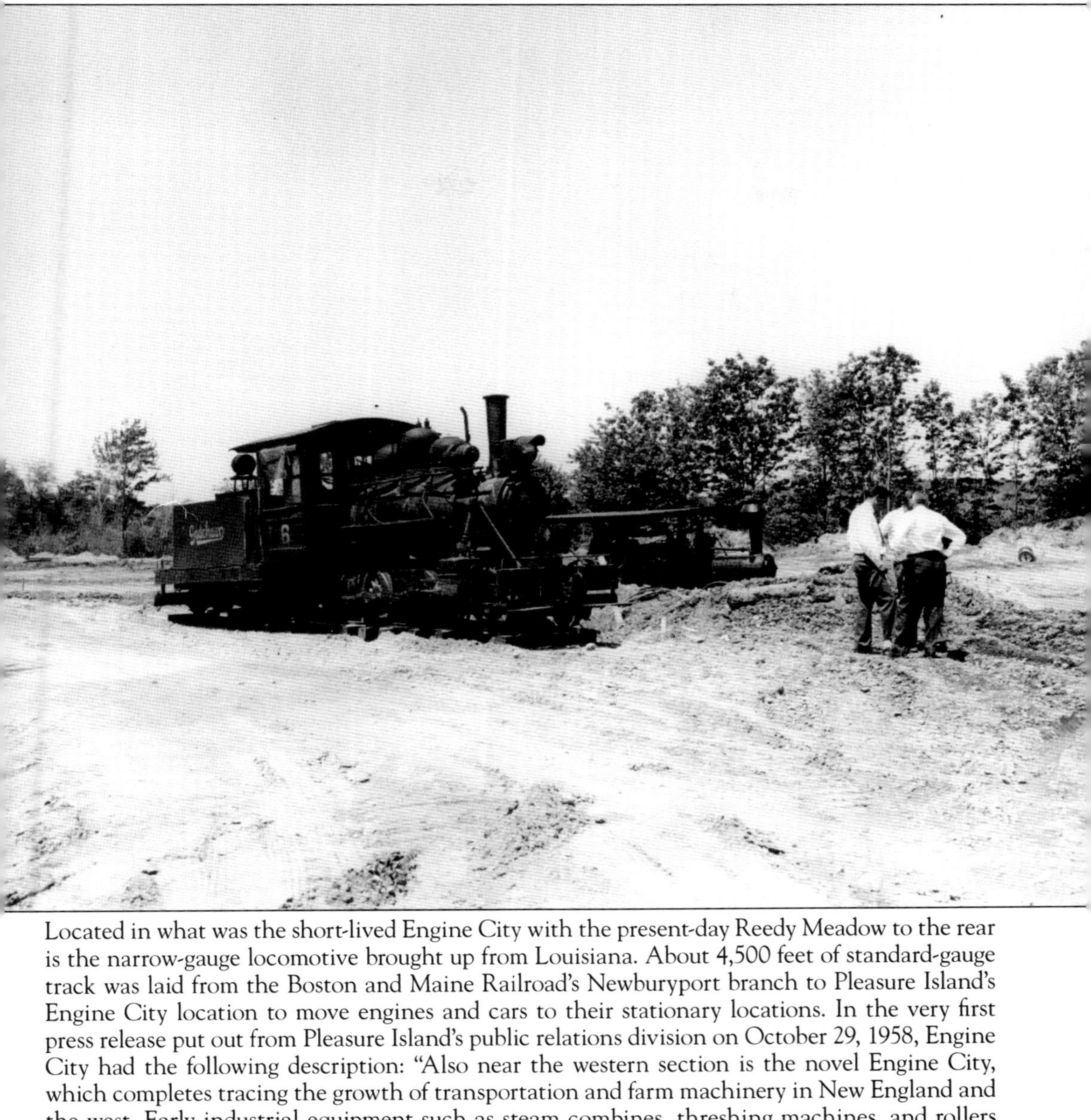

Located in what was the short-lived Engine City with the present-day Reedy Meadow to the rear is the narrow-gauge locomotive brought up from Louisiana. About 4,500 feet of standard-gauge track was laid from the Boston and Maine Railroad's Newburyport branch to Pleasure Island's Engine City location to move engines and cars to their stationary locations. In the very first press release put out from Pleasure Island's public relations division on October 29, 1958, Engine City had the following description: "Also near the western section is the novel Engine City, which completes tracing the growth of transportation and farm machinery in New England and the west. Early industrial equipment such as steam combines, threshing machines, and rollers will be on display." Most of the equipment did not materialize, but the trains certainly did. (Courtesy of FOPI archives.)

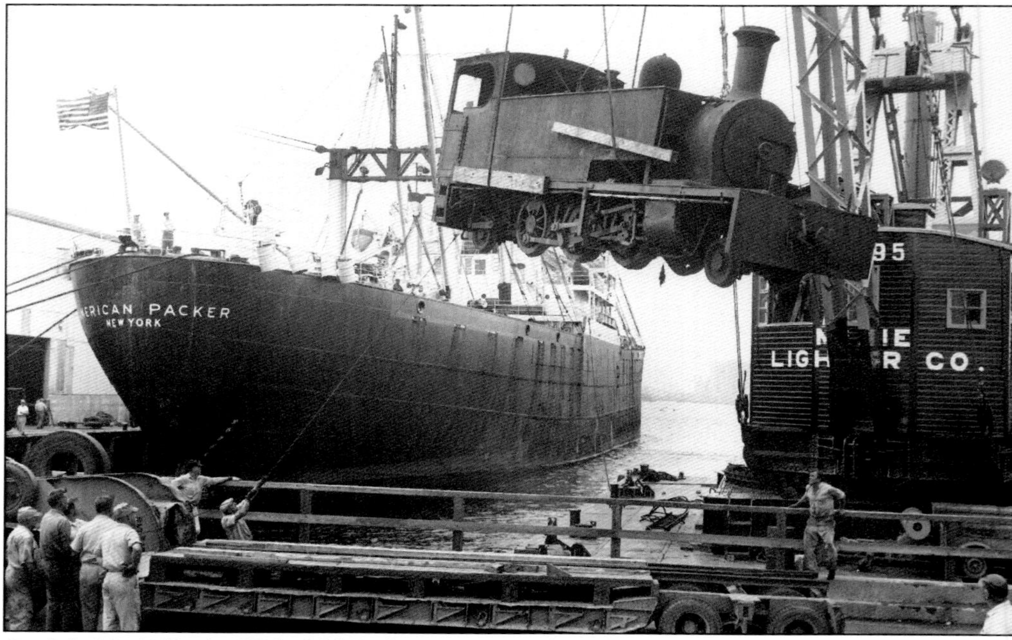

On July 23, 1959, the *Wakefield Daily Item* reported, "A bit of Ireland has been transplanted to Pleasure Island's Engine City, the 'Lady Edith,' a 72 year old steam locomotive and a tiny 50 year old passenger coach. This equipment is owned by the Lady Edith Society, a group of American and Irish men, including writers, bankers and businessmen, who collect and preserve ancient railroad engines and cars for exhibition. The locomotive was originally constructed by Robert Stevenson and Company of New Castle-on-Tyne in England for the Cavan and Leitrim Railway in Ireland. The passenger car was built for the famous Tralee and Dingle Light Railway in county Kerry. Both pieces of equipment were loaned to Pleasure Island's Engine City." (Above, courtesy of House of Photography; below, courtesy of Bourdon Studios.)

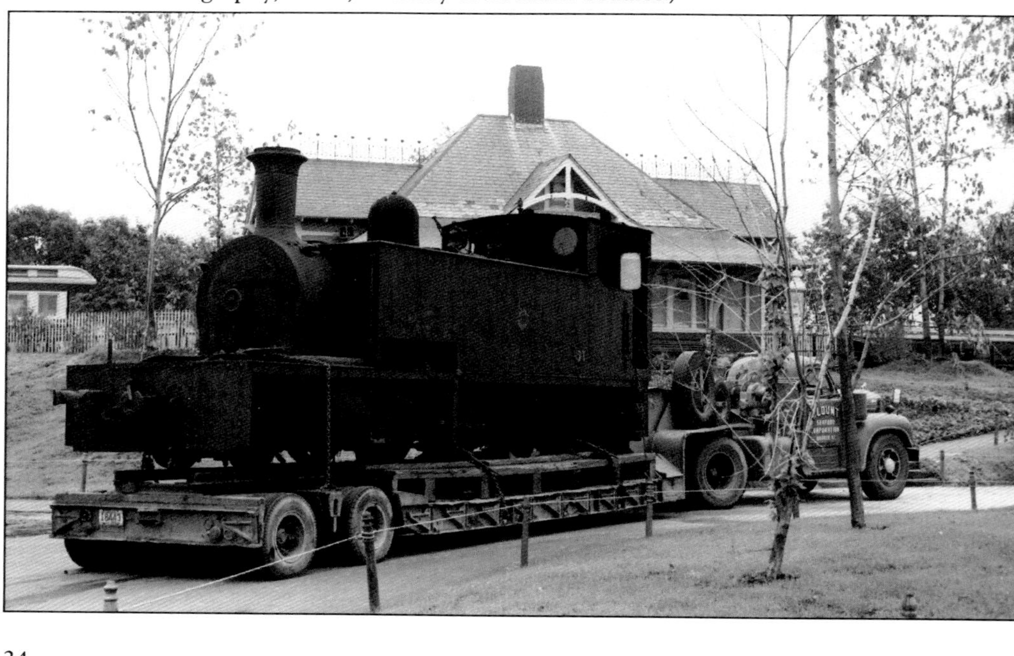

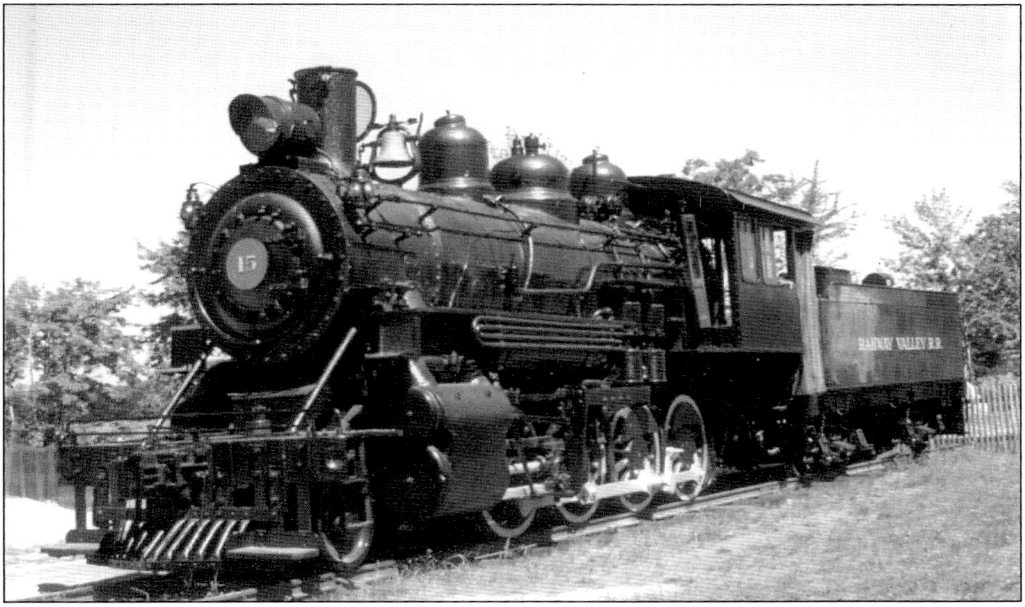

Baldwin Locomotive Works delivered this engine, a 2-8-0 consolidation-type locomotive, to the Oneida and Western Railroad in 1916. In 1937, the engine was sold to the Rahway Valley Railroad for use on its New Jersey short line. Last used in service in 1953, the Rahway Valley No. 15 is shown above at Engine City on August 26, 1960. (Photograph by Harold W. Boothroyd; courtesy of Walker Transportation Collection, Beverly Historical Society.)

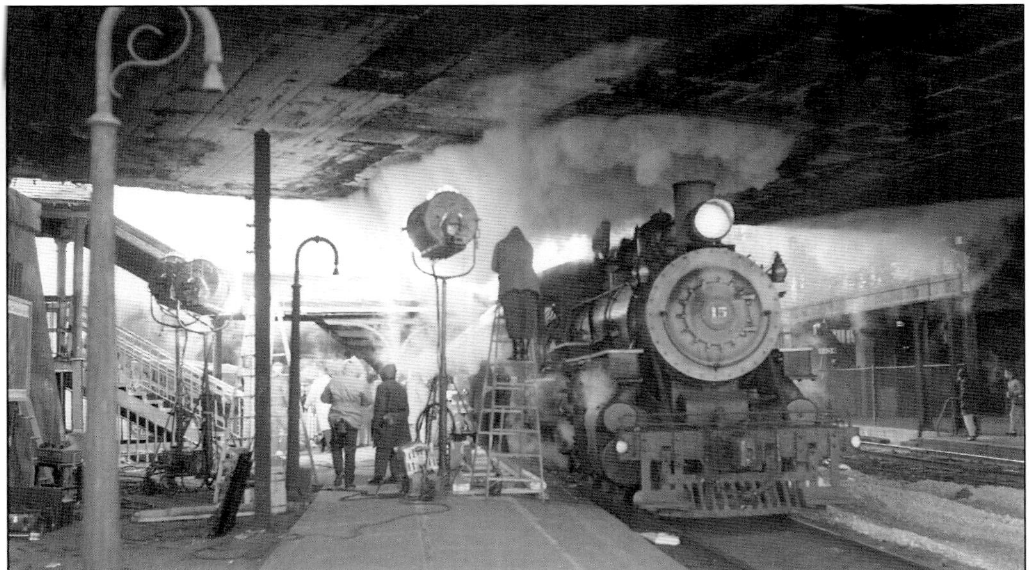

Word got out, so Richard W. Symmes, a local train buff and historian, along with some buddies, were on hand to watch *The Cardinal* being filmed. This scene was shot at Trinity Place station in Boston on February 16, 1963. The Massachusetts Turnpike is on this site today. Rahway Valley Railroad No. 15 traveled down from Steamtown USA in Bellows Falls, Vermont, to share credits in Otto Preminger's film. (Photograph by Russell F. Munroe; courtesy of Walker Transportation Collection, Beverly Historical Society.)

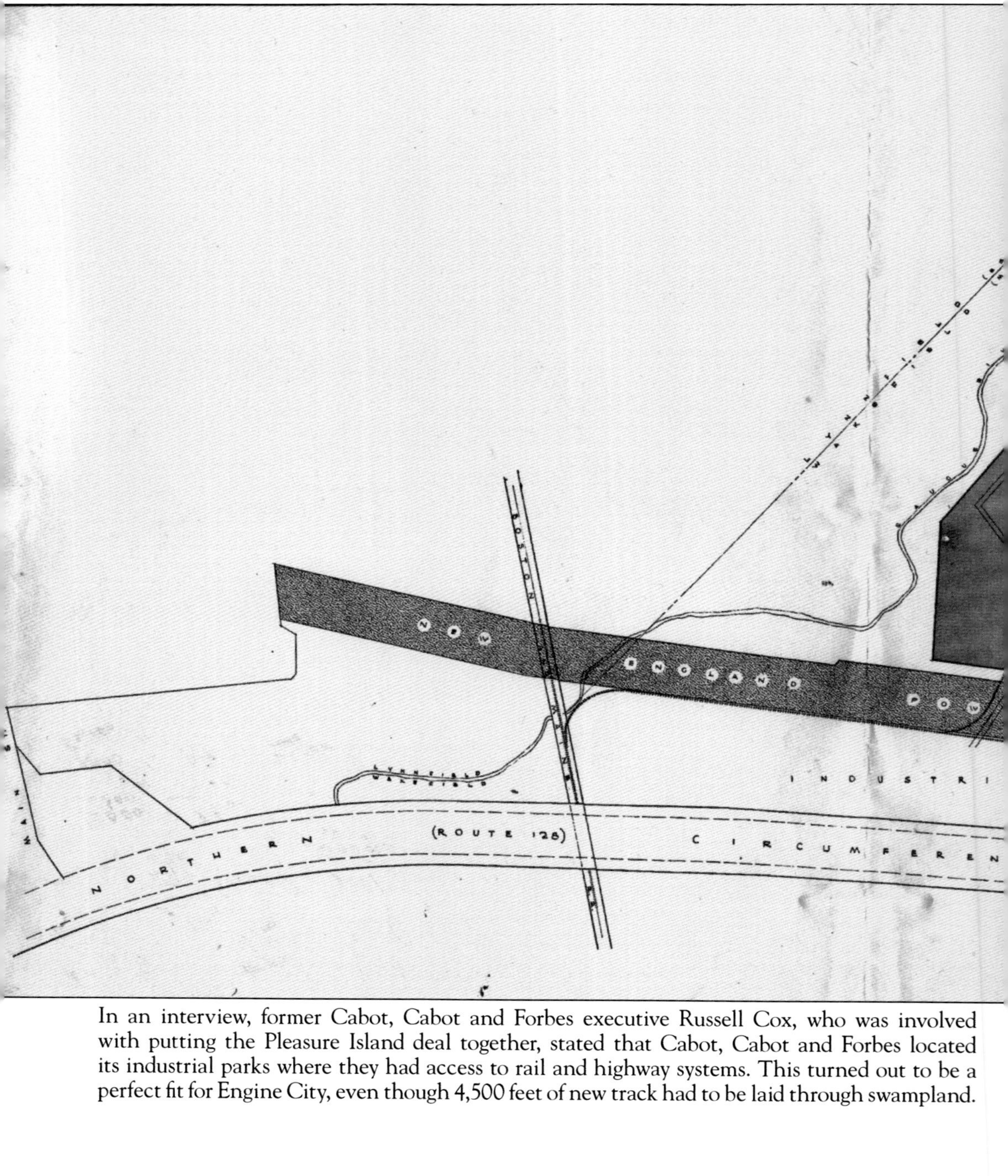

In an interview, former Cabot, Cabot and Forbes executive Russell Cox, who was involved with putting the Pleasure Island deal together, stated that Cabot, Cabot and Forbes located its industrial parks where they had access to rail and highway systems. This turned out to be a perfect fit for Engine City, even though 4,500 feet of new track had to be laid through swampland.

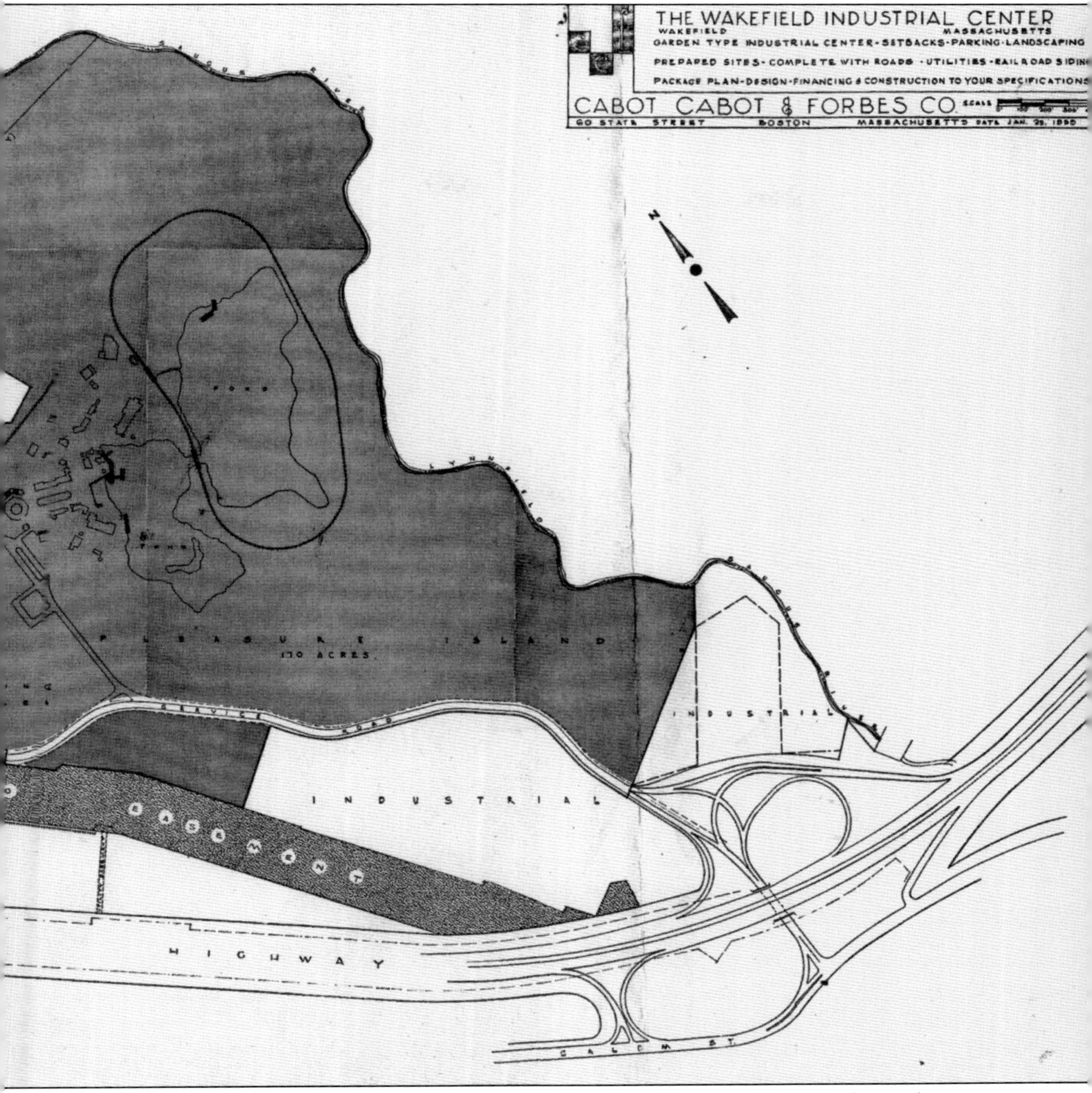

This Pleasure Island layout by Cabot, Cabot and Forbes, dated January 29, 1959, shows the route of the spur line from the Boston and Maine Railroad line to Engine City at the end. Also shown is the narrow-gauge layout minus the siding section. The tracks along the New England Power Company easement are still visible today. (Courtesy of FOPI archives.)

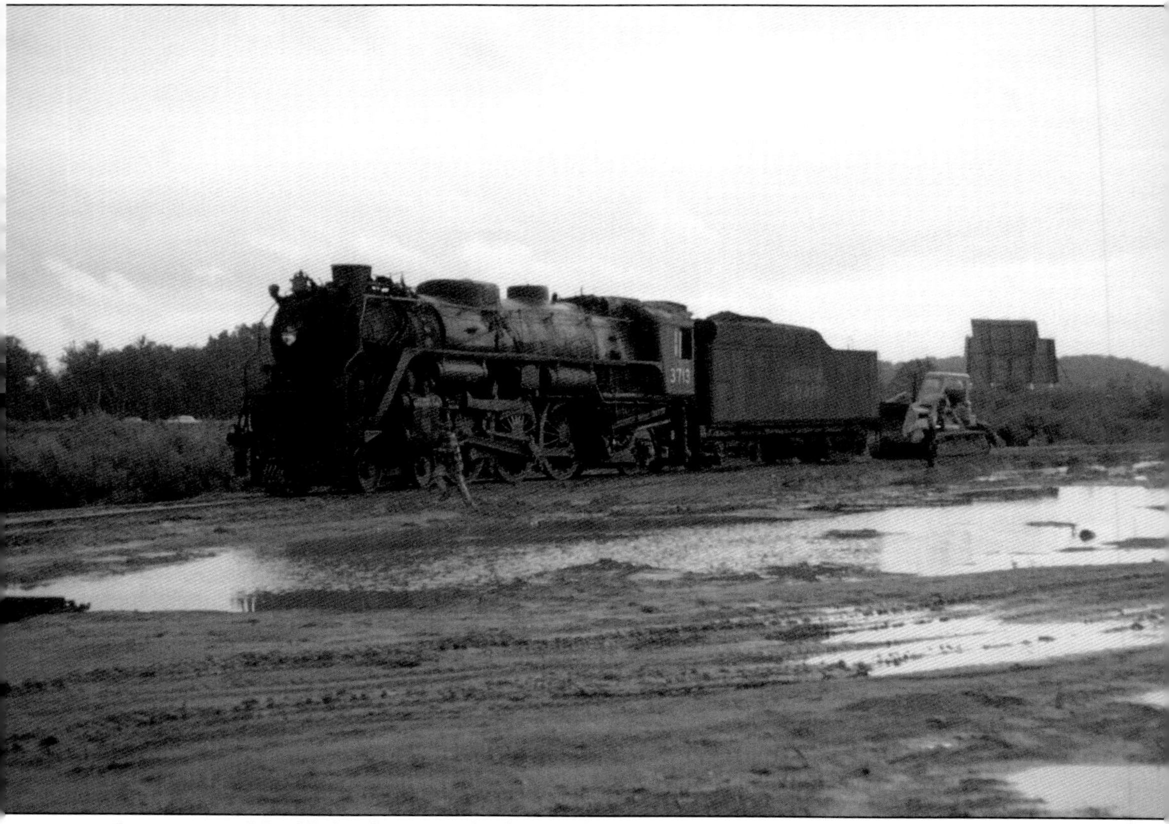

Locomotive No. 3713 is being pushed toward Engine City. The Pleasure Island billboard is to the right, facing Route 128. Patrick McKnight is the historian for Steamtown National Historic Site in Scranton, Pennsylvania. He has written an in-depth developmental history of the Boston and Maine Railroad's locomotive No. 3713. The following is a summary of his report: The No. 3713 was purchased from Boston and Maine Railroad by F. Nelson Blount (owner of the Edaville Railroad) on June 11, 1958. Reportedly, the purchase price was $1. By the summer of 1959, it was on display at Engine City in Pleasure Island. On December 16, 1961, it was moved to North Walpole, New Hampshire. By 1964, it went to Blount's Steamtown USA in Bellows Falls, Vermont. The next stop was the front lawn of Boston's Museum of Science on October 16, 1969. By February 1985, the No. 3713 went to Scranton, the new home of Steamtown, which eventually became a national historic site. (Courtesy of FOPI archives.)

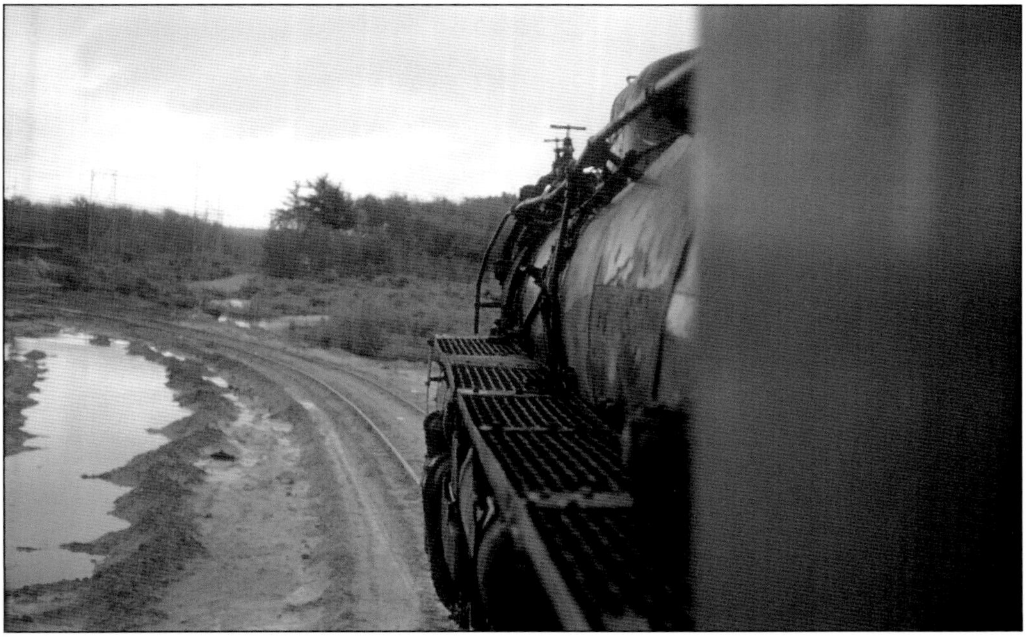

With above-normal rainfall and construction work behind schedule, locomotive No. 3713 is heading to its next stop, Engine City at Pleasure Island. Sold to Blount, it was the last steam engine owned by the Boston and Maine Railroad, according to train historian Richard W. Symmes. (Courtesy of FOPI archives.)

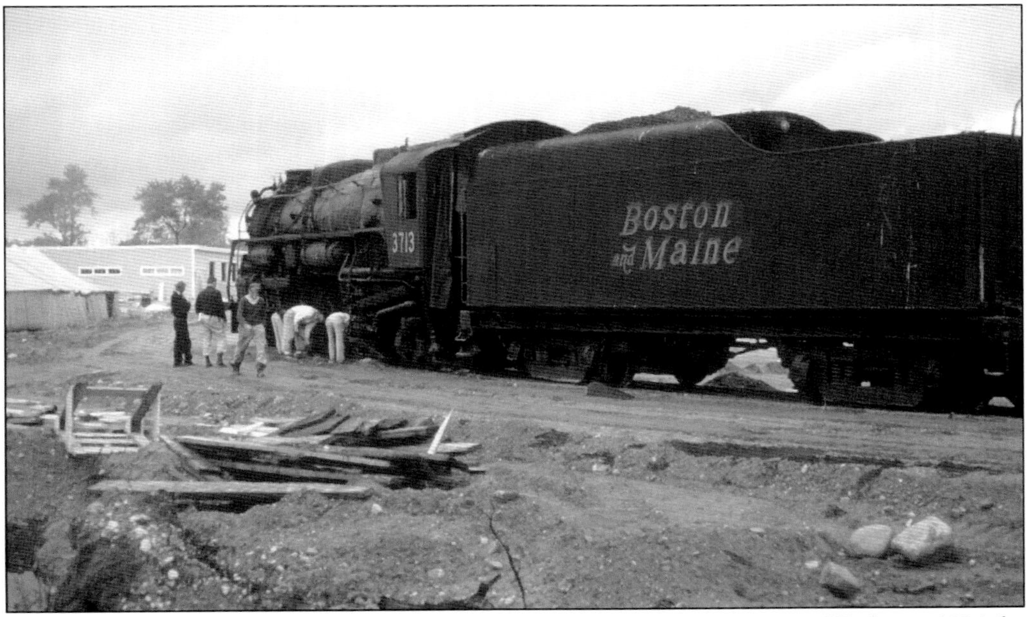

Locomotive No. 3713 was a 4-6-2 Pacific type built by Lima Locomotive Works in 1934 for the Boston and Maine Railroad. It weighed 250 tons in working order. According to Symmes, No. 3713 is one of the largest Pacific-type passenger locomotives built in the United States. To the left is a personnel training tent for new employees and the Pleasure Island maintenance building on the edge of present-day Reedy Meadow. (Courtesy of FOPI archives.)

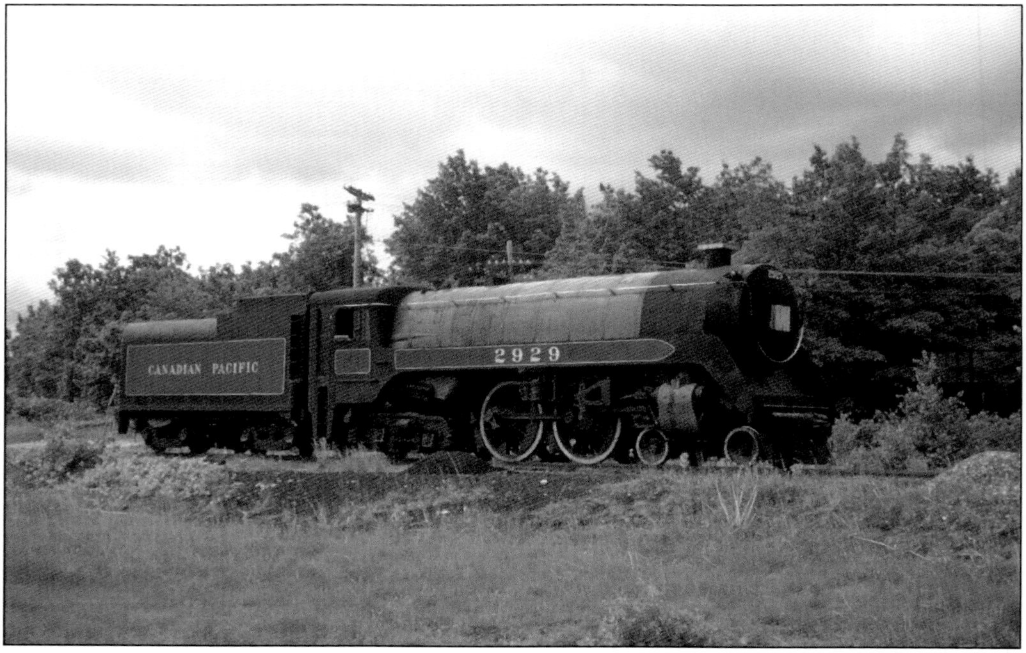

The Canadian Pacific Railway No. 2929 commuter engine was purchased by F. Nelson Blount and brought to Engine City at Pleasure Island. According to train historian Richard W. Symmes, No. 2929 had a rare wheel arrangement of 4-4-4, almost unheard of in North America. It was built in 1936, and its tender carried coal and water. No. 2929 is at an unknown location in the photograph above. The photograph below has it on the spur line heading toward Engine City. (Courtesy of FOPI archives.)

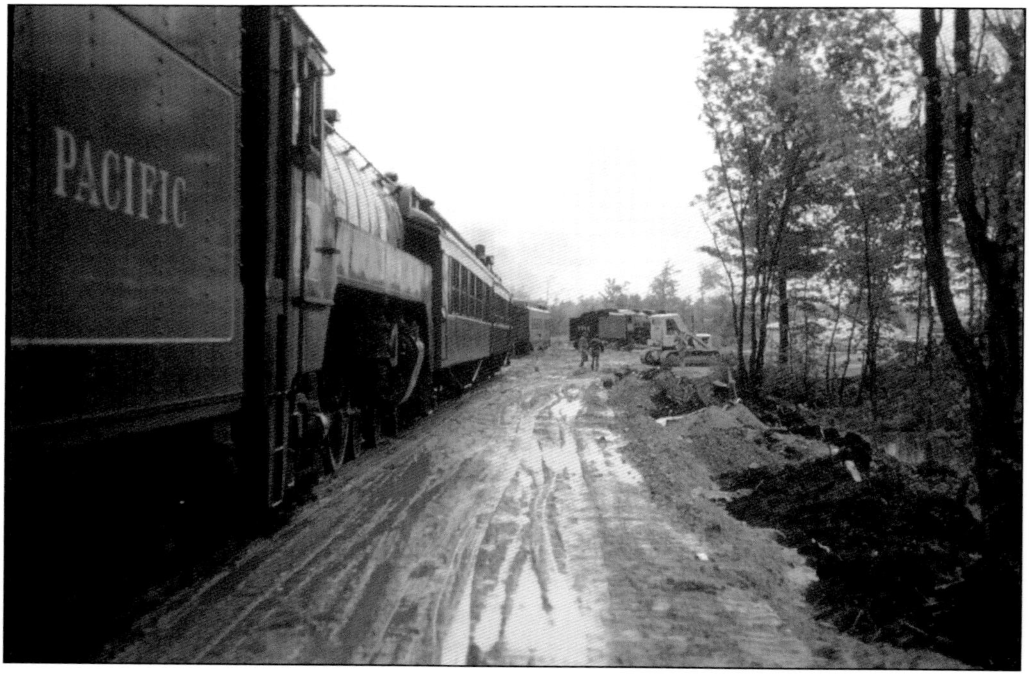

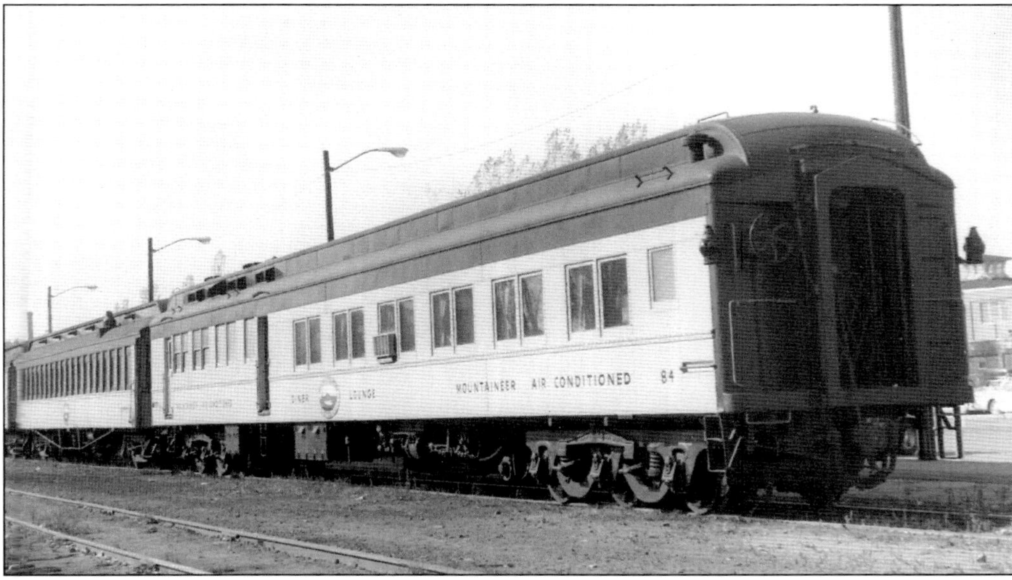

This 1962 photograph is of the former Boston and Maine Railroad diner/lounge car *Mountaineer* on the end of the Monadnock Northern Railroad (Steamtown) excursion train at Keene, New Hampshire. Built in the 1920s, this was the last car of a train with service for just the passengers of the diner/lounge car. This car is currently unrestored and located at the Steamtown National Historic Site in Scranton, Pennsylvania. (Courtesy of Walker Transportation Collection, Beverly Historical Society.)

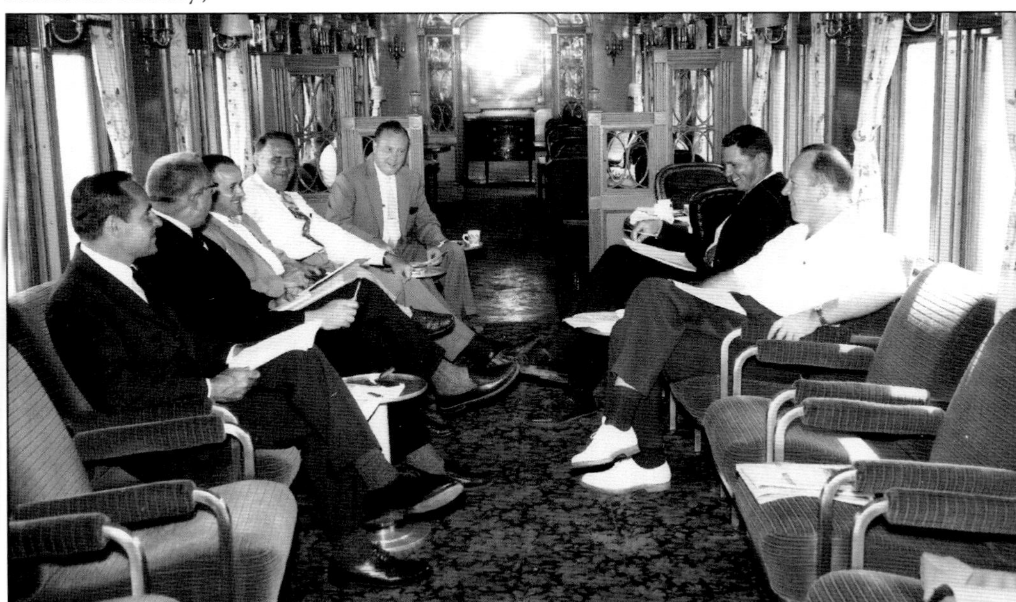

The *Mountaineer* was part of Pleasure Island's Engine City exhibit owned by Blount. From left to right at a 1959 board of directors meeting are members Gerald Blakeley Jr., unidentified, Cabot, Cabot and Forbes treasurer John King (not a board member), F. Nelson Blount, Robert Linnell, Bill Hawkes, and unidentified. Board members Luther Breck Jr. and G. Walter Laborie are probably the two unidentified gentlemen. (Courtesy of Bourdon Studios.)

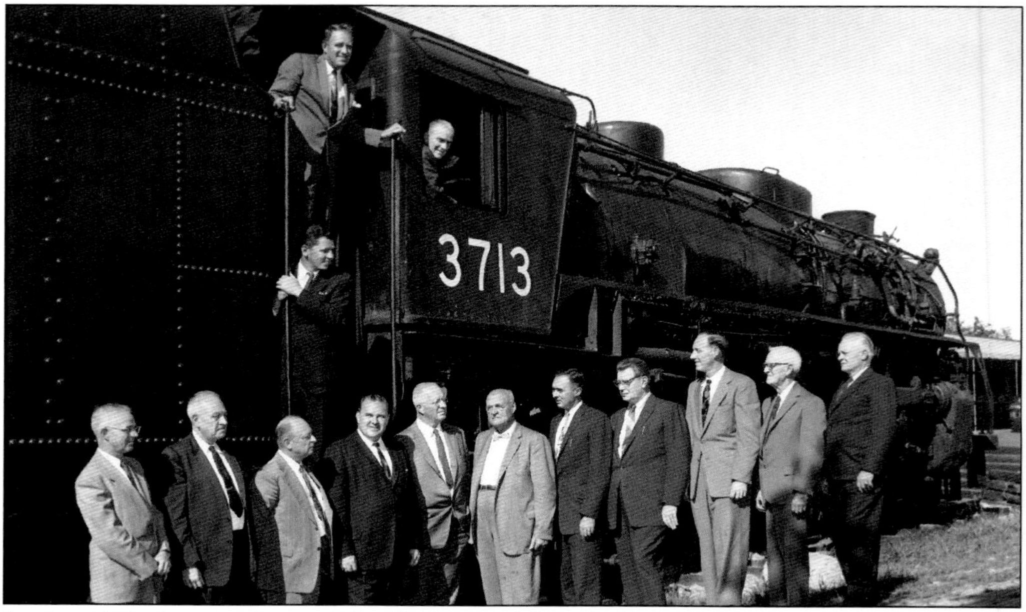

In this 1959 photograph, the Edaville Railroad Board of Directors is in front of No. 3713 at Pleasure Island. In the cab window is president of the Boston and Maine Railroad Patrick B. McGinnis. In the gangway is F. Nelson Blount (top). Below Blount is Bill Hawkes. The fifth man from the right is Fred Richardson, Blount's business partner and general manager of the Edaville Railroad. (Courtesy of Russ Adams Productions.)

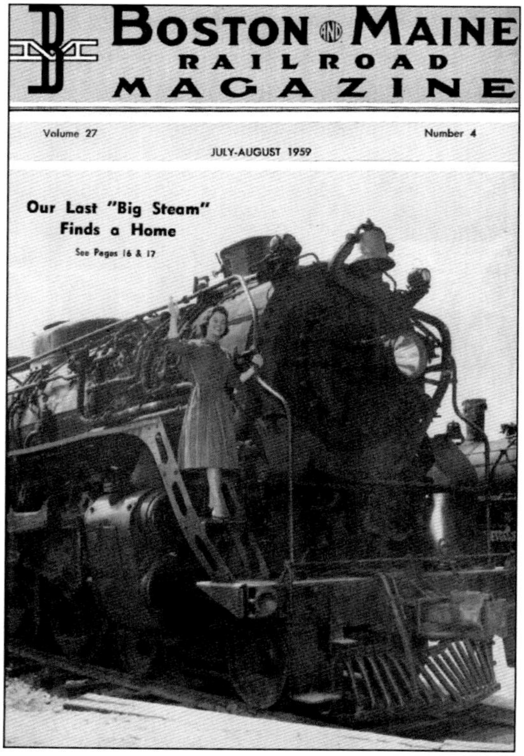

Patricia (Nordling) Rowe Douglass, Miss Massachusetts 1958, is featured on the Boston and Maine Railroad No. 3713. She was Pleasure Island's park hostess for the 1959 season. (Courtesy of FOPI archives.)

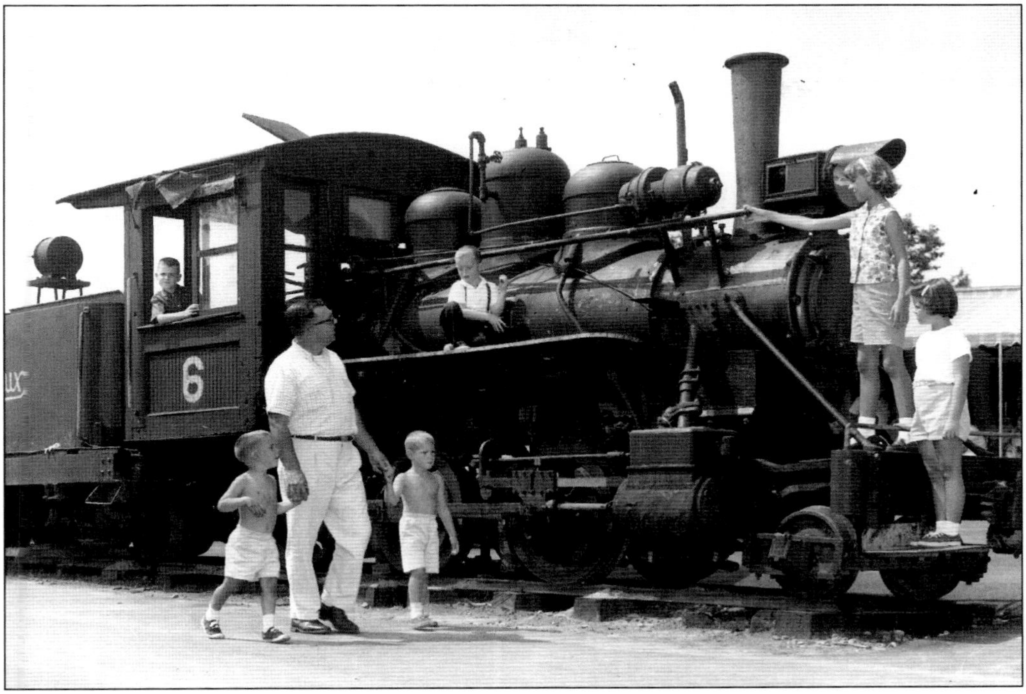

Going back to the conceptual stages of Hawkes's plan to build a family entertainment center, two pieces had to come together for his vision—fun and education. That is what both photographs represent. It must have been fun for kids and grown-ups to be able to climb in and over the trains at Engine City. On December 16, 1961, the locomotives displayed at Engine City started the journey to North Walpole, New Hampshire, thus ending a three-year run of this popular attraction. (Courtesy of Russ Adams Productions.)

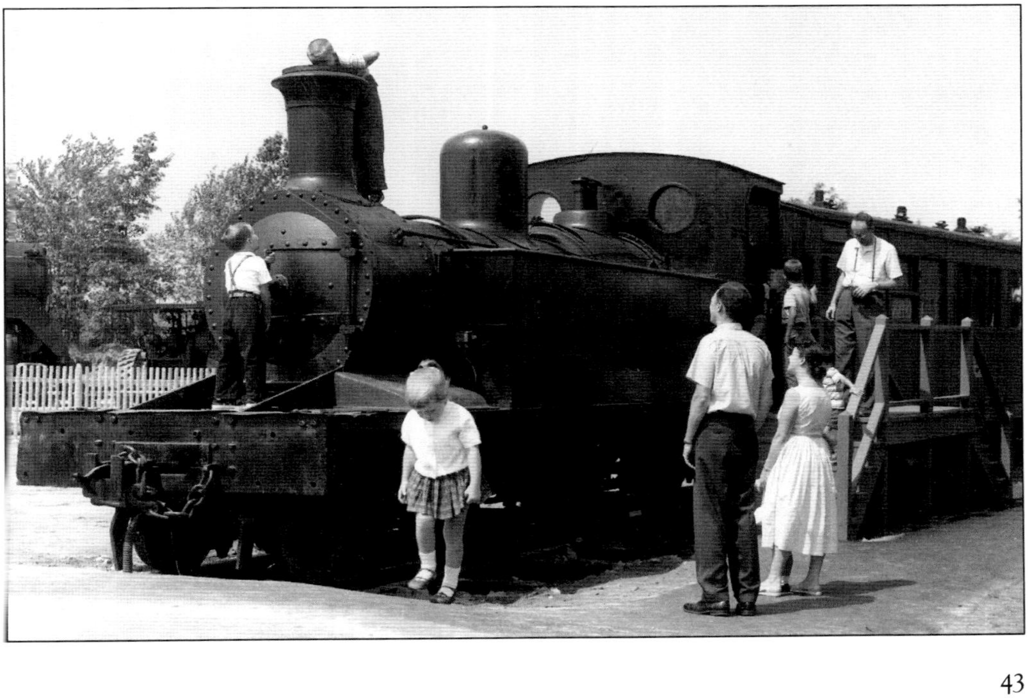

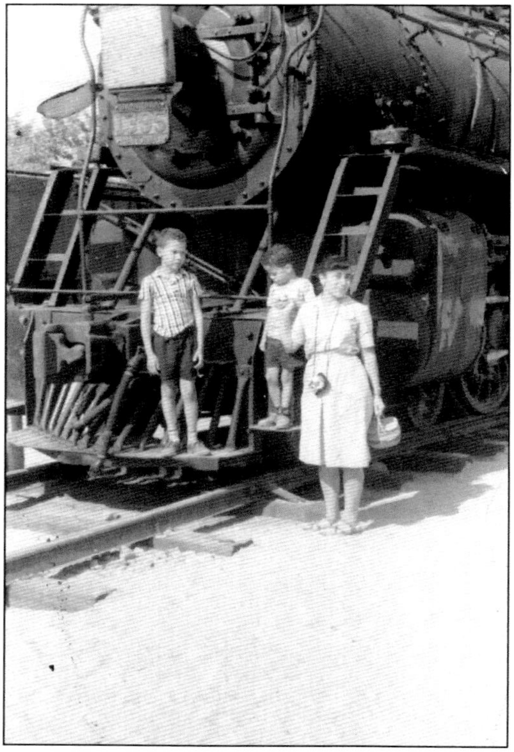

Standing on Canadian National Railway No. 1395, a 4-6-0, are William Kydd III (left), age eight, and Douglas F. Kydd, age five, with their mom, as dad takes this 1959 photograph. Engine City had an everlasting effect on young Douglas. According to him, at age five, he had his very first taste of a lifetime aboard locomotives when he first sat in the Boston and Maine Railroad's No. 3814 engineer's seat. By age 18, he was working in the railroad industry. By age 26, he was an engineer, and he is presently working the Amtrak Acela Boston-to-New York route. (Courtesy of Douglas F. Kydd.)

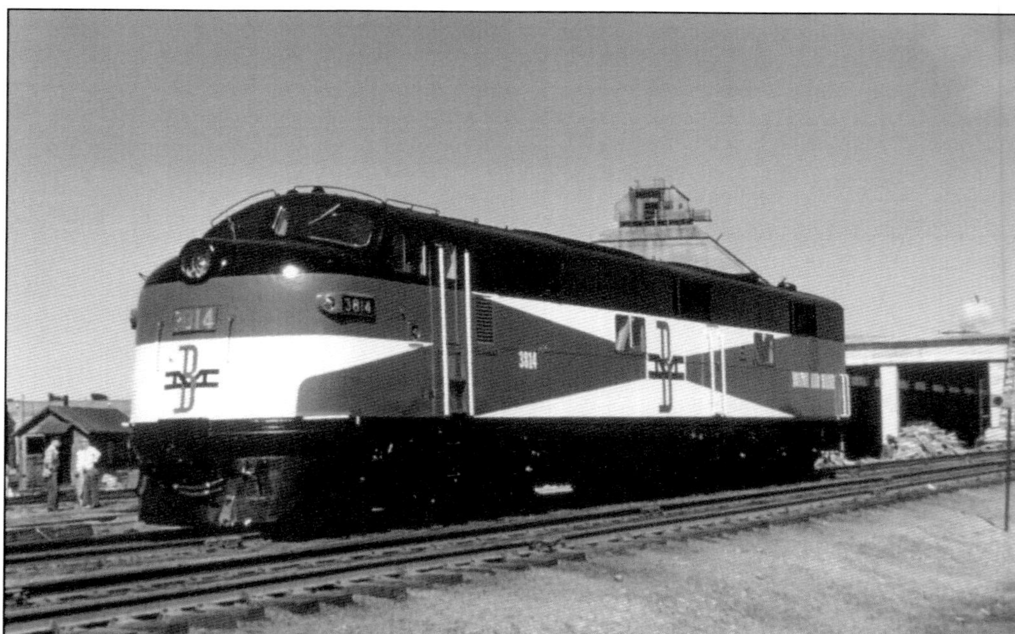

Boston and Maine Railroad No. 3814, an Electro-Motive Corporation model E-7 2,000-horsepower diesel locomotive, was painted in a pattern known as the McGinnis blue, black, and white style. Loaned to Engine City, this post–World War II diesel was sold for scrap by the Boston and Maine in April 1962. (Courtesy of Donald G. Hills.)

Fay Foto Service was hired by Pleasure Island to document construction prior to the park opening. With Old Smoky No. 3 approaching the Goldpan Gulch station on what appears to be a test run, two individuals are below checking the trestle bridge. Below the bridge to the right is the Burro Trail. (Courtesy of Fay Foto Service.)

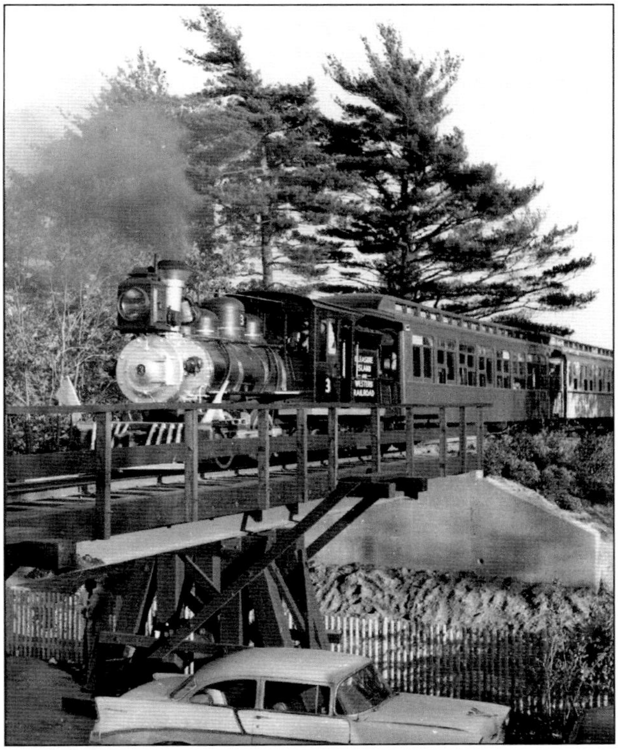

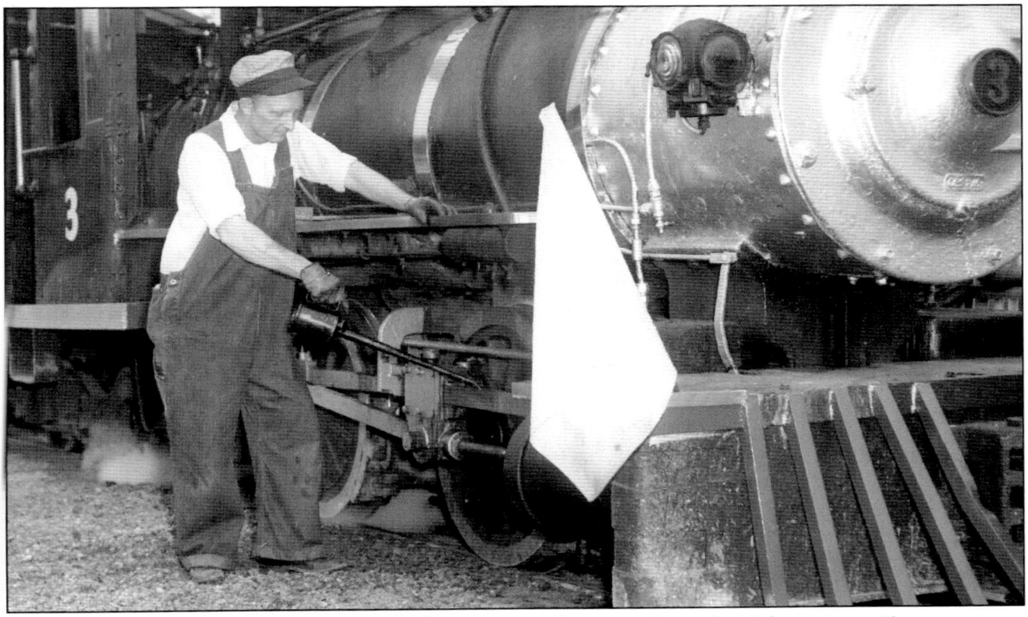

According to Pleasure Island's 1959 public relations division, "Number Three is an 18-ton narrow gauge locomotive built in 1917 by the Vulcan Iron Works. This locomotive is the tank type which carries water and fuel on the same structure and burns either coal or coke. Originally number three was used on the Monson Railroad in Central Maine for daily runs of six miles to and from slate quarries with both freight and passengers." (Courtesy of Russ Adams Productions.)

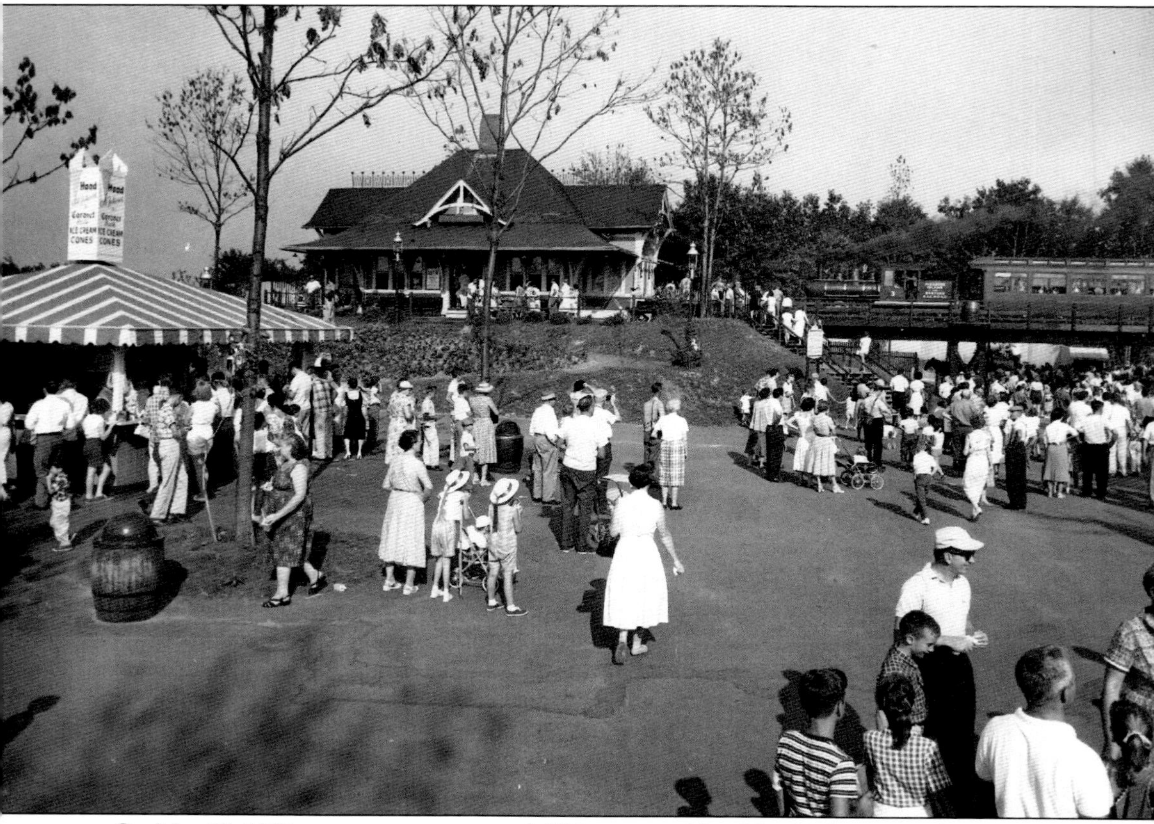

On May 27, 1959, a newspaper reported, "Gloucester, May 26—It's been standing room only for commuters at the Boston and Maine Railroad Station since yesterday. An indication that the commuting business is picking up? No such luck. The answer is much simpler—no benches. Yesterday, workers took out all the benches, loaded them on a truck and took them to Pleasure Island in Wakefield where they would be used for the railroad station. When the Gloucester Station was sold, a clause was inserted for part of the site to be reserved as a waiting station. But apparently it didn't say anything about benches." No. 3 ran only during the 1959 season before being returned to service at the Edaville Railroad in South Carver, Massachusetts. It is currently in Phillips, Maine, at the Sandy River and Rangeley Lakes Railroad. (Courtesy of Russ Adams Productions.)

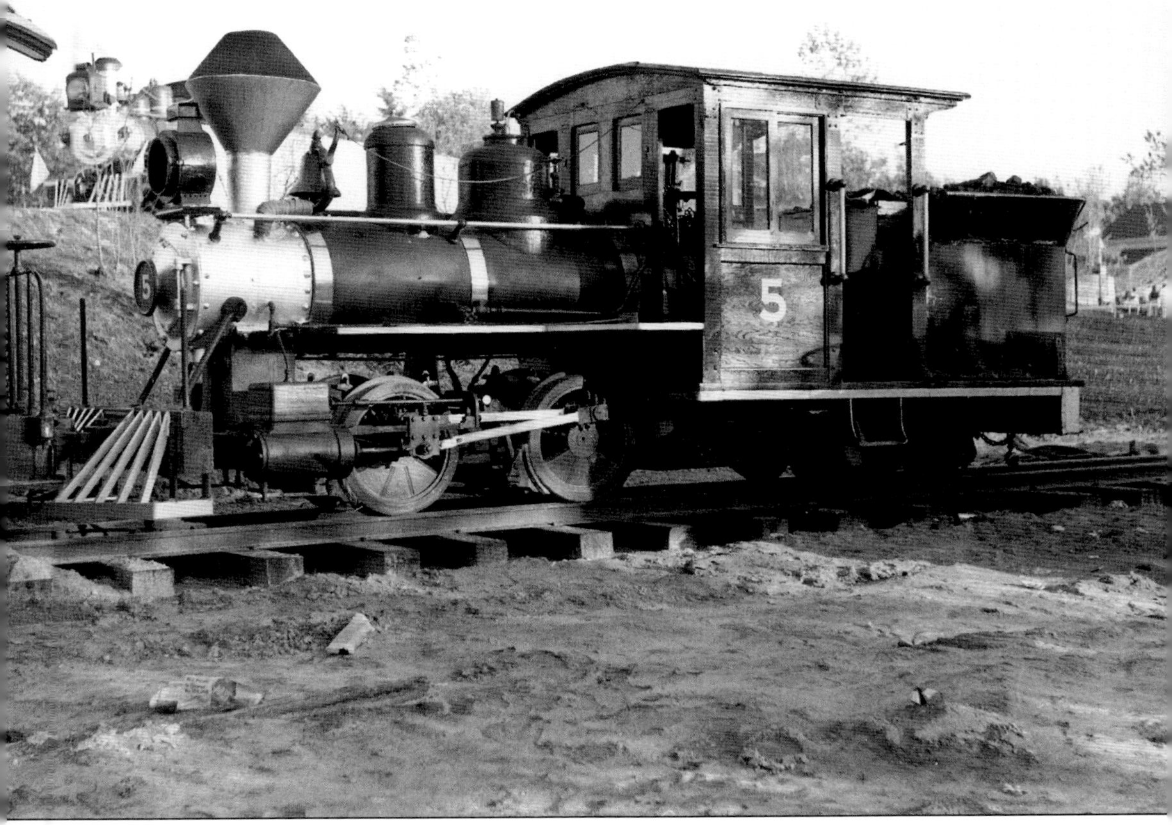

According to Pleasure Island's public relations department, "Number Five was a 12-ton engine which served for many years in the Sugarcane Fields of Louisiana. Originally, Number Five was a 30-gauge model but has been rebuilt to operate on 24 inch gauge tracks." David R. Barnes, No. 5's former engineer at Pleasure Island, wrote a letter about some of his experiences at the park to the Wiscasset, Waterville and Farmington (WW&F) Railway Museum in Alna, Maine. Here is one of his memories: "The Station was atop a 30-foot hill and the track left the station counter clockwise on the loop, and went over a timber trestle. A string of donkeys passed beneath this trestle for the Burro Trail. We had to be careful not to stampede them when our train rumbled over the bridge." No. 5 operated at Pleasure Island from 1960 until the park closed in 1969. (Courtesy of Fay Foto Service.)

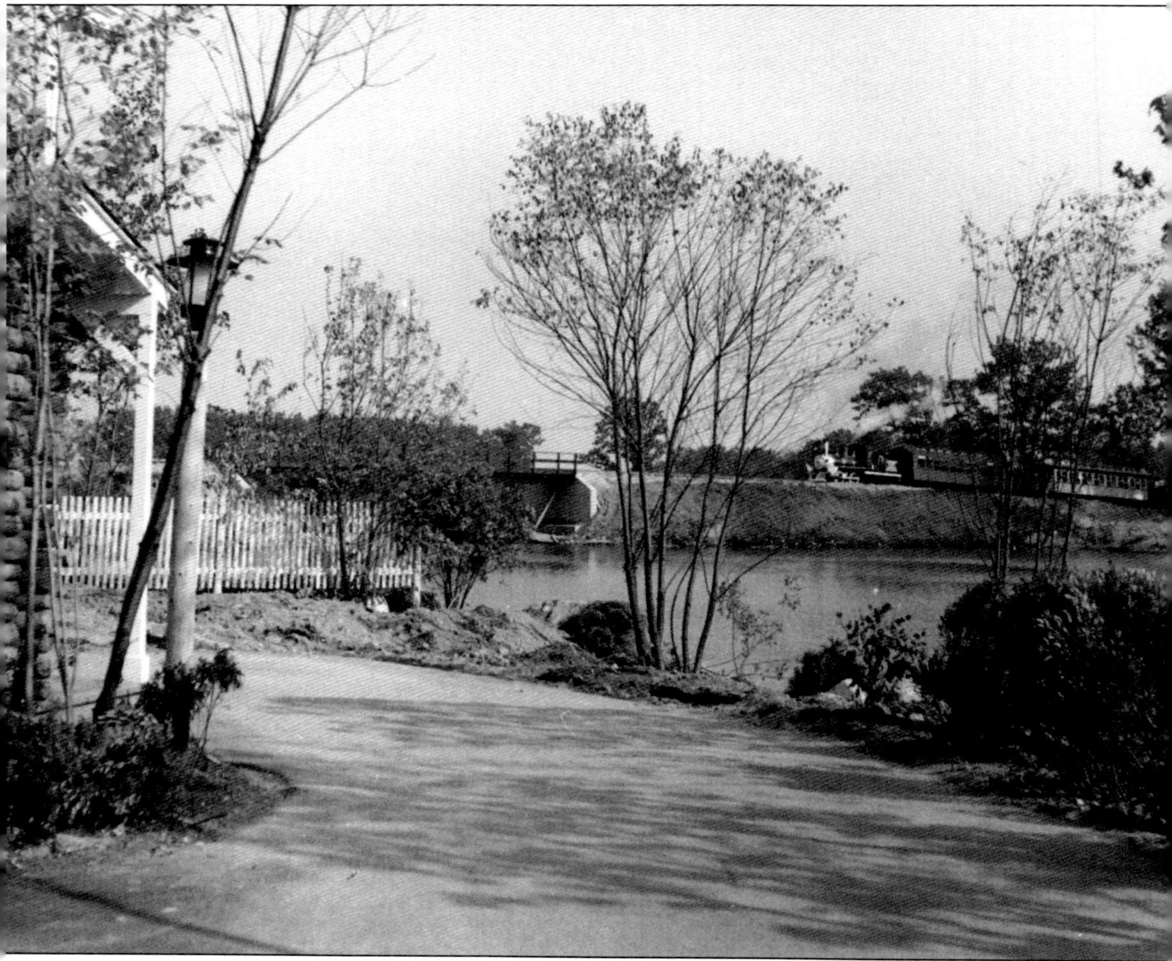

This photograph from 1959 features the No. 3 engine. During some portion of the train ride, bandits on horseback halted the train and attempted to hold up the passengers. However, armed guards overpowered the bad men and saved the day. Several versions of these stunts took place throughout the life of the park, and some were quite dangerous for the actors. The following excerpts are from a letter to the WW&F Railway Museum from former Edaville Railroad employee William Robie: "When I became fireman during my second and third years (1963–1964), I usually arrived around 8:30 AM in order to bring up steam, shovel coal into the tender bunker, bring Number Five around backwards from the storage siding to the depot, fill the tank, and couple to the three-car train, all by the 10:00 AM opening time. By that time, Paul Correa, an Edaville Engineer who commuted from South Carver, had arrived, and after checking things over, we were ready to begin the day's operation." (Courtesy of Fay Foto Service.)

Three

The 1959 Season

At only 37 years old, Bill Hawkes succeeded in realizing his dream to build a family recreation center. At 10:00 a.m. on Monday, June 22, 1959, Pleasure Island opened to the public. On Saturday, June 20, at 2:00 p.m., approximately 4,500 invited guests and members of the press, radio, and television got a special preview of the park. The following day at 2:00 p.m., there was a special benefit premiere with all proceeds going to the Boys Club of Boston. Tickets for this event were $25 for adults and $5 for children. According to a front-page story in the local newspaper the following day, 2,000 people attended the charity premiere. "Pleasure Island officials estimated that 13,000 people were turned away from the park yesterday afternoon. A mix-up in radio and television releases had the park open to the public Sunday instead of today, June 22." A dozen Hollywood and television stars were on hand for the two-day occasion, signing autographs and talking with patrons. Built at a cost of nearly $4 million (in 1958–1959 dollars), Pleasure Island was a first-class operation. A personal-training expert was brought in by Marco Engineering. He set up a training program for the reportedly 400 new employees.

On opening day, 5,000 people visited Pleasure Island. Admission was $1 for adults and 50¢ for children. Individual tickets for the attractions were priced separately. The Diamond Lil Show was free, as was parking. Park hours were 10:00 a.m. until 8:00 p.m., Monday through Saturday, and 1:00 p.m. to 8:00 p.m. on Sundays. By August, extended hours to 10:00 p.m. were approved by the board of selectmen, although the train whistle and bell and the shooting in the western section would not be permitted after 8:00 p.m.

In a study done before Pleasure Island was constructed, 750,000 guests were projected for the first season. According to an interview with Bill Hawkes, only about half of that number went through the turnstiles. In the Northeast, 1959 was the wettest year since 1927, which had a negative effect on the outdoor entertainment industry. Pleasure Island suffered by not reaching the attendance numbers the exhibitors, like H. P. Hood and Sons and Pepsi-Cola, had expected.

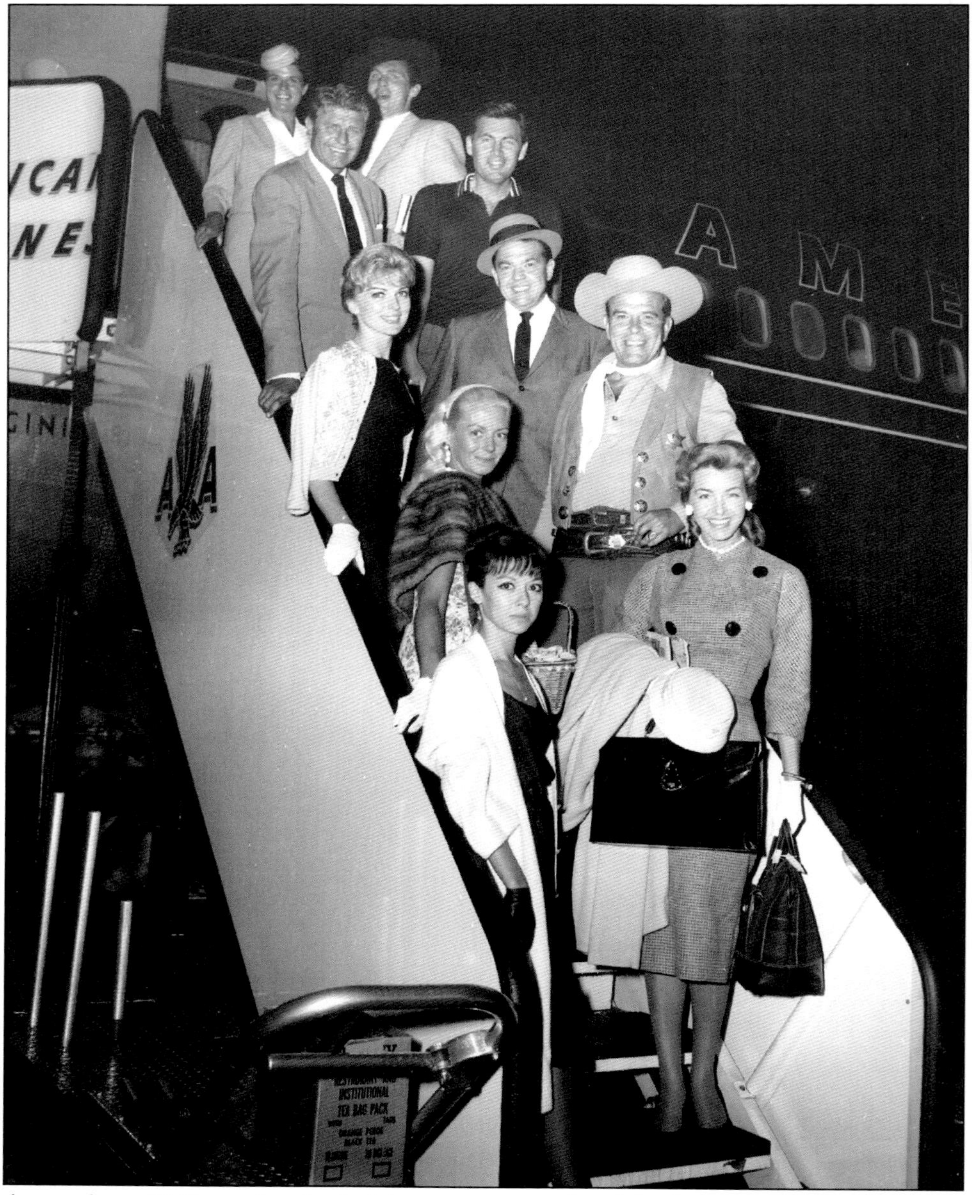

At least a dozen Hollywood and television stars were on hand for the two-day preopening events at Pleasure Island. They signed autographs and talked with patrons, according to local news accounts. This author had the opportunity to interview Fess Parker (pictured on the right, second from top) in 2007 at his office in Los Olivos, California. Parker remembered his weekend at Pleasure Island, which included a party for the stars at a local state senator's home. Also in this photograph are Marvin Miller (just below Parker) from the television show *The Millionaire* and Rita Moreno (bottom left). Moreno was one of the very few and very first performers to win an Oscar, an Emmy, a Tony, and a Grammy. She was 27 years old in this photograph. By 1961, she had won an Oscar for best supporting actress in *West Side Story*. Other stars, according to the *Boston Herald* and the *Wakefield Daily Item*, attending were Will Rogers Jr., Doug Kennedy, Pat Conway, Leo Carrillo, Marsha Hunt, and others. (Courtesy of FOPI archives.)

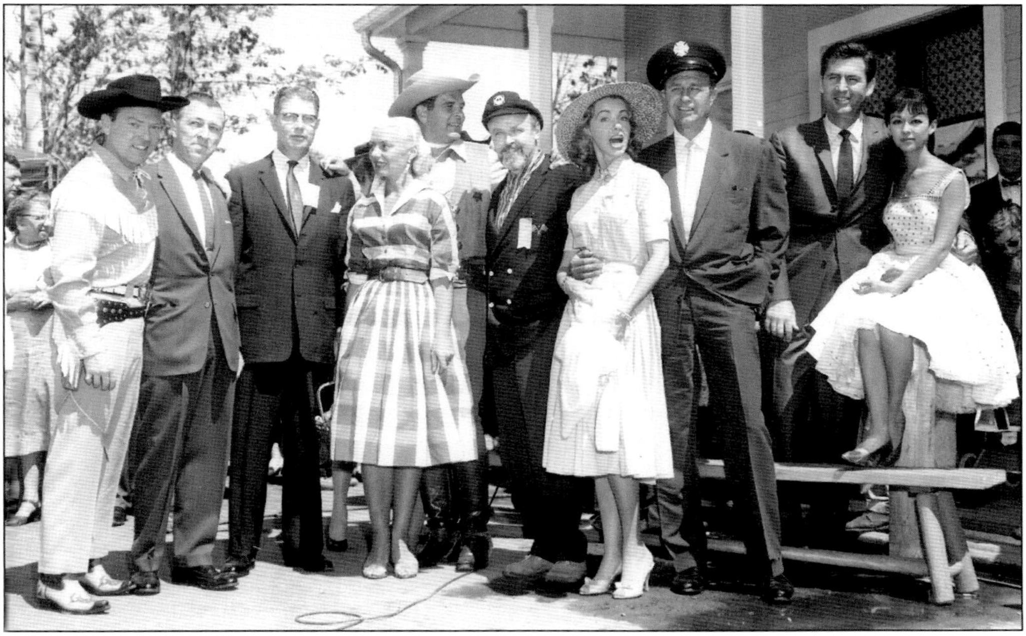

Among the stars in front of the Diamond Lil Saloon is Robert Cottle (sixth from the left). He was Boston's "Captain Bob." One of his first shows, *The Nature World of Captain Bob*, began in Hartford, Connecticut. Later in 1953, the show moved to Boston, where it ran for another 14 years. Cottle died in 1999 in San Mateo, California. (Courtesy of FOPI archives.)

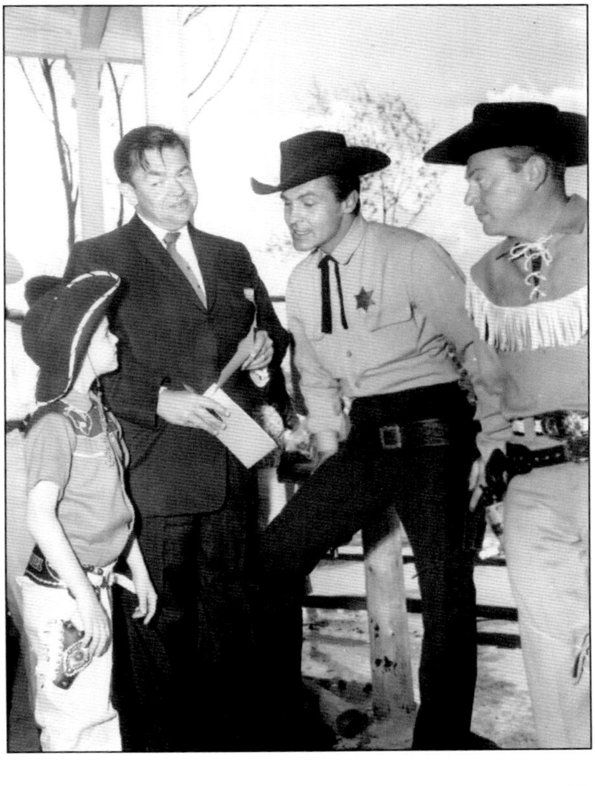

Outside Pleasure Island's Diamond Lil Saloon are Miller (left) and Champ Butler (right). Notice that Miller is handing out checks. His character's name was Michael Anthony, the executive secretary to the mysterious billionaire John Beresford Tipton, on *The Millionaire*. Each episode of the series, which first aired in 1955, began with Miller's character giving a $1 million check to a startled recipient. Miller died in 1985 at the age of 71. (Courtesy of FOPI archives.)

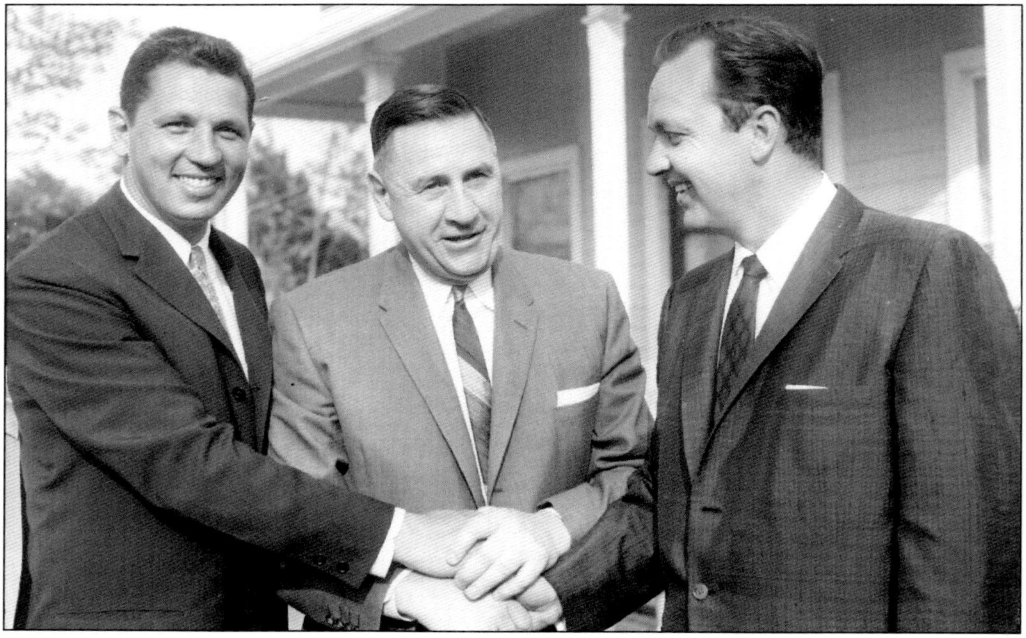

Bill Hawkes (left) and C. V. Wood (right) are shaking hands with Massachusetts governor Foster Furcolo. This photograph was taken at the charity premiere held on June 21, 1959. Furcolo was elected governor of Massachusetts in 1956 and reelected in 1958, serving from 1957 to 1961. He died on July 5, 1999, at the age of 83. (Courtesy of FOPI archives.)

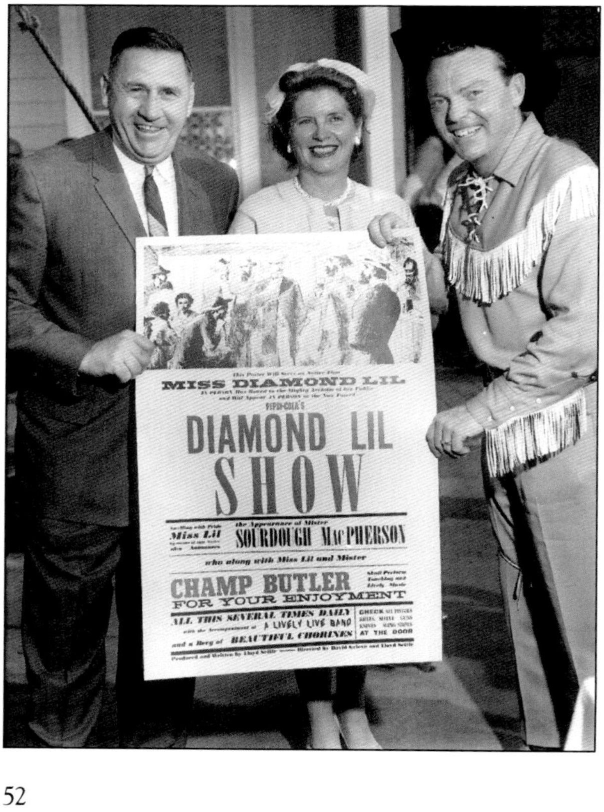

Standing on the front porch of the Diamond Lil Saloon are Gov. Foster Furcolo and wife Kathryn. Champ Butler (right) was one of the stars at the Diamond Lil Saloon. He was brought in from Pacific Ocean Park, California, by Lloyd D. Settle, producer for the Diamond Lil Show. Butler's 1951 recording of "Down Yonder" can be heard on YouTube. He sang this song as part of the show. (Courtesy of FOPI archives.)

PEPSI-COLA'S

Diamond Lil Show®

Written and Produced by Lloyd Settle

MUSIC CONDUCTED AND ARRANGED BY TED GRAHAM CHOREOGRAPHER: GUS SOLOMONS

Directed by David Grieve and Mr. Settle

STARRING

Champ Butler
AS RAGTIME COWBOY JOE

Charmaine Harma
AS DIAMOND LIL

AND

Buddy Farnan *as Sourdough MacPherson*

FEATURING THE DISGRUNTLED THREESOME AND TWO BILBOUS BARTENDERS

TECHNICAL DIRECTOR:
Lemar Bledsoe

Settings and draperies by: Francis Mahard

Costumes designed and executed by: Ellie Groper, Esther Small, Gus Bowen and Lucy Cornice

© The Diamond Lil Show is the copyrighted property of Lloyd D. Settle

This is the first page of Pepsi-Cola's Diamond Lil Show program. Not only was Settle the marketing director for Pleasure Island, he also wrote and produced the show. New songs written for the show included "Pleasure Island," "War Song of the Texas Rangers," and "Moby Dick Is Sick." (Courtesy of FOPI archives.)

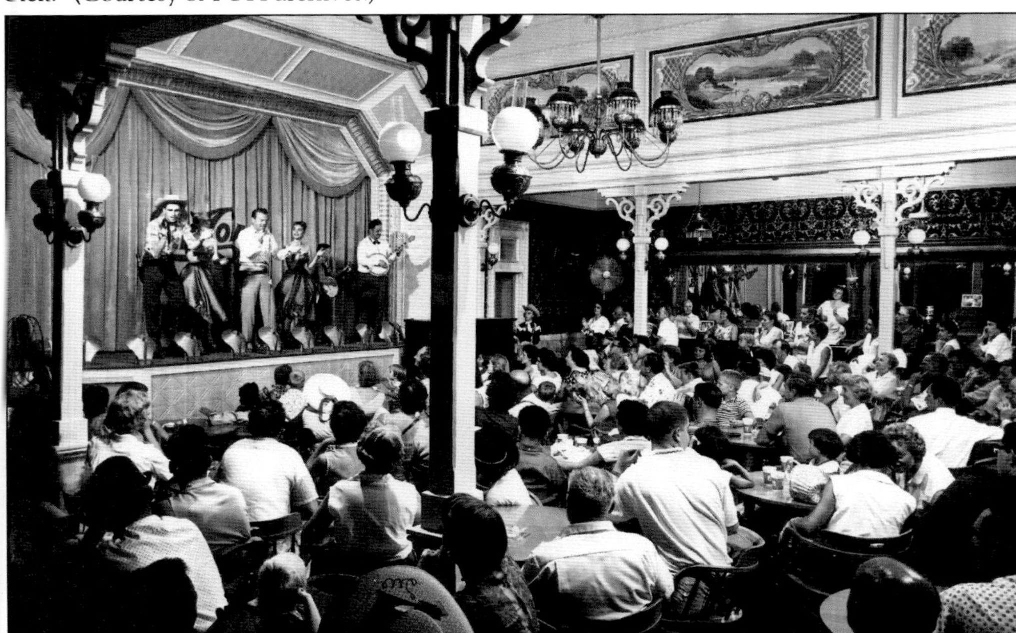

Onstage at the Diamond Lil Saloon are Buddy Farnan (left), Butler (center), and Pat Terry, Sr. and his son, Pat Terry, Jr. (right). Terry and his son ended up playing their banjos at Disney World later in their careers. To the right of the stage is the Diamond Lil Bar. (Courtesy of Russ Adams Productions.)

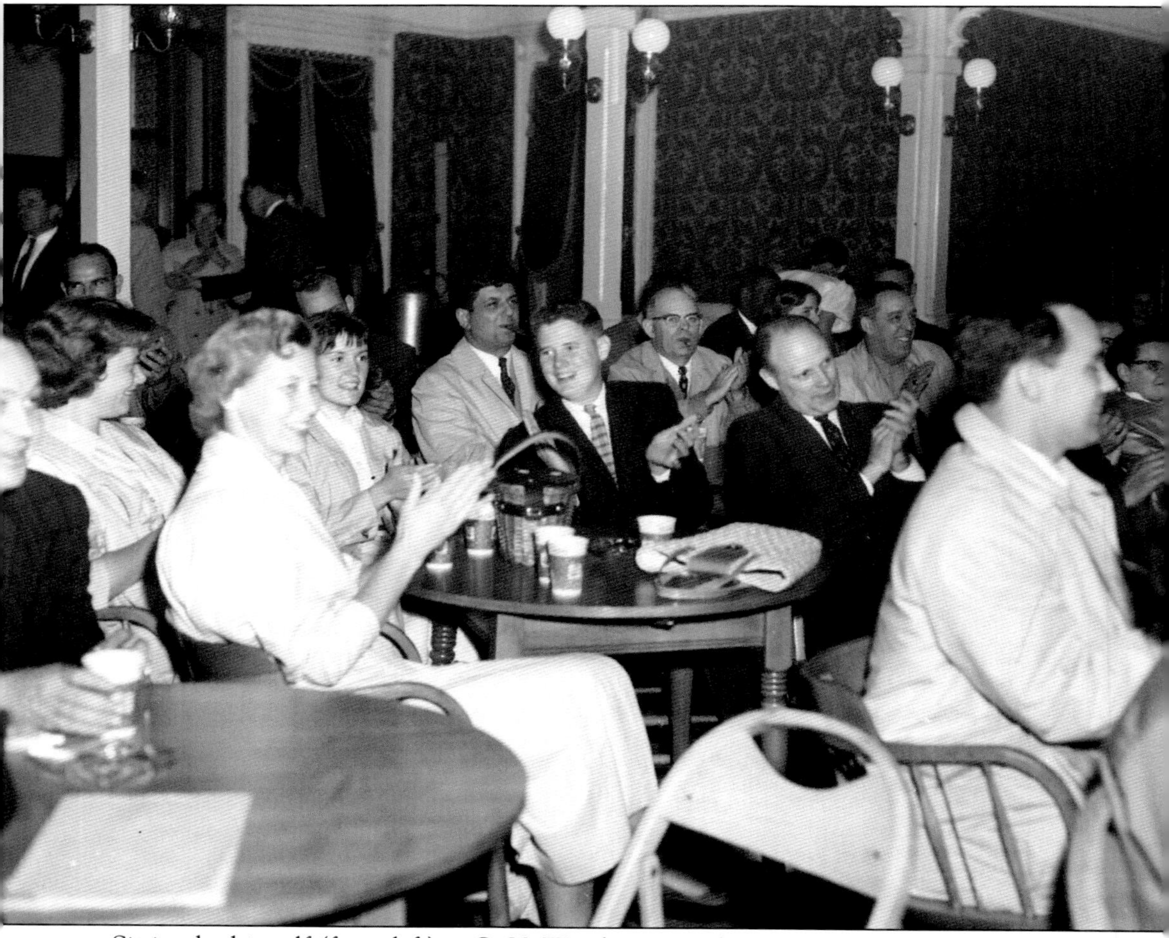

Sitting by himself (front left) is C. V. Wood, owner of Marco Engineering, whose company designed Pleasure Island. Marco Engineering provided market research, design, and engineering to the leisure industry. In the late 1950s, Robert McCulloch was looking for a site to test outboard motors that his company produced. By the early 1960s, Marco Engineering merged with McCulloch Properties. McCulloch and Wood created Lake Havasu City in Arizona with construction starting in 1964. In 1968, Wood achieved worldwide recognition when he arranged for the purchase of the London Bridge with McCulloch and had it dismantled and shipped to Lake Havasu City. Wood was hired by Warner Brothers to pioneer its entry into the studio-tour attraction business. He was the master planner who built and opened the company's first attraction, Warner Brothers Movie World, on the Gold Coast of Australia in 1991. Wood, with automobile racer and car designer Carroll Shelby, cofounded the International Chili Society, which sanctioned cook-offs around the world each year, benefiting numerous charitable organizations. Wood was married to screen actress Joanne Dru. At the time of his death on March 16, 1992, he was 71. (Courtesy of Russ Adams Productions.)

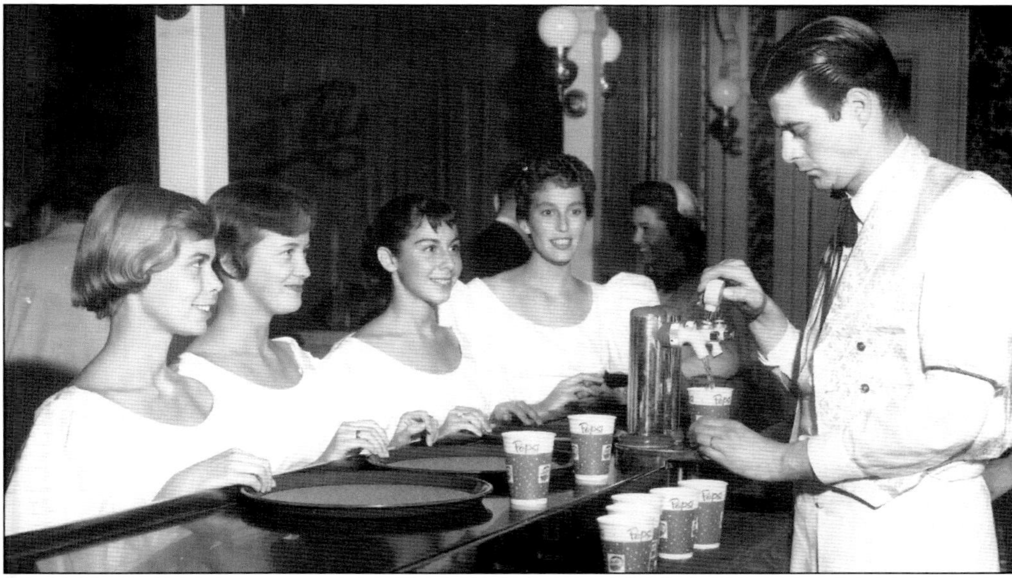

Using the same concept and sponsor as Disneyland's Golden Horseshoe, the Diamond Lil Show was a hit during the 1959 season. Pleasure Island gave a lot of local high school and college students and some of the area teachers summer employment. The Diamond Lil Saloon was approximately 2,700 square feet in area. The interior fixtures and decorations were constructed at a cost of about $50,000, of which Pepsi-Cola paid one-half and Pleasure Island paid the other half. (Courtesy of Russ Adams Productions.)

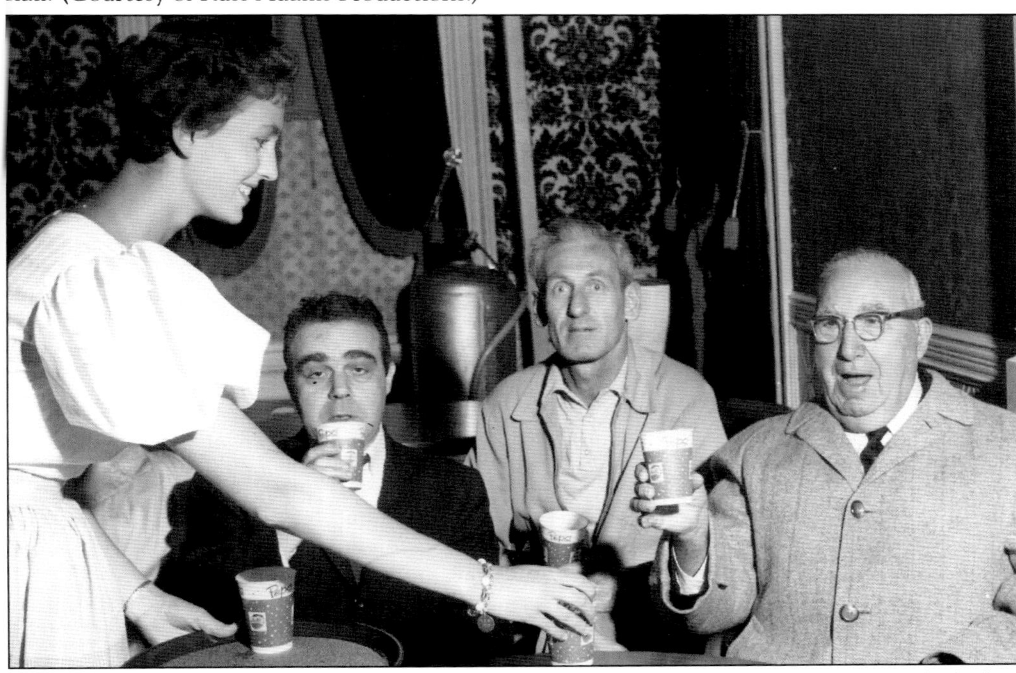

These three gentlemen are attending one of the five free shows sponsored by Pepsi-Cola daily at the Diamond Lil Saloon. One has to ask, what is in the drinks at their table? (Courtesy of Russ Adams Productions.)

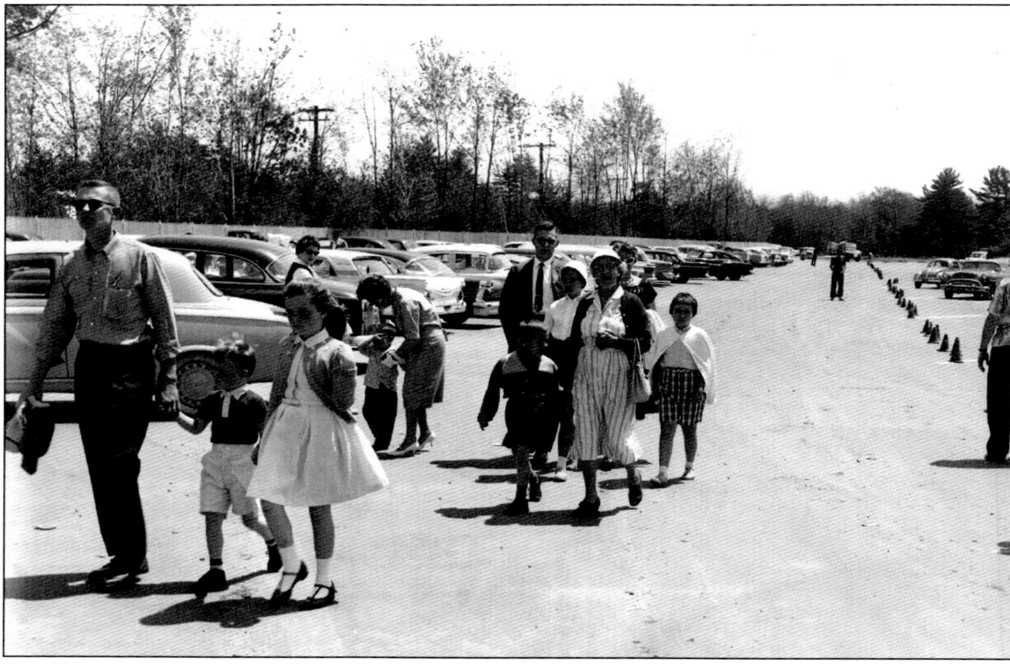

According to interviews conducted over the last nine years, people who visited Pleasure Island as children remember one common thing: the trip there seemed a lot farther away than it actually was, even though some families might have come from just a few towns away. (Courtesy of House of Photography.)

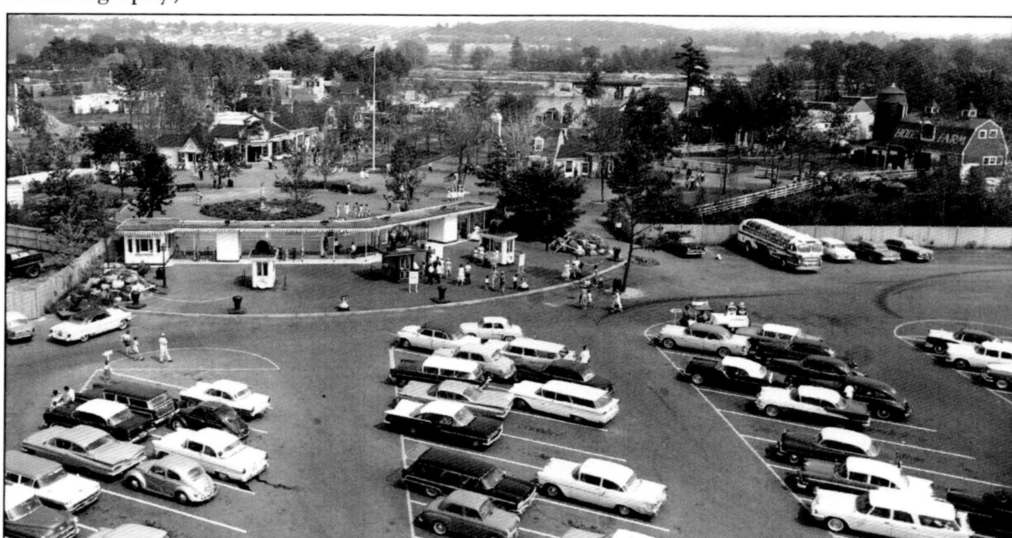

Pleasure Island's parking lot reportedly could hold 3,000 cars, and parking was free. While guests were in the park, employees would attach cardboard Pleasure Island advertisements by wiring them to the rear bumpers. Following a public hearing on July 7, 1959, the Wakefield Board of Selectmen granted permission to the Lynnfield community bus line to operate up to the ticketing area inside the park for picking up or dropping off guests. (Courtesy of Russ Adams Productions.)

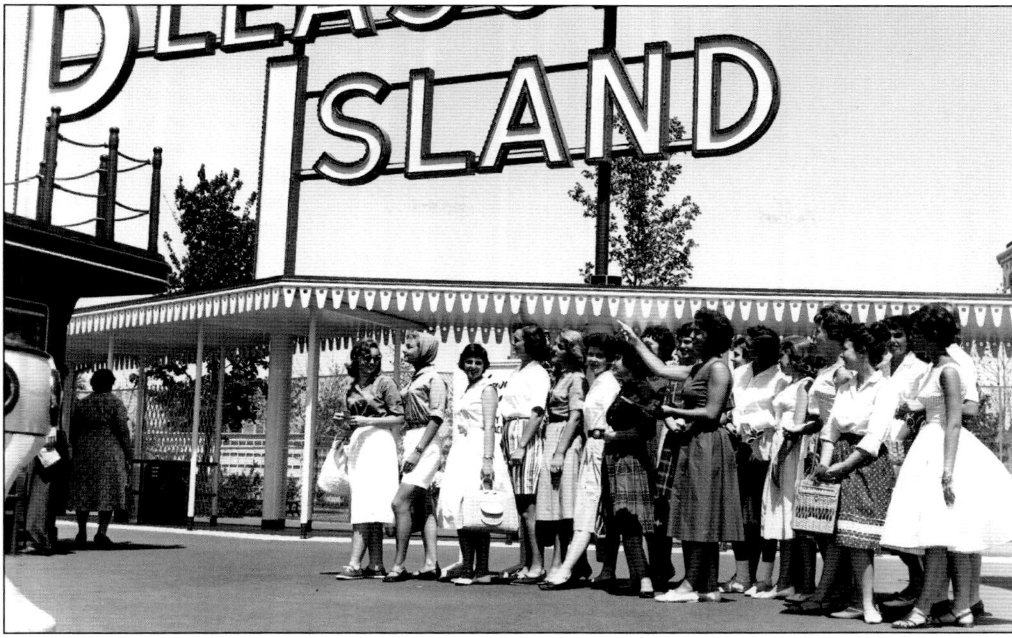

In the center of this group of young ladies, with her arm pointing up, is the official hostess at Pleasure Island, Patricia (Nordling) Rowe Douglass. She came from Lexington and was Miss Massachusetts in 1958. She had a great job guiding groups through the park and even singing now and then at the Diamond Lil Saloon. (Courtesy of House of Photography.)

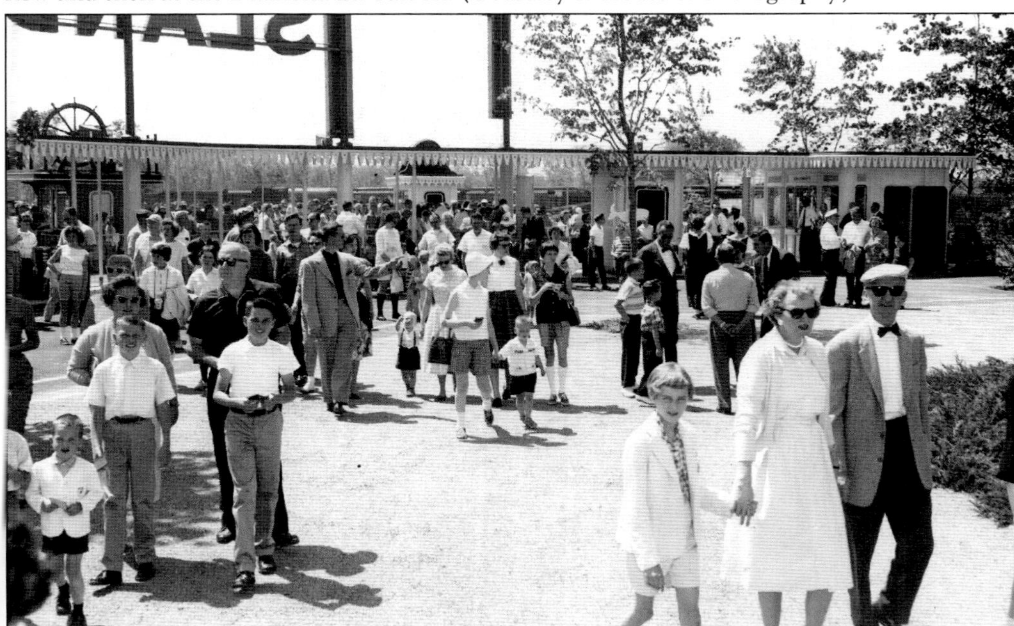

Entering Pleasure Island had to be exciting for both young and old. According to a story in the *Wakefield Daily Item* on July 15, 1959, "About 8,300 people visited Pleasure Island last Sunday, the largest attendance for a single day." Sunday, July 12, was only the third Sunday since Pleasure Island was opened to the public. (Courtesy of House of Photography.)

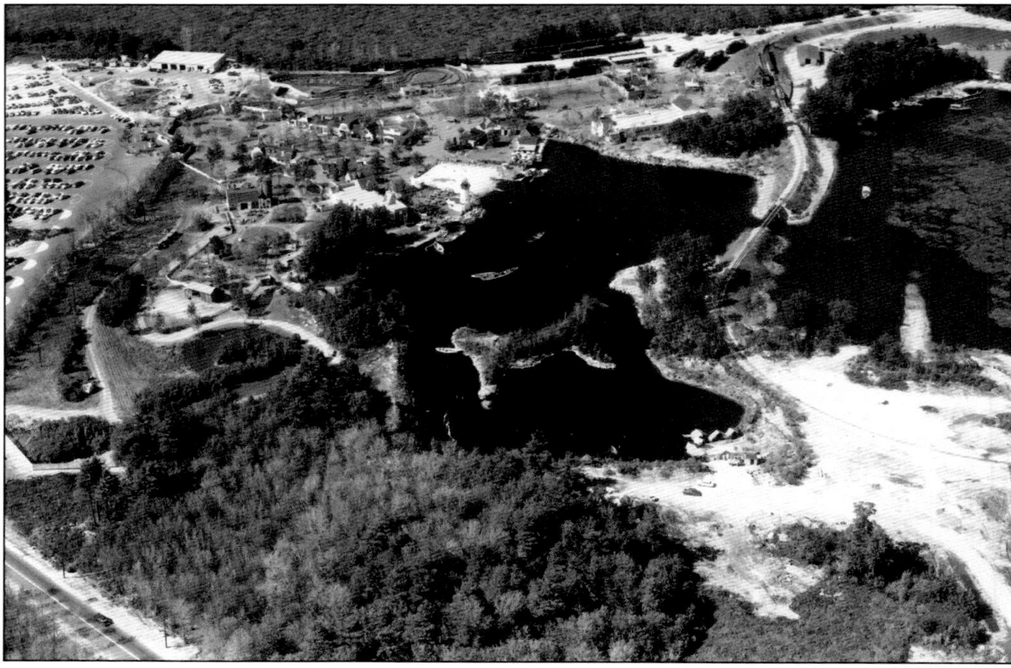

The following four photographs were taken by Laurence Lowry on Friday, August 14, 1959. At the top is the present-day Reedy Meadow. Moby Dick is resting under water located in the lagoon south of the island. (Courtesy of Laurence Lowry.)

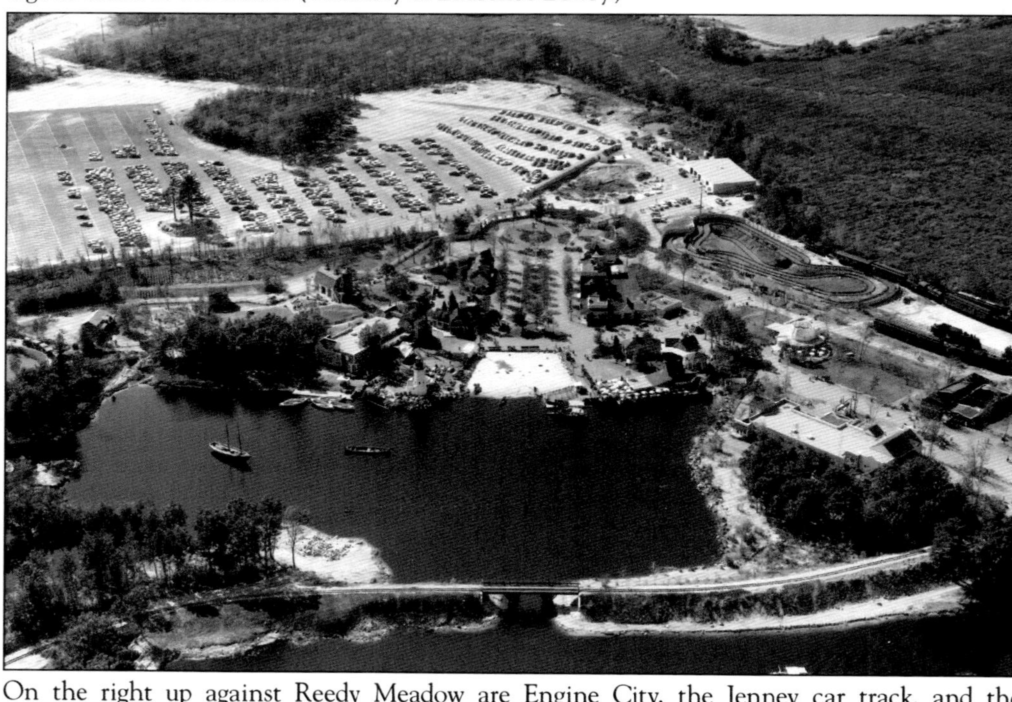

On the right up against Reedy Meadow are Engine City, the Jenney car track, and the maintenance building. In the center are the narrow-gauge trestle, the beach, Main Street, and the parking lot. (Courtesy of Laurence Lowry.)

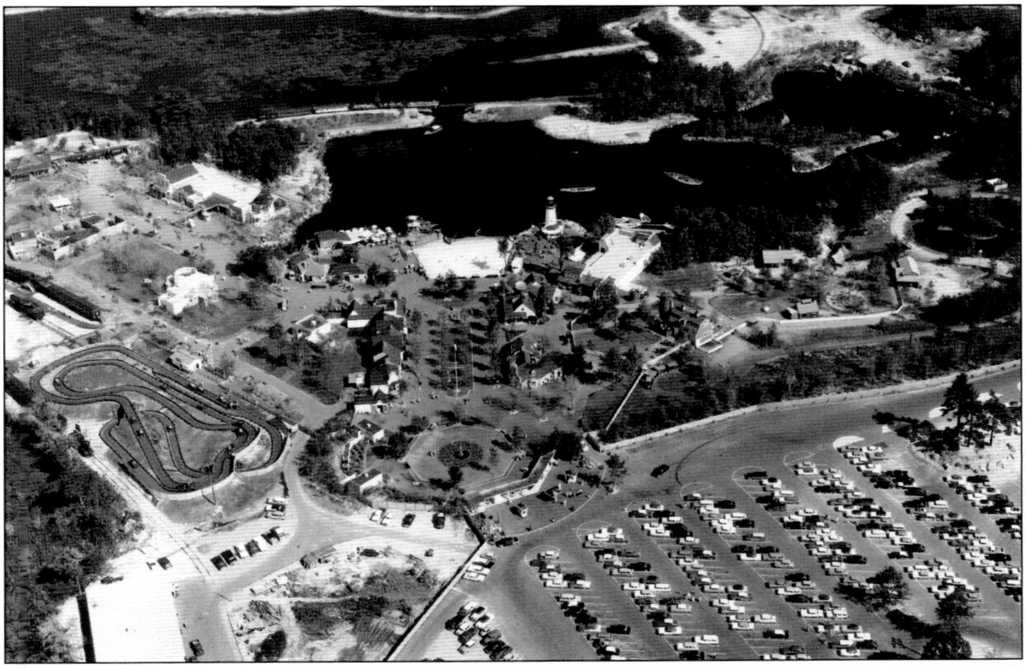

The area at the bottom left eventually became the go-kart track. Past the Jenney car track are Hood's Ice Cream Parlor and the western section. In the center is Main Street, leading to Clipper Cove. On the right is the Hood Farm. (Courtesy of Laurence Lowry.)

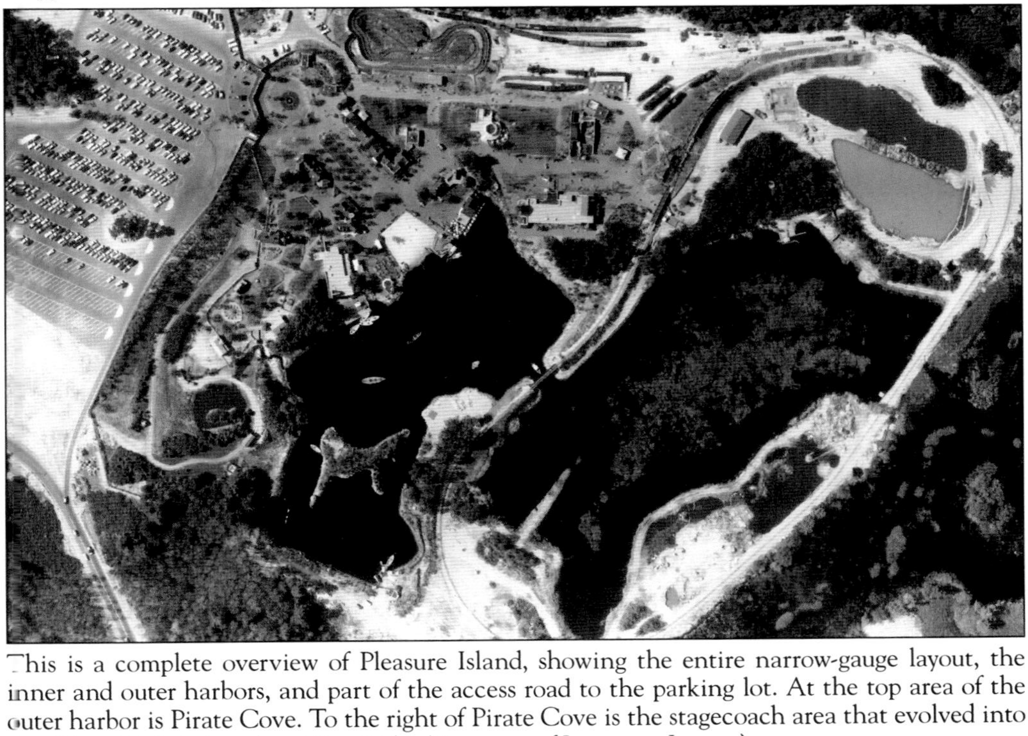

This is a complete overview of Pleasure Island, showing the entire narrow-gauge layout, the inner and outer harbors, and part of the access road to the parking lot. At the top area of the outer harbor is Pirate Cove. To the right of Pirate Cove is the stagecoach area that evolved into the Water Buffalo Land and Sea Ride. (Courtesy of Laurence Lowry.)

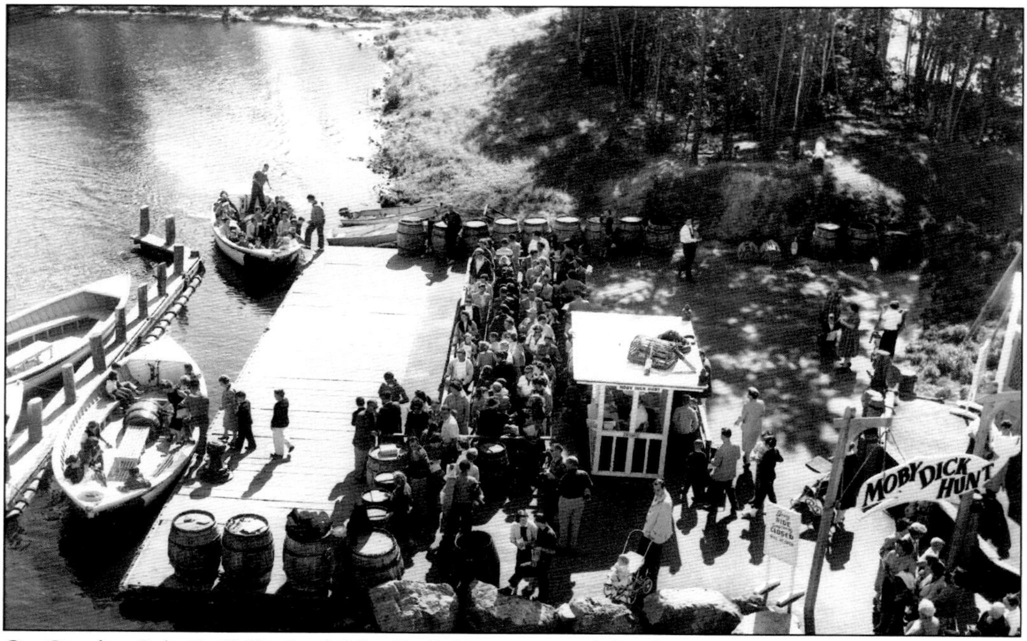

On Sunday, July 5, 1959, the Moby Dick Hunt opened for the first time. Plagued by weeks of bad weather and technical problems, scores of specialists worked day and night to perfect the intricate installation. Shown above are guests loading and off-loading at the Clipper Cove dock. (Courtesy of Russ Adams Productions.)

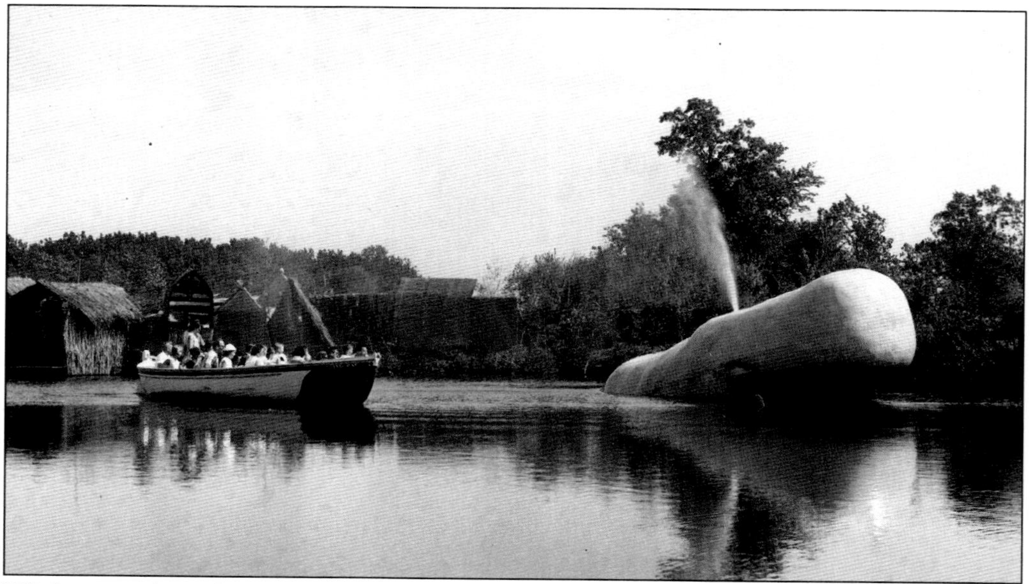

While researching this attraction, there is only one conclusion that makes sense: it is no wonder many adults who were exposed to the Moby Dick Hunt as a child have a problem going on a whale watch. The Moby Dick Hunt had several great special effects leading up to Moby Dick's rise from the sea and more while returning to the safety of Clipper Cove. There were timed sound effects, a charging rhinoceros, animated gimmicks, and professional narration from the whaleboat fleet captains. (Courtesy of Russ Adams Productions.)

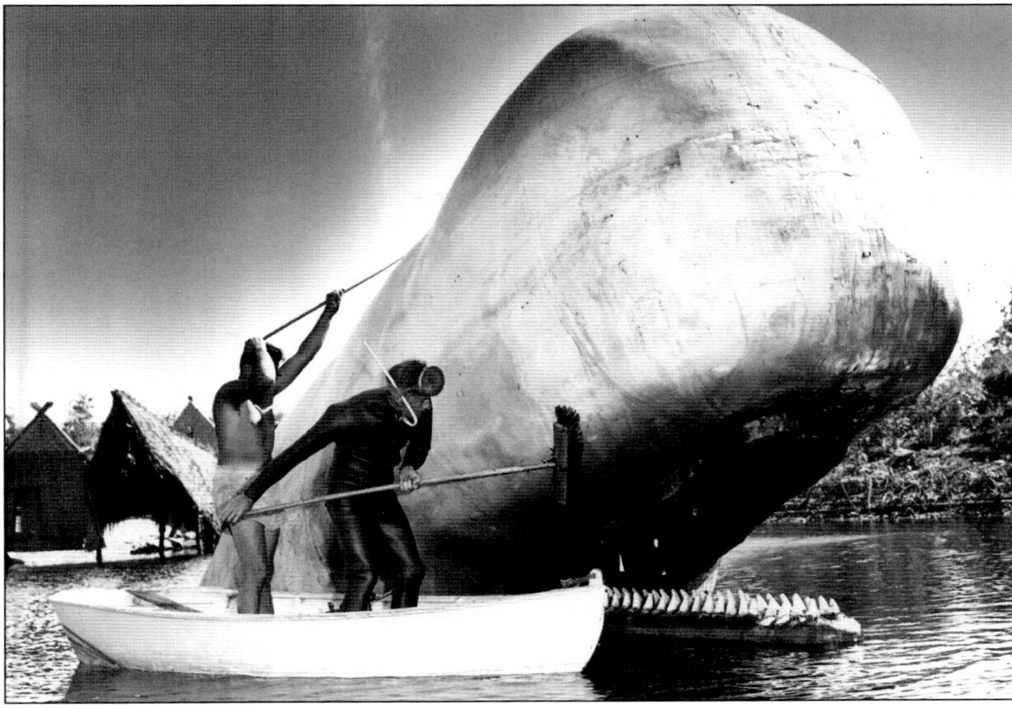

Both of these photographs have Moby Dick getting cleaned up for his upcoming performances. After all, he was "the great white whale." Staying white was a problem. Parks such as Disney were able to control, filter, and drain their water-related special effect areas. Pleasure Island did not have the ability to do this, which led to constant maintenance problems throughout the life of the park. (Courtesy of Russ Adams Productions.)

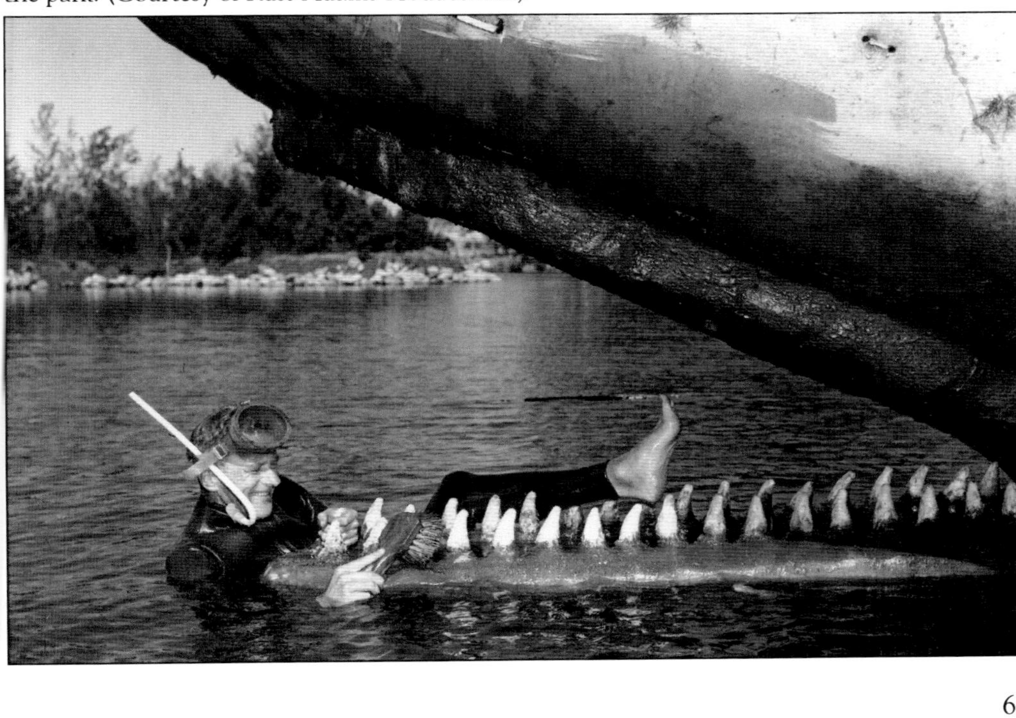

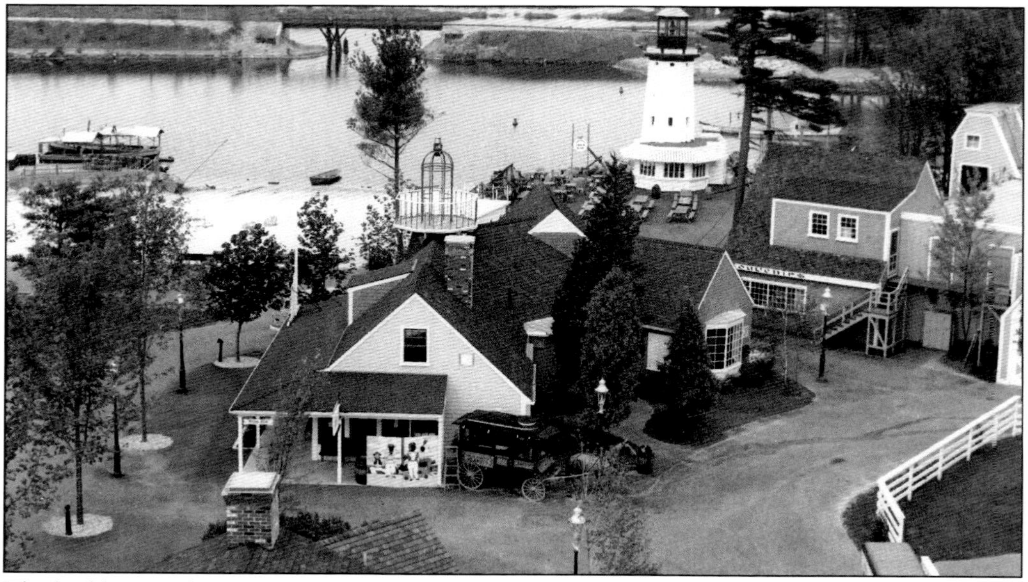

The building in the center housed Bourdon's, the official camera shop at Pleasure Island. Notice the cut-out panels for taking photographs. The building to the far right has a set of stairs leading to the operation center. From there, announcer Ken Saunders kept guests updated throughout the day of showtimes and events. Also, all sound effects for the Moby Dick Hunt, the dark rides, and more came from the operation center's 1959 high-tech equipment. (Courtesy of Russ Adams Productions.)

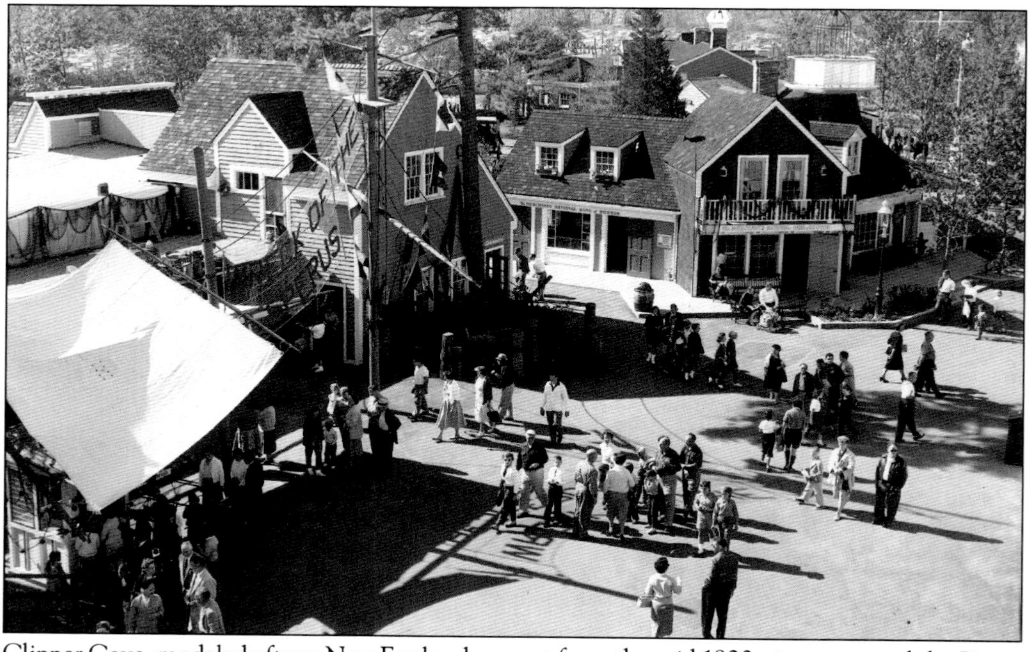

Clipper Cove, modeled after a New England seaport from the mid-1800s, incorporated the Pirate Cove and Moby Dick Hunt attractions as well as the Wreck of the Hesperus dark ride, where guests were transported in cars shaped like ships through a sea of special effects. (Courtesy of Russ Adams Productions.)

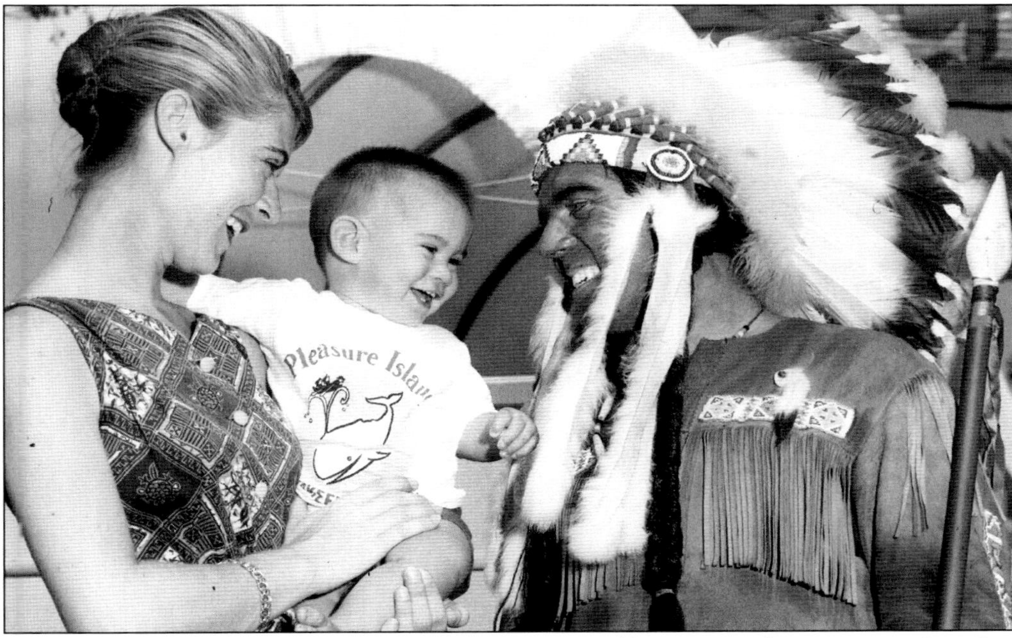

According to an untitled newspaper clip, "Gregory Gillis, 10 months, in arms of mother, Mrs. Stephen Gillis of Los Angeles, seems to be enjoying a powwow with Big Chief Thunderbird, Indian sheriff of Goldpan Gulch." Chief Thunderbird was played by Herb Sauve, who was one of the longest-working performers at Pleasure Island. (Courtesy of Russ Adams Productions.)

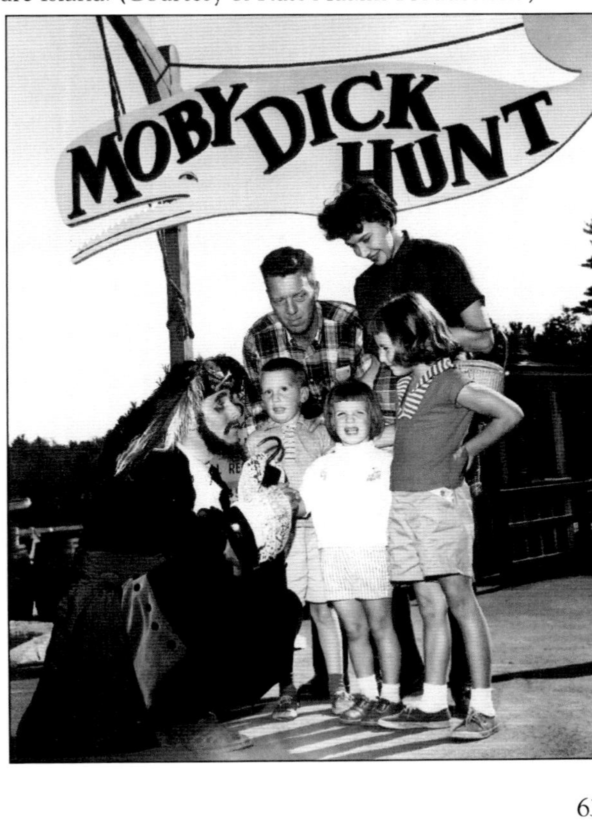

Pleasure Island wanted very much to be educational and entertaining. By hiring Richard Freniere, it got even more. In his character, the Barbados Mute, he acted but did not speak. The late Freniere had many passions; one was his jazz music collection. His 78s, LPs, CDs, tapes, books, and videos made up one of the largest private jazz collections in New England. He passed away on June 22, 2008, at 87 years old. (Courtesy of Russ Adams Productions.)

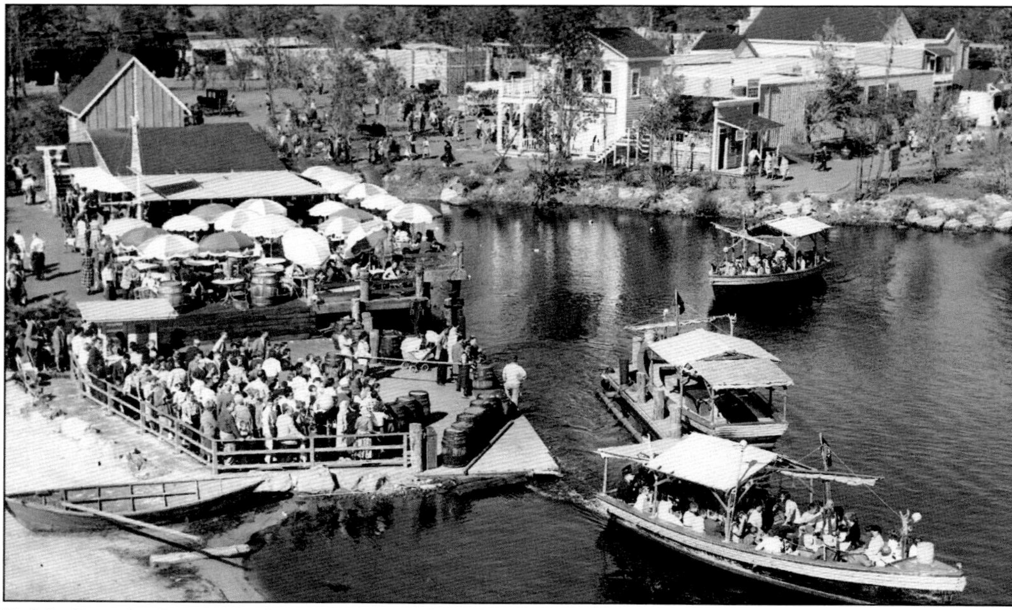

F. H. Snow's Canning Company was founded in 1920 when Capt. Fred Snow began selling fresh clams in Pine Point, Maine. By 1959, the company was sold to the Borden Company. As an exhibitor within the park, Snow's followed the playbook of industrial advertising set by Disneyland. Cap'n Snow's Chowder House is to the left, and the building with the flat roof (top right) is the dark ride the Chisholm Trail. (Courtesy of Russ Adams Productions.)

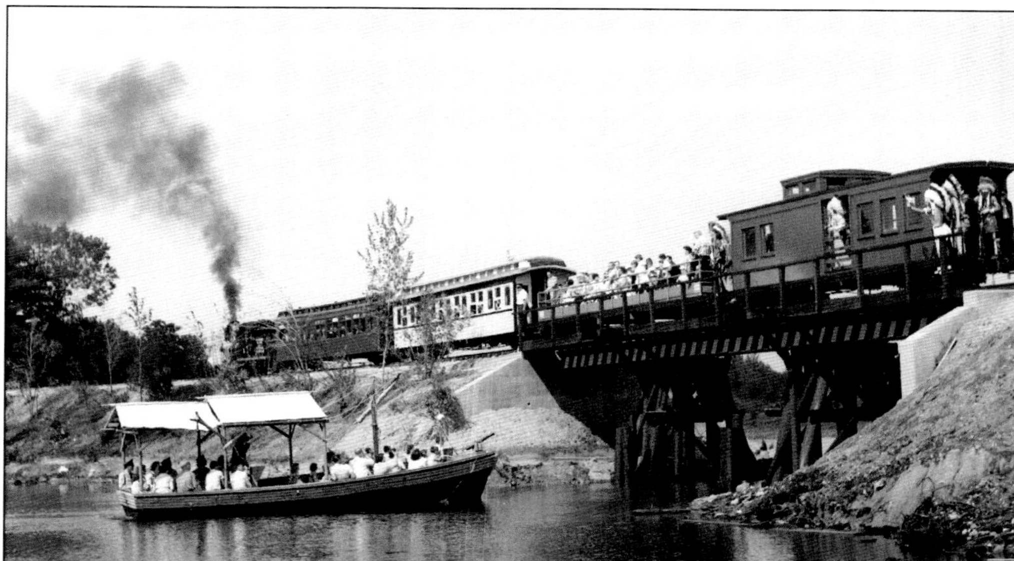

Heading out to Pirate Cove was just half the fun, and riding on Old Smoky was the other half. Pleasure Island was the result of one man's dream to create a recreation center for the whole family, and that man was Bill Hawkes. (Courtesy of Russ Adams Productions.)

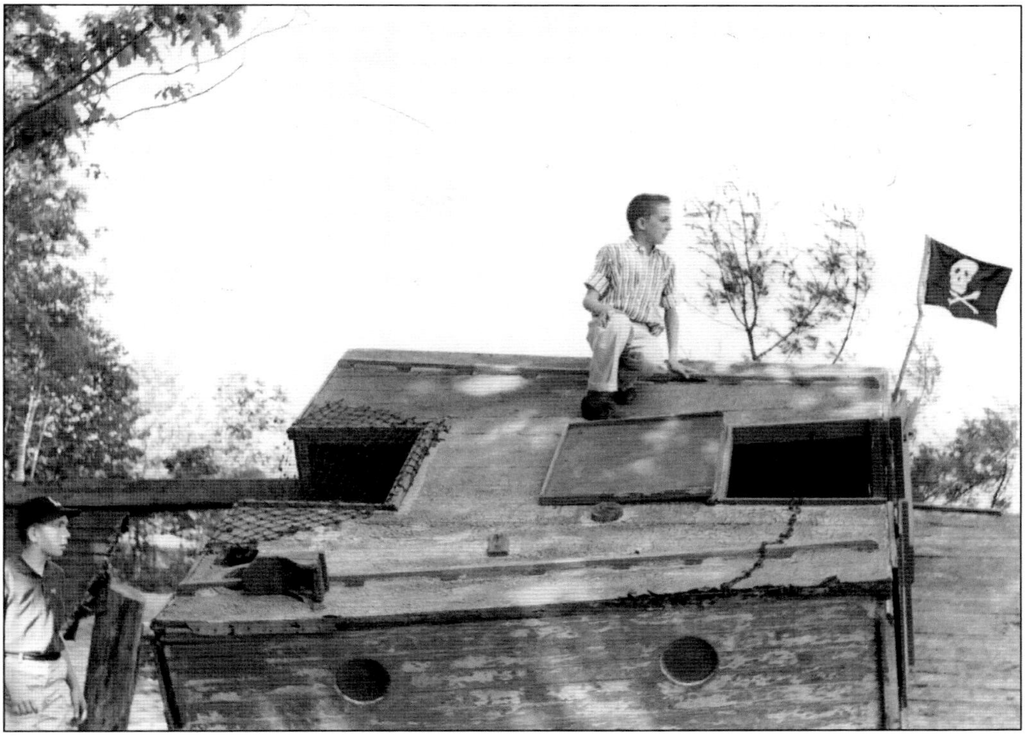

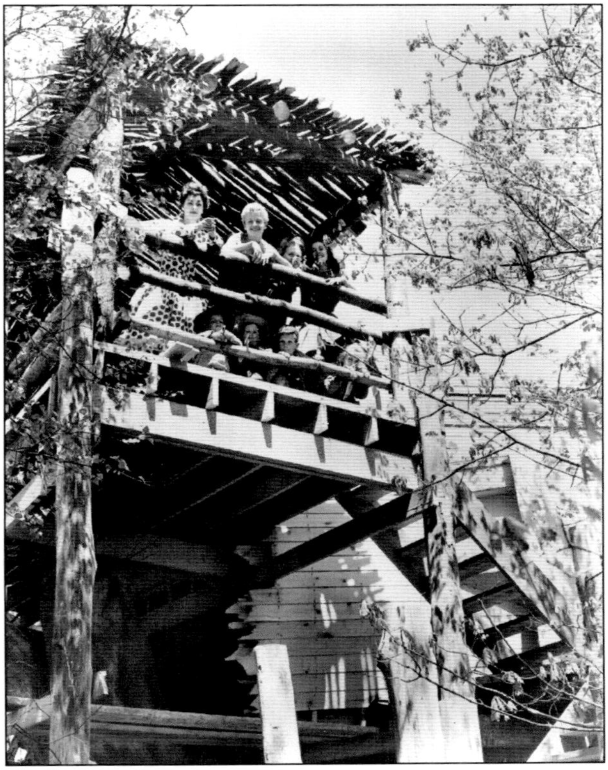

Taking a boat ride to Pirate Cove was every child's dream come true. First, visitors were greeted by live pirate Cap'n Kidd, and then they could explore a shipwreck and climb what was billed as "the largest tree house in the world." Other activities on the make-believe island enhanced the experience, and then guests got to go on a boat ride again back to Clipper Cove. (Above, courtesy of FOPI archives; right, courtesy of Russ Adams Productions.)

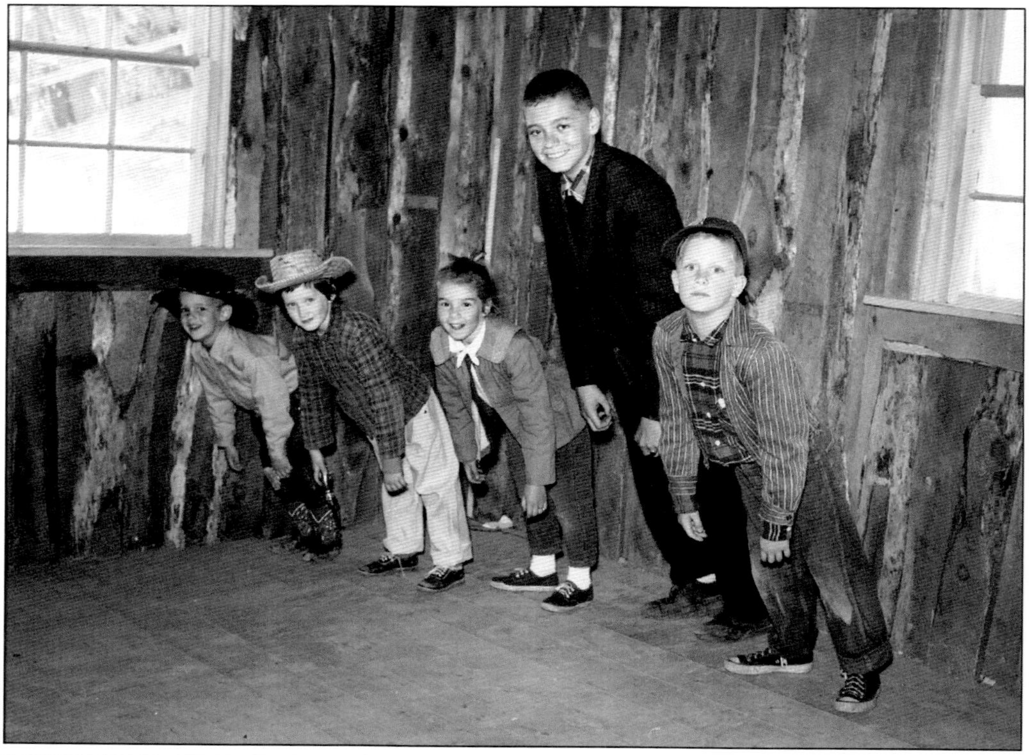

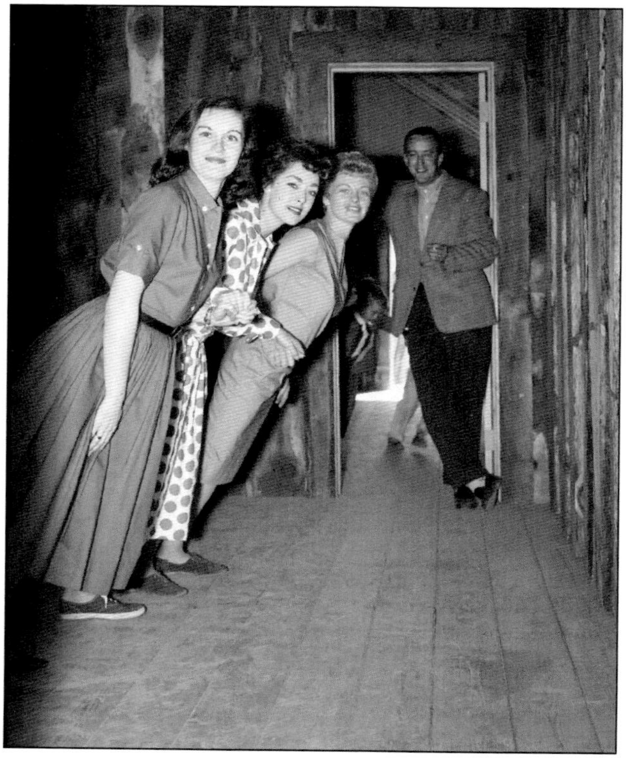

The Slanty Shanty has had many names, including the Magnetic House and the Strange Shanty. Built to defy the laws of gravity, this walk-through attraction was a hit at Pleasure Island. Bill Hawkes's wife, Jean, with three young children and one on the way, helped Marco Engineering's art director Randy Duell decorate the attraction, "where water ran uphill." While entering through Diamond Lil Saloon's mine tunnel, the guests entered an optical illusion, consisting of two rooms of a rundown western mine shack. Of course, the Slanty Shanty hostess enhanced the visit with a scripted and possibly ad-libbed spiel. (Courtesy of Bourdon Studios.)

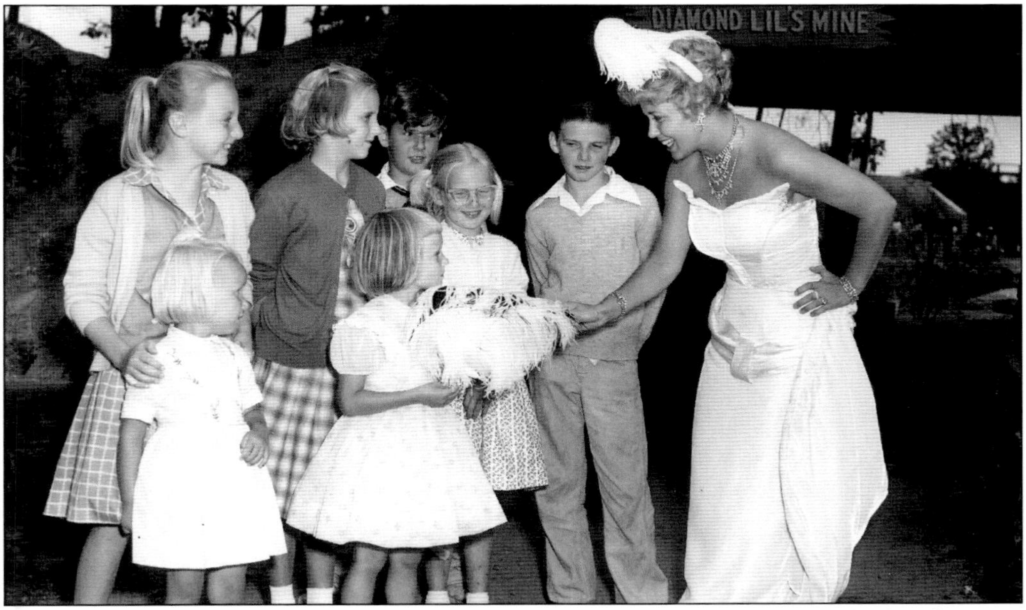

Charmaine Harma was Pleasure Island's 23-year-old "Diamond Lil," as one of the headliners at the saloon. Lloyd D. Settle, the show's producer, brought her here from Pacific Ocean Park in California. Harma was reportedly an up-and-coming opera star. While at Pleasure Island, she rented a house in the middle of Pillings Pond, accessible by rowboat, in Lynnfield. This photograph was taken at the entrance to the Slanty Shanty. (Courtesy of Russ Adams Productions.)

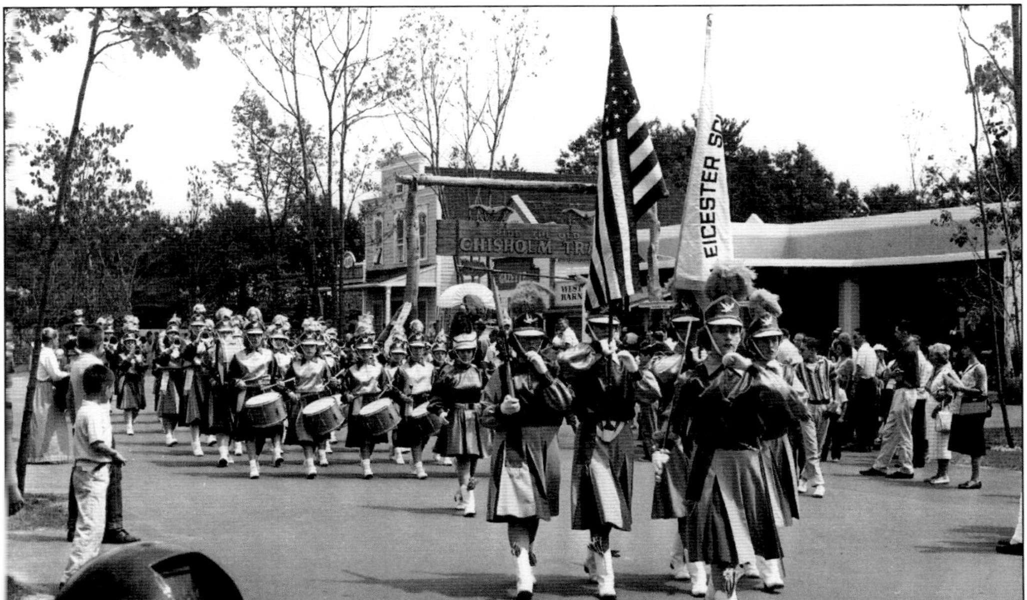

Part of Pleasure Island's appeal, beyond the attractions, was the spontaneity of day-to-day events. Whether it was a gunfight outside the saloon, a train robbery, or, as in this photograph, a marching band, every day at Pleasure Island was designed to be special for both young and old. (Courtesy of Russ Adams Productions.)

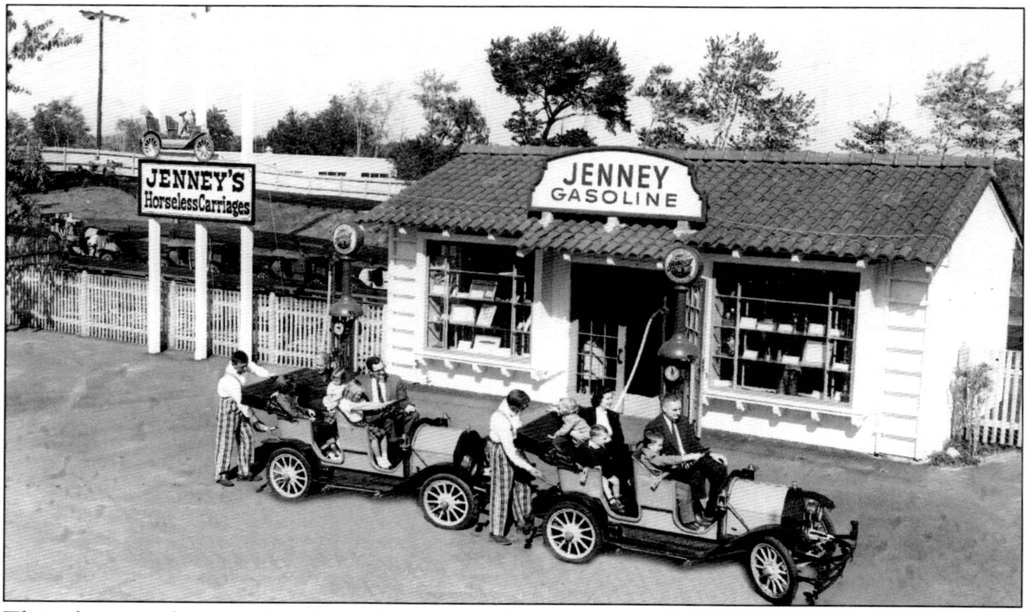

This photograph was taken for publicity use. The pumps were just props, according to Dave Mitchell, a former mechanic at Pleasure Island. The Jenney station was reportedly a replica of the first Jenney gasoline station ever built. The Jenney cars were one of the most popular attractions at Pleasure Island. Former employee Sid Hodson is behind the left car. (Courtesy of Russ Adams Productions.)

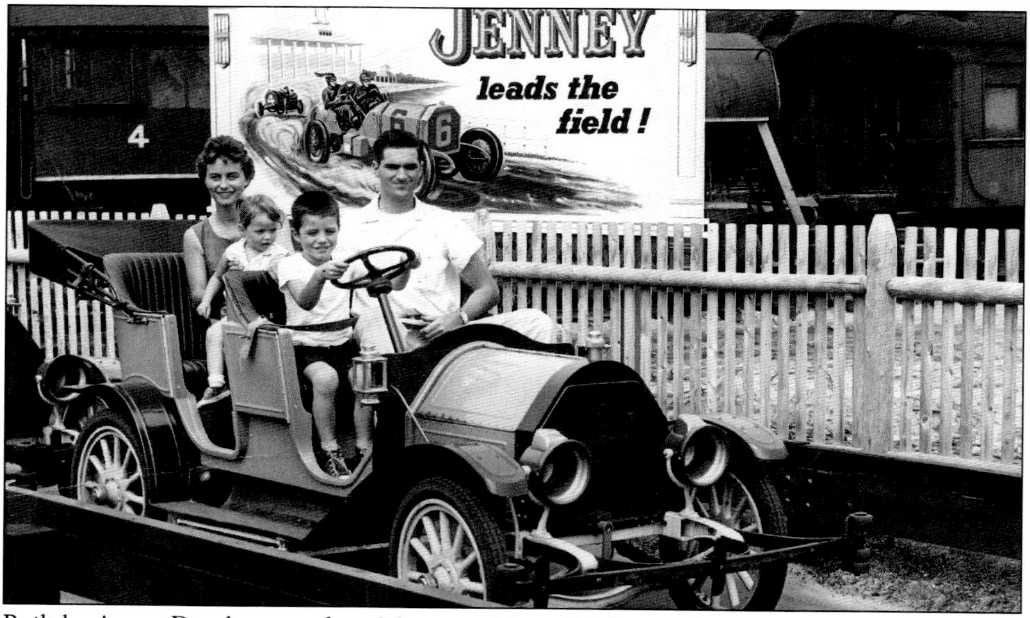

Built by Arrow Development from Mountain View, California, the Jenney cars were four-seater scale-model reproductions of 1911 Cadillacs. They operated on one-cylinder, seven-horsepower gasoline engines and had one pedal. Arrow also built the scaled-down cars for Disneyland. Children had to pass a height test to be able to drive their own car. Engine City can be viewed alongside the Jenney horseless carriage ride. (Courtesy of Russ Adams Productions.)

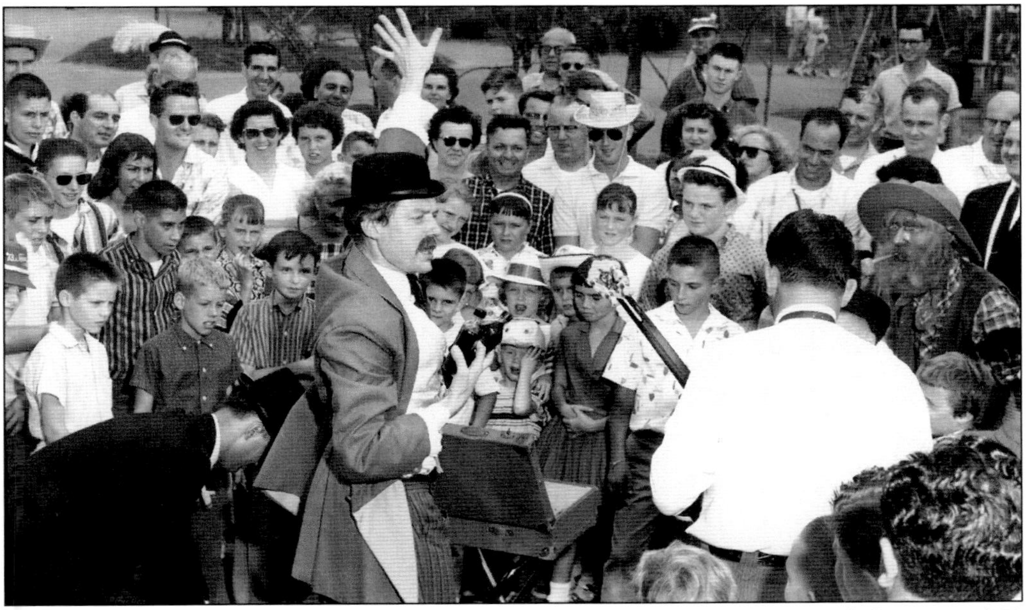

Played by park actor Bob Harmon (center), the character in this skit is Col. Beauregard T. Beauregard, the snake oil salesman. On the right facing the crowd is Pat Terrio, Pleasure Island's resident banjo player. Ormond Davis (right) played the Old Prospector. Anytime and almost anywhere throughout the park, the actors set up and performed various skits. (Courtesy of Russ Adams Productions.)

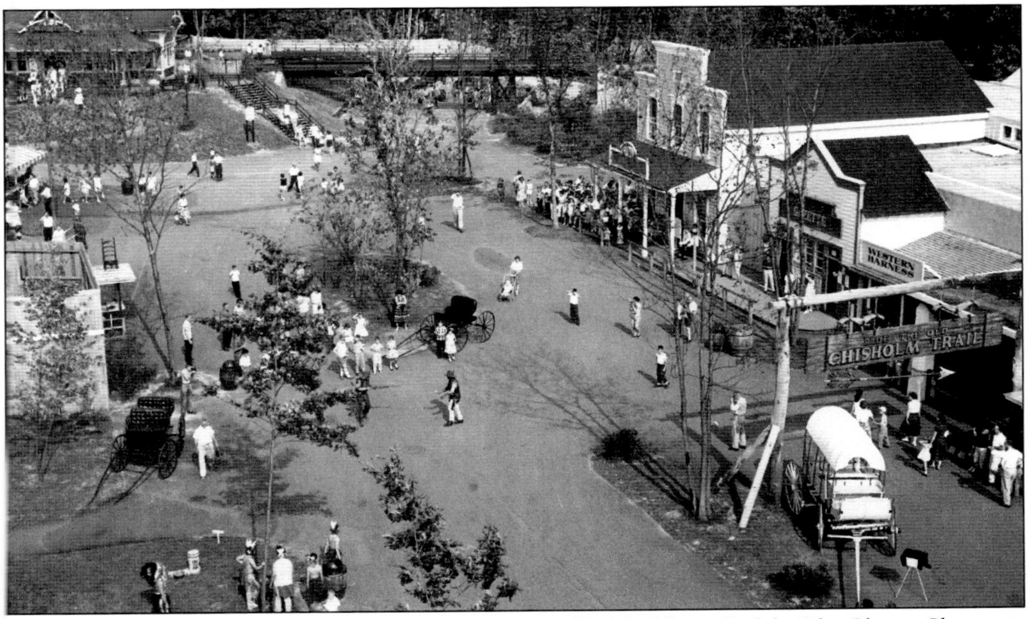

This photograph shows part of the western section called Goldpan Gulch. The Slanty Shanty is on the left. Guests boarded Old Smoky at the Goldpan Gulch station. There is a crowd waiting for the next show at the Diamond Lil Saloon. Next door is the print shop. The Chisholm Trail ride was a simulated buckboard tour of the Old West, with animated western characters and animals. (Courtesy of Russ Adams Productions.)

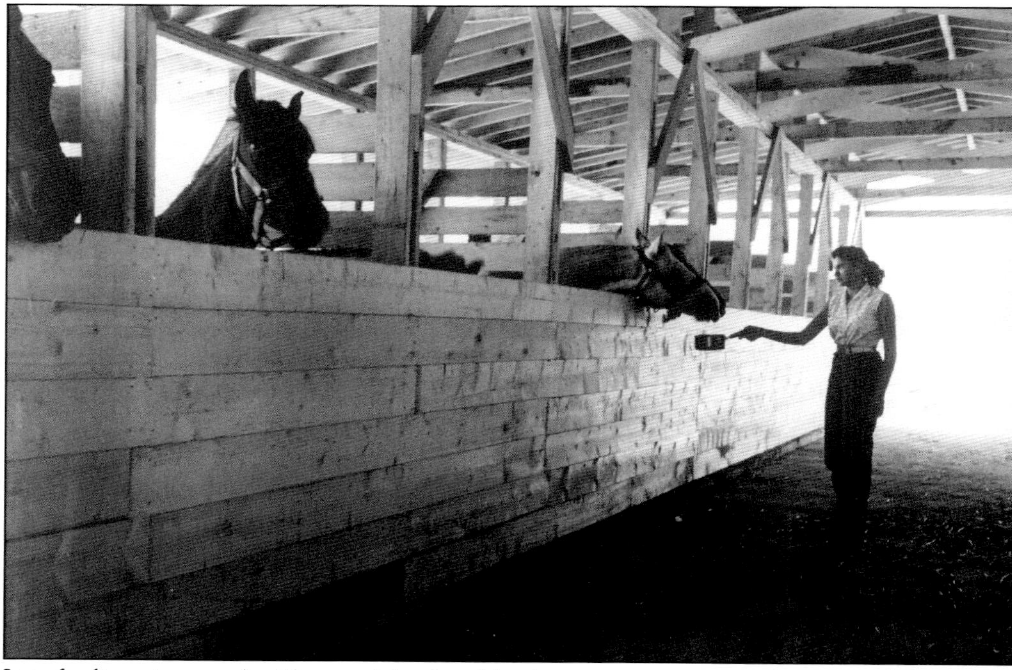

It is feeding time at the Pleasure Island stable. A preopening press release stated facts about Pleasure Island: "The horses, ponies and burros in the Pleasure Island Corral were transported from Magic Mountain in Denver, Colorado." (Courtesy of Fay Foto Service.)

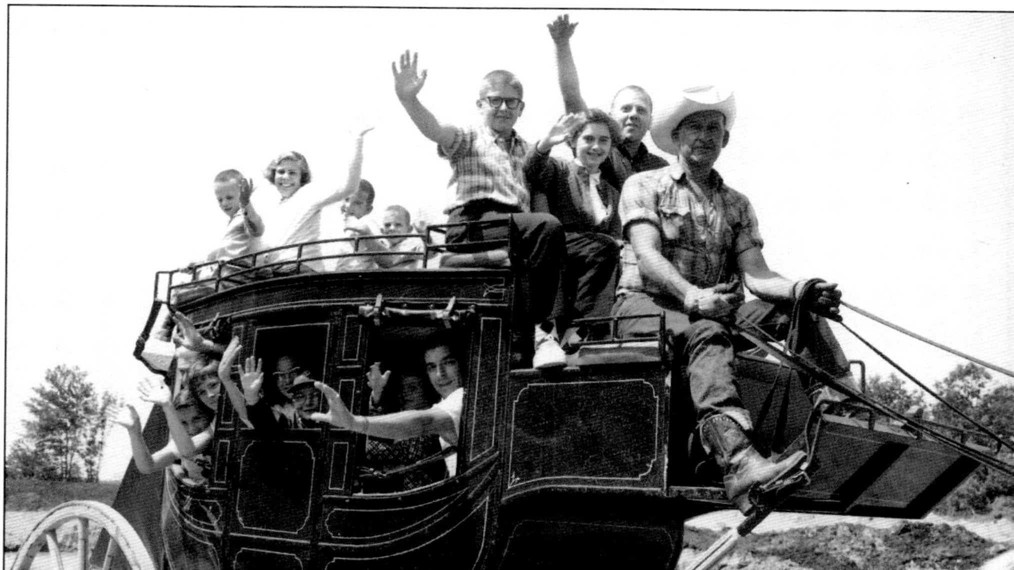

This photograph features a replica of an overland stagecoach, Abbot and Downing style, from the 1880s. As stated in the 1959 *Clipper Cove Chronicle*, "Riders will bump away from a regular depot in Goldpan Gulch and travel alongside a portion of the Old Smoky Line." (Courtesy of Bourdon Studios.)

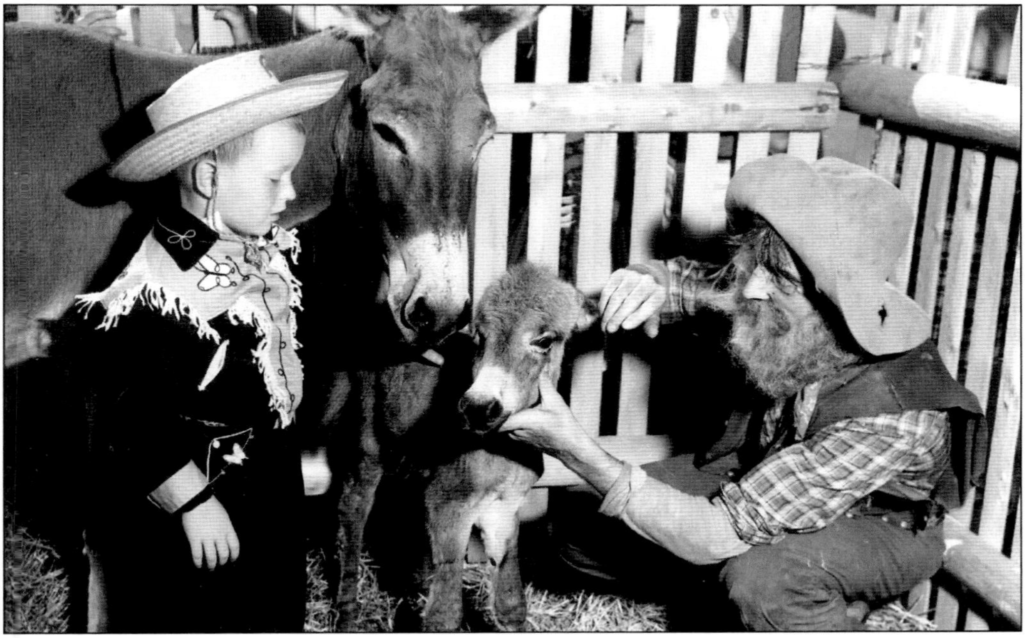

The Old Prospector character, played by Ormond Davis, checks out the baby burro with his little cowboy helper. The burro ride started out from the same depot as the stagecoach. A park employee led a string of eight burros along a trail, which included going under the trestle bridge that was between the inner and outer harbors. (Courtesy of Russ Adams Productions.)

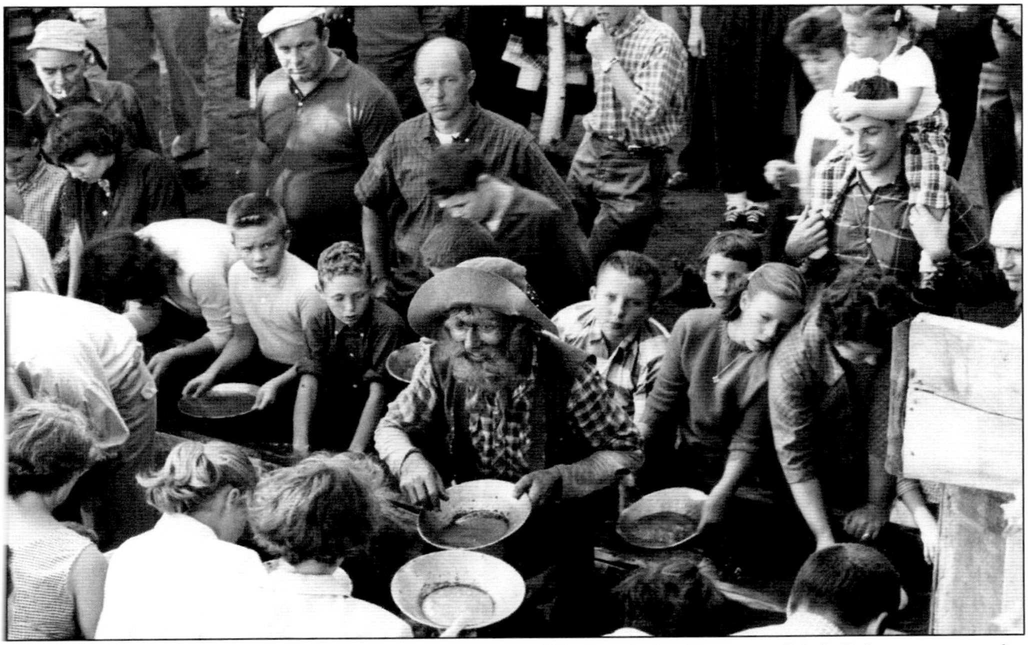

Davis tries his hand at panning for gold. Located behind the Diamond Lil Saloon, water for the sluicing operation was fed to a flume by a huge donkey-operated wheel lift. Prospectors of all ages could discover a certain amount of fake gold, which they could keep or have assessed at Merchants Bank in Clipper Cove. (Courtesy of Russ Adams Productions.)

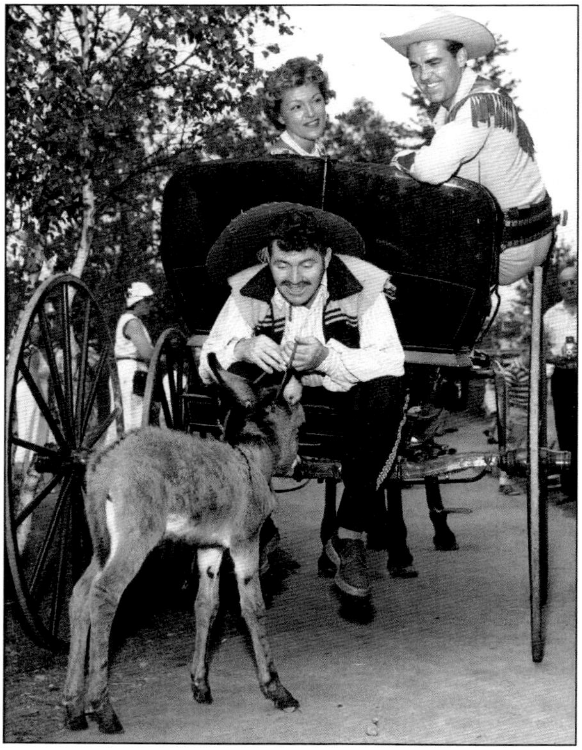

Appearing with Rex Trailer at Pleasure Island is Pablo, played by the late actor Richard Kilbride. Pablo played Trailer's sidekick on the television show *Boomtown* from 1956 to 1967. The swan puppet Hubert was also handled by Kilbride. Michael Bavaro, a local filmmaker, produced a documentary on *Boomtown* that aired on WBZ-TV on June 18, 2005. Bavaro estimates that more than four million baby boomers grew up watching *Boomtown* and that nearly 250,000 children appeared in the live audiences. (Courtesy of Russ Adams Productions.)

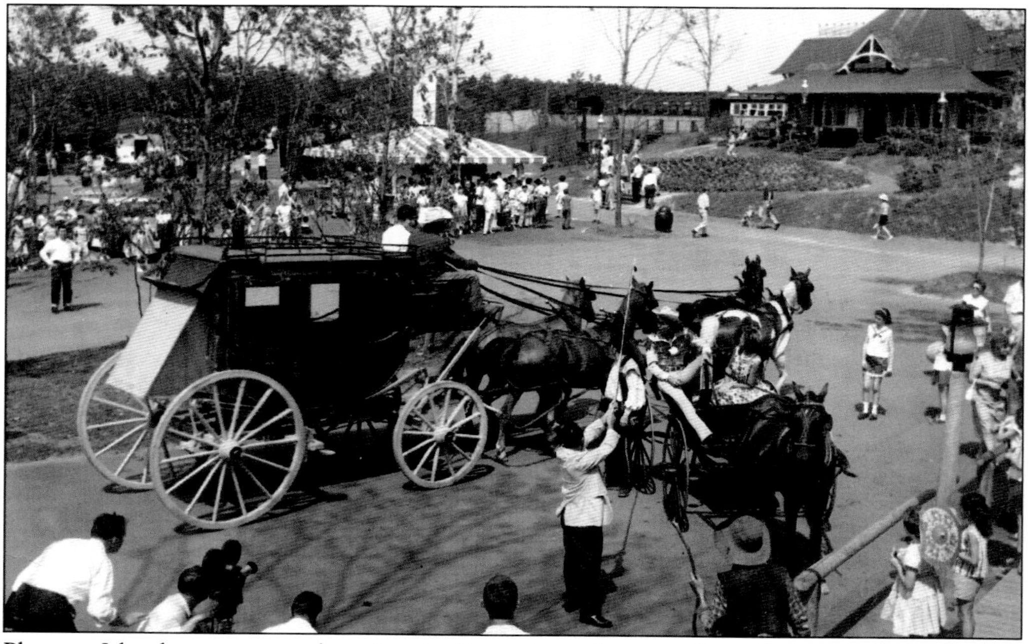

Pleasure Island was a natural setting for Boston's cowboy star Rex Trailer. Trailer and Pablo are filming a scene in front of the Diamond Lil Saloon. Trailer occasionally originated his live *Boomtown* show, which ran on WBZ-TV from 1956 to 1974, from Pleasure Island. (Courtesy of Russ Adams Productions.)

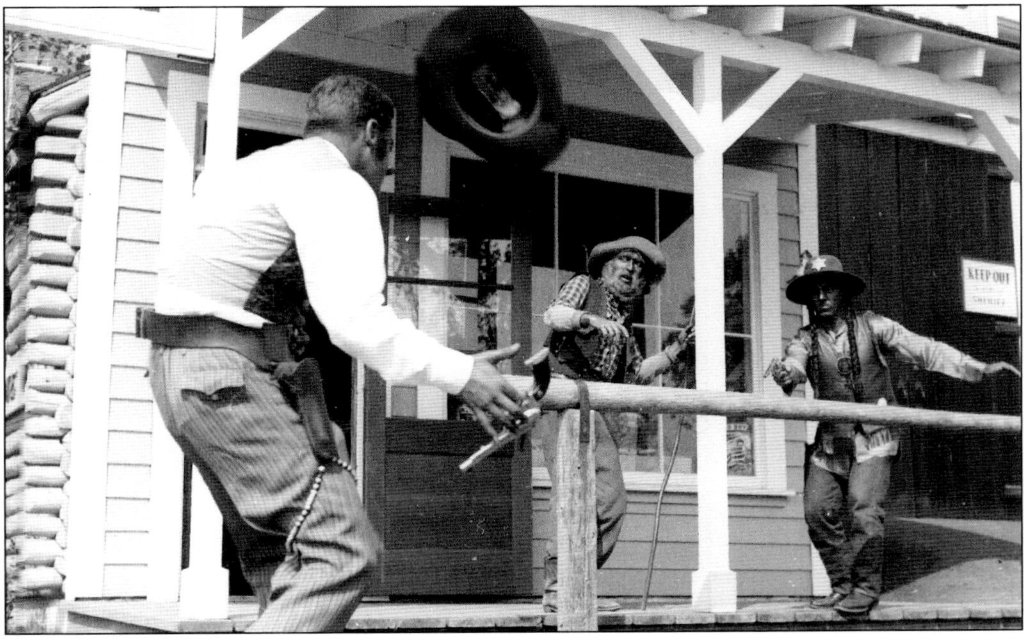

In front of the sheriff's office are Dangerous Dan (left), played by Bob Harmon; the Old Prospector (center), played by Ormond Davis; and Chief Thunderbird, the Native American sheriff, played by Herb Sauve. It must have been fun to play these characters all day and get paid for it to boot. (Courtesy of Bourdon Studios, Herb Sauve collection.)

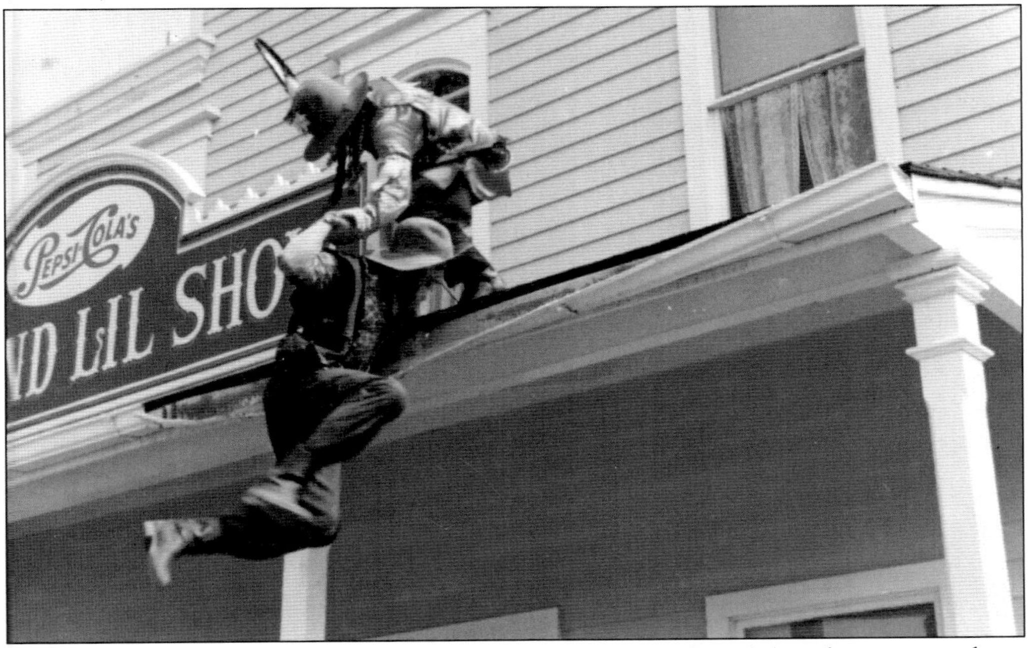

There were two stages at the Diamond Lil Saloon; one was inside and the other was outside on the porch roof. Stunts like this one were performed daily by various actors throughout the life of the park. In this photograph, Sauve's character Chief Thunderbird is helping the Old Prospector back up on the roof. (Courtesy of Herb Sauve.)

IF YOU DON'T SEE WHAT YOU LIKE... NAME WHAT YOU LIKE ... WE'LL MAKE IT FOR YOU!

Our counter men are daring. You can't stymie them. Just tell the waitress what you'd like to have created, and we'll go to work on it.

HOOD' ICE CREAM P GAY NINETIES FOUN

YOUR CHOICE OF CORONET ICE CREAM
IN A VARIETY OF NATURAL FLAVORS

Vanilla
Chocolate
Strawberry
Coffee
Frozen Pudding
Maple Walnut
Peppermint Stick
Chocolate Chip
Banana
Peach
Orange Pineapple
Pistachio
Black Raspberry
Butter Pecan

.25 and .15

CORONET SHERBETS

Orange Lemon Lime Raspberry

.25 and .15

SUNDAES SUPREME

Flavor Favorites of the Gaslight Era
Served in sparkling Tulip Glasses

GAY NINETIES
Two dips Peppermint Stick Ice Cream, Creamy Caramel Fudge Sauce, Pink Whipped Cream topped with Maraschino Cherry .40

APPLE BLOSSOM TIME
Two dips Vanilla Ice Cream, topped with ladle of Fresh Fruit Salad, crowned with a pinnacle of Whipped Cream and garnished with Chopped Nuts and Maraschino Cherry .40

CRACKER BARREL
Two dips Chocolate Ice Cream, Chocolate Fudge Sauce, crushed Macaroons, Whipped Cream and Maraschino Cherry .40

CAROUSEL
Two dips Pistachio Ice Cream, Hot Chocolate Fudge Sauce, a circle of 4 Banana Quarters on top with Whipped Cream and Maraschino Cherry .45

Sweet Adeline
One dip Strawberry Ice Cream, one dip Banana Ice Cream, a ladle of tangy fresh Pineapple, crown of Banana halves and billowy Whipped Cream .45

Sugar 'n Spice
Two dips Vanilla Ice Cream, ladle of plump fresh Strawberries rolled in Confectioners Sugar, a rosette of Whipped Cream, peaked with more Frosted Strawberries .40

Charmaine
Two dips Peach Ice Cream swimming in fresh Peach Quarters, topped with Nabisco Wafers, Whipped Cream and Maraschino Cherry .45

GIBSON GIRL
Two dips Chocolate Ice Cream, Marshmallow Sauce, Hot Fudge Sauce, a billow of Whipped Cream and an avalanche of Toasted Nuts .40

MERRY WIDOW
Two dips Strawberry Ice Cream, ladle of Fresh Fruit Salad, topped with half of Banana, Whipped Cream and Chopped Nuts .40

Crinoline Days
Two dips Peppermint Stick Ice Cream, Marshmallow Sauce, Hot Fudge Sauce, Whipped Cream, Chopped Nuts topped with a Peppermint Stick .45

AULD LANG SYNE
Two dips Frozen Pudding Ice Cream, Caramel Fudge Sauce, Marshmallow Sauce, Macaroon Crumbs and a billowy peak of Whipped Cream .45

ICED DRINKS

Hood Florida Fresh Orange Juice .20

Pepsi-Cola .10 and .15 Root Beer .10 and .15

The delectable fountain treats you enjoy in this establishment are created from the finest ice cream in the world — Old-Fashioned CORONET by Hood.
This ice cream of elegance is made from pure, heavy whipping cream masterfully blended with natural flavors, then patiently frozen to luxuriously smooth perfection. Coronet Ice Cream is the echo of bygone

days . . . a
used to ma
Whatever
taste thrill
flavor alon
era . . . tha
enjoyed at

Frappes Deluxe
GAY NINETIES STYLE

16 DIFFERENT, DELICIOUS CONCOCTIONS
Check Ice Cream Soda List for Flavor of Your Choice

We blend more than ice cream in our frappes. We mix in a lot of adventure, a dash of daring and a pinch of romance. We start with a container of fresh, rich Hood Homogenized Milk, we add two big scoops of Coronet Old-Fashioned Ice Cream, add plenty of pure, natural syrup and then frappe it lovingly into a smooth, mellow and memorable delight .40

WE MAKE "CUSTOM FRAPPES" . . . WE'LL MIX TOGETHER ANY COMBINATION OF INGREDIENTS THAT DOESN'T EXPLODE!

SYRUPS, TOPPINGS and GARNISHES THAT ADD to the and GOODNESS of OUR ICE CRE

SYRUPS

Vanilla Chocolate Coffee Strawberry Maple
Egg Nog Cherry Orange Lemon
Lime Raspberry Creme de Menthe Coffee Brandy
Checkerberry Mint

TOPPINGS

Fresh Strawberries Fresh Fruit Salad Fresh Peaches
Fresh Bananas Pineapples Oranges
Lemons Limes Rich Hot Fudge Sauce
Creamy Caramel Fudge Sauce Marshmallow Sauce
Whipped Cream Cherries (Red and Green)

Crushed
Pe
N
Licorice
Crus

Mis
Lac

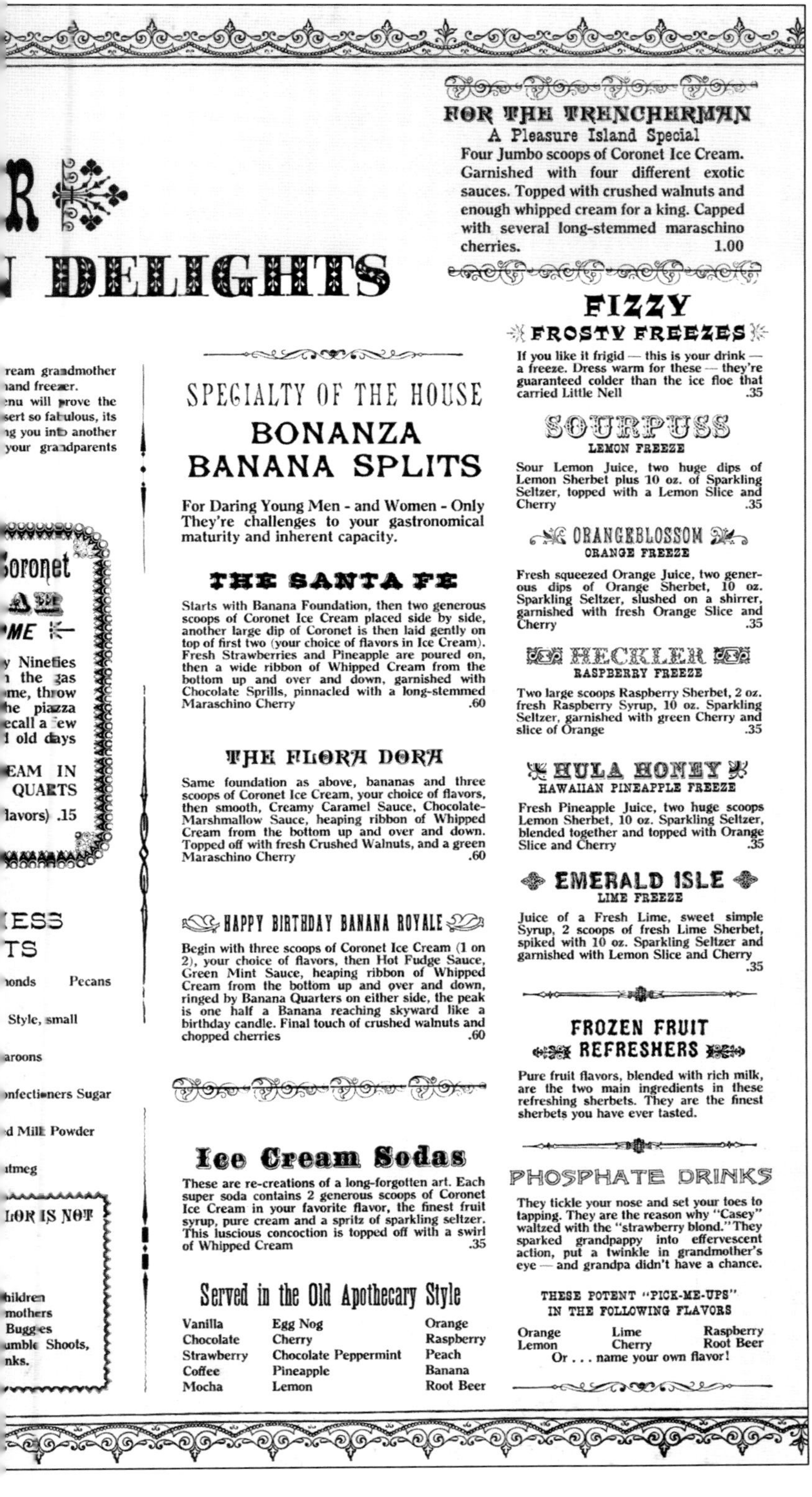

R

DELIGHTS

ream grandmother
hand freezer.
nu will prove the
sert so fabulous, its
ng you into another
your grandparents

Coronet

ME

y Nineties
the gas
me, throw
he piazza
ecall a few
l old days

EAM IN
QUARTS
lavors) .15

ESS
TS

nonds Pecans

Style, small

aroons

nfectioners Sugar

d Milk Powder

tmeg

LOR IS NOT

hildren
mothers
Buggies
umble Shoots,
nks.

SPECIALTY OF THE HOUSE

BONANZA BANANA SPLITS

For Daring Young Men - and Women - Only They're challenges to your gastronomical maturity and inherent capacity.

THE SANTA FE

Starts with Banana Foundation, then two generous scoops of Coronet Ice Cream placed side by side, another large dip of Coronet is then laid gently on top of first two (your choice of flavors in Ice Cream). Fresh Strawberries and Pineapple are poured on, then a wide ribbon of Whipped Cream from the bottom up and over and down, garnished with Chocolate Sprills, pinnacled with a long-stemmed Maraschino Cherry .60

THE FLORA DORA

Same foundation as above, bananas and three scoops of Coronet Ice Cream, your choice of flavors, then smooth, Creamy Caramel Sauce, Chocolate-Marshmallow Sauce, heaping ribbon of Whipped Cream from the bottom up and over and down. Topped off with fresh Crushed Walnuts, and a green Maraschino Cherry .60

HAPPY BIRTHDAY BANANA ROYALE

Begin with three scoops of Coronet Ice Cream (1 on 2), your choice of flavors, then Hot Fudge Sauce, Green Mint Sauce, heaping ribbon of Whipped Cream from the bottom up and over and down, ringed by Banana Quarters on either side, the peak is one half a Banana reaching skyward like a birthday candle. Final touch of crushed walnuts and chopped cherries .60

Ice Cream Sodas

These are re-creations of a long-forgotten art. Each super soda contains 2 generous scoops of Coronet Ice Cream in your favorite flavor, the finest fruit syrup, pure cream and a spritz of sparkling seltzer. This luscious concoction is topped off with a swirl of Whipped Cream .35

Served in the Old Apothecary Style

Vanilla	Egg Nog	Orange
Chocolate	Cherry	Raspberry
Strawberry	Chocolate Peppermint	Peach
Coffee	Pineapple	Banana
Mocha	Lemon	Root Beer

FOR THE TRENCHERMAN

A Pleasure Island Special

Four Jumbo scoops of Coronet Ice Cream. Garnished with four different exotic sauces. Topped with crushed walnuts and enough whipped cream for a king. Capped with several long-stemmed maraschino cherries. 1.00

FIZZY FROSTY FREEZES

If you like it frigid — this is your drink — a freeze. Dress warm for these — they're guaranteed colder than the ice floe that carried Little Nell .35

SOURPUSS

LEMON FREEZE

Sour Lemon Juice, two huge dips of Lemon Sherbet plus 10 oz. of Sparkling Seltzer, topped with a Lemon Slice and Cherry .35

ORANGEBLOSSOM

ORANGE FREEZE

Fresh squeezed Orange Juice, two generous dips of Orange Sherbet, 10 oz. Sparkling Seltzer, slushed on a shirrer, garnished with fresh Orange Slice and Cherry .35

HECKLER

RASPBERRY FREEZE

Two large scoops Raspberry Sherbet, 2 oz. fresh Raspberry Syrup, 10 oz. Sparkling Seltzer, garnished with green Cherry and slice of Orange .35

HULA HONEY

HAWAIIAN PINEAPPLE FREEZE

Fresh Pineapple Juice, two huge scoops Lemon Sherbet, 10 oz. Sparkling Seltzer, blended together and topped with Orange Slice and Cherry .35

EMERALD ISLE

LIME FREEZE

Juice of a Fresh Lime, sweet simple Syrup, 2 scoops of fresh Lime Sherbet, spiked with 10 oz. Sparkling Seltzer and garnished with Lemon Slice and Cherry .35

FROZEN FRUIT REFRESHERS

Pure fruit flavors, blended with rich milk, are the two main ingredients in these refreshing sherbets. They are the finest sherbets you have ever tasted.

PHOSPHATE DRINKS

They tickle your nose and set your toes to tapping. They are the reason why "Casey" waltzed with the "strawberry blond." They sparked grandpappy into effervescent action, put a twinkle in grandmother's eye — and grandpa didn't have a chance.

THESE POTENT "PICK-ME-UPS" IN THE FOLLOWING FLAVORS

Orange	Lime	Raspberry
Lemon	Cherry	Root Beer

Or . . . name your own flavor!

According to the *Clipper Cove Chronicle*, "Midway between Clipper Cove and Goldpan Gulch is the beautiful Victorian-styled Hood's Gay Nineties Ice Cream Parlor. The attractive circular building is almost completely surrounded with a shaded porch and affords a view of both the New England and western sections of the park." (Courtesy of Raymond DiPirro.)

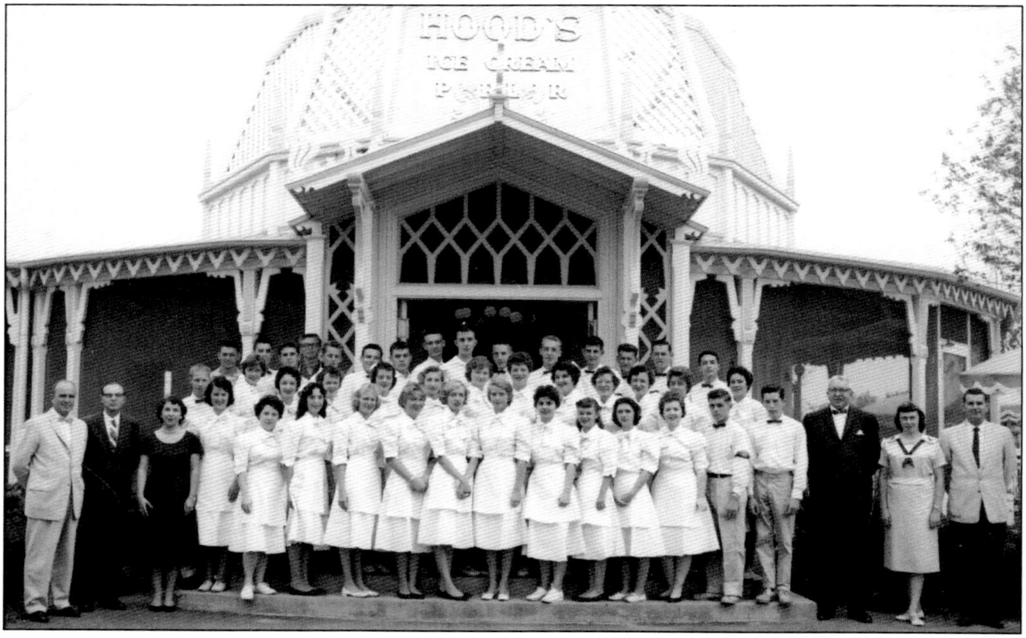

H. P. Hood and Sons had a big presence and investment at Pleasure Island. According to a February 12, 1959, story in the *Wakefield Daily Item*, "Hood was the first company to sign a lease for the supply of products to the Recreational Center." This photograph is on the Friends of Pleasure Island Web site with some of the employees identified. (Courtesy of Donald G. Graham.)

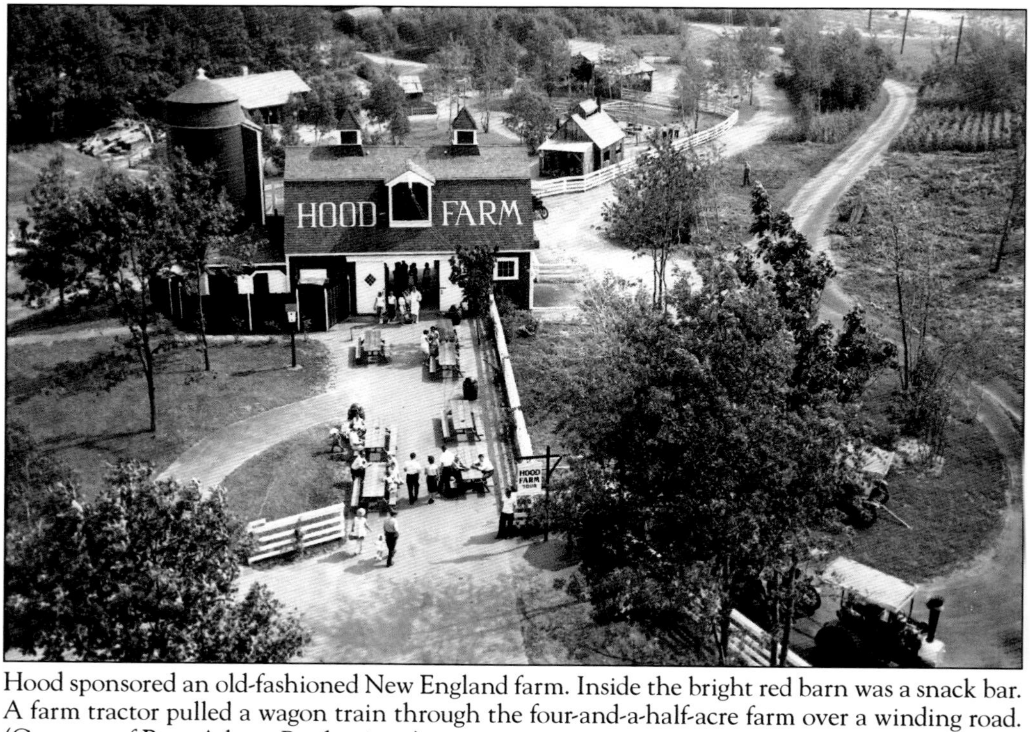

Hood sponsored an old-fashioned New England farm. Inside the bright red barn was a snack bar. A farm tractor pulled a wagon train through the four-and-a-half-acre farm over a winding road. (Courtesy of Russ Adams Productions.)

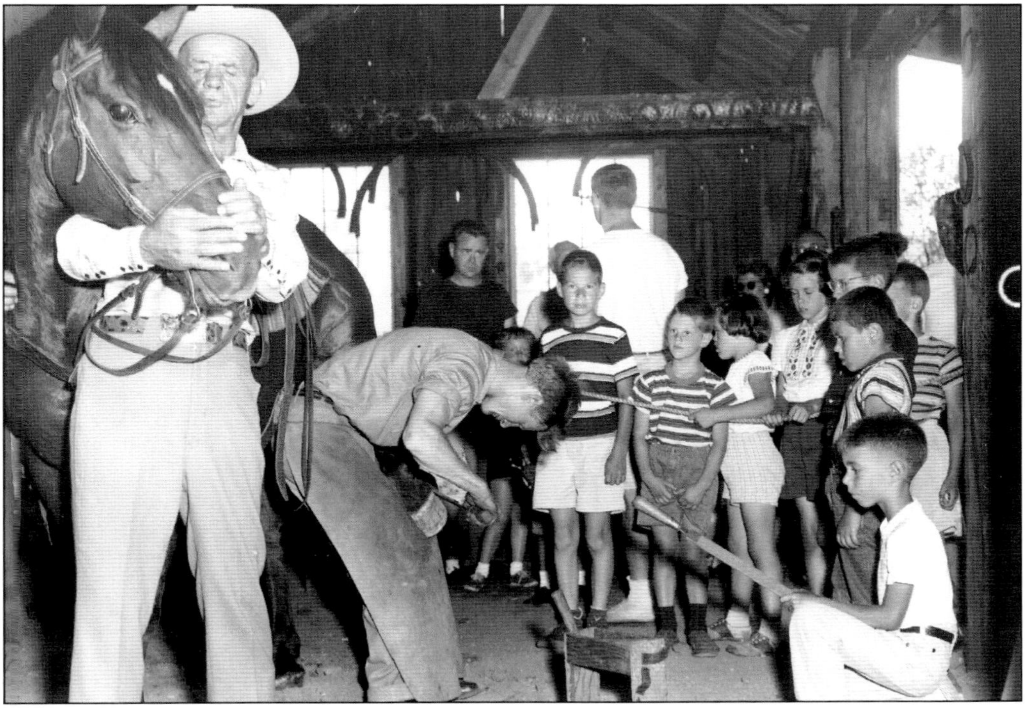

Also at the Hood Farm was a blacksmith shop (above) with the smithy actually shoeing a horse. Souvenir horseshoes with a "Pleasure Island 1959" plaque attached were made at the shop and sold at the park. The Maple Sugar House (below), where syrup was boiled for guests to capture the New England farm experience, was also located there. (Above, courtesy of House of Photography; below, courtesy of Russ Adams Productions.)

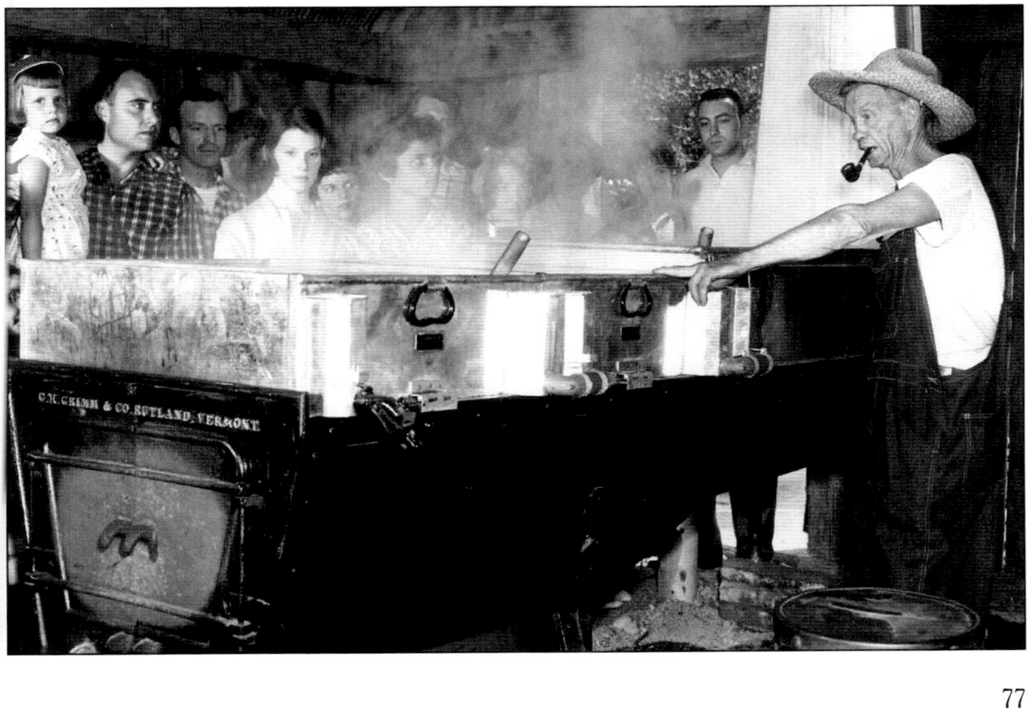

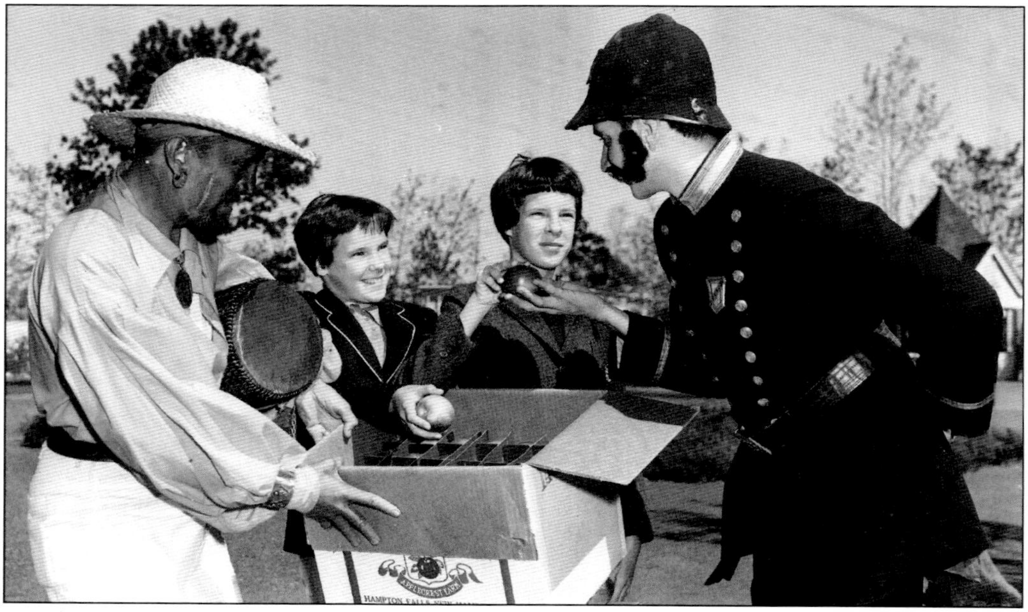

Winding down for the 1959 season, two events occurred. On Saturday, September 19, admission and rides were discounted for Wakefield and Lynnfield residents, and Sunday, September 20, was the apple festival. Upon leaving the park, visitors received a McIntosh apple from Jasper, first mate to Captain Ahab (played by the late Richard Freniere) and Clancy the Cop (Apollo Dukakis). October 3 and 4 were Pleasure Island's last weekend days for the season. (Courtesy of Russ Adams Productions.)

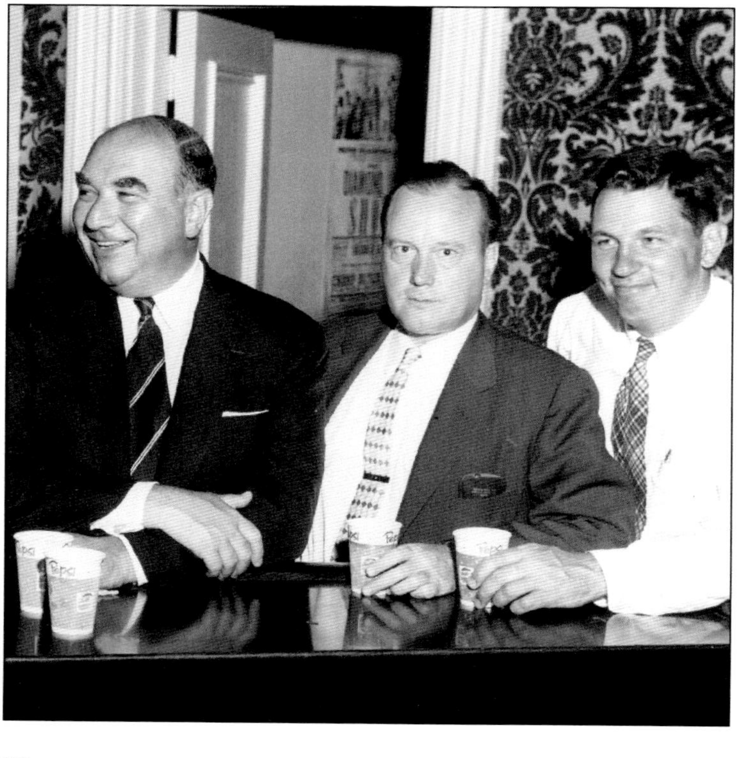

These gentlemen are in for some business changes in 1960. Standing at the Diamond Lil Bar are William Zeckendorf (left), Robert Linnell (center), and Bill Hawkes. This photograph was probably taken on Pleasure Island's opening weekend in 1959. (Courtesy of Russ Adams Productions.)

Four

From 1960 to 1969

When Pleasure Island closed at the end of its first season, the corporation that built Pleasure Island, led by Bill Hawkes, also ended in bankruptcy. Many factors led to this end, and creditors reportedly received only 20¢ on the dollar. Three Boston businessmen purchased the park and opened it on June 18, 1960, Walter Smith Jr., Pleasure Island's new general manager; Herbert Lee; and Robert Linnell. That year saw big changes at the park. Exhibitors H. P. Hood and Sons and Pepsi-Cola were out. Also, a new trend-setting policy replaced individual tickets for attractions with a one-price entry fee for all rides and shows. The popular Diamond Lil Show was out, and a brand-new amphitheater named the Show Bowl was in. Opening week brought the Three Stooges to the new stage, with the local press reporting nearly 20,000 guests the first weekend alone. On the weekend of August 26 and 27, 1960, Newport Jazz Festival promoter George Wein took the festival to Pleasure Island with a reported crowd of 12,000 concertgoers. A program of this concert is on the Friends of Pleasure Island Web site. An impressive lineup of television and movie stars, recording artists, circus performers, animal acts, and local talent entertained guests throughout most of the life of Pleasure Island, winding down in the later seasons. It was reported locally on May 13, 1964, that Pleasure Island would be leased for the 1964 season. Boston Ventures, a corporation made up of investors and headed by famed orchestra leader Ruby Newman took over the operation of Pleasure Island. Al Longo and the late Sandy Giampapa were the hands-on managers and also partners among others in Boston Ventures. Boston Ventures bought the park in 1965. During its five-year run, slacking attendance and rising maintenance problems had the owners looking for options, and by the spring of 1969, the park was sold to Fairbanks Amusement Corporation, which closed it down for good at the end of the 1969 season.

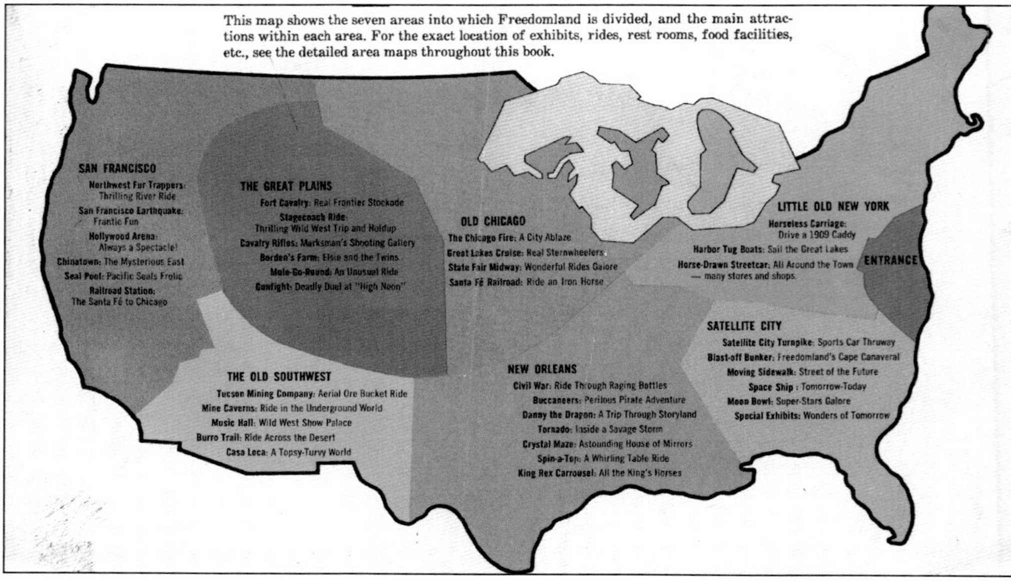

One day after Pleasure Island opened for its 1960 season, Freedomland, located in the Bronx in New York City, opened for its first season. Built in the shape of the United States and themed accordingly, it was the largest of the parks designed by C. V. Wood. It was also billed as the "Disneyland of the East." With a lawsuit from Disney over misrepresentation and other factors, this was the last of a planned 12 Disneyland copycat parks for Wood's company. (Author's collection.)

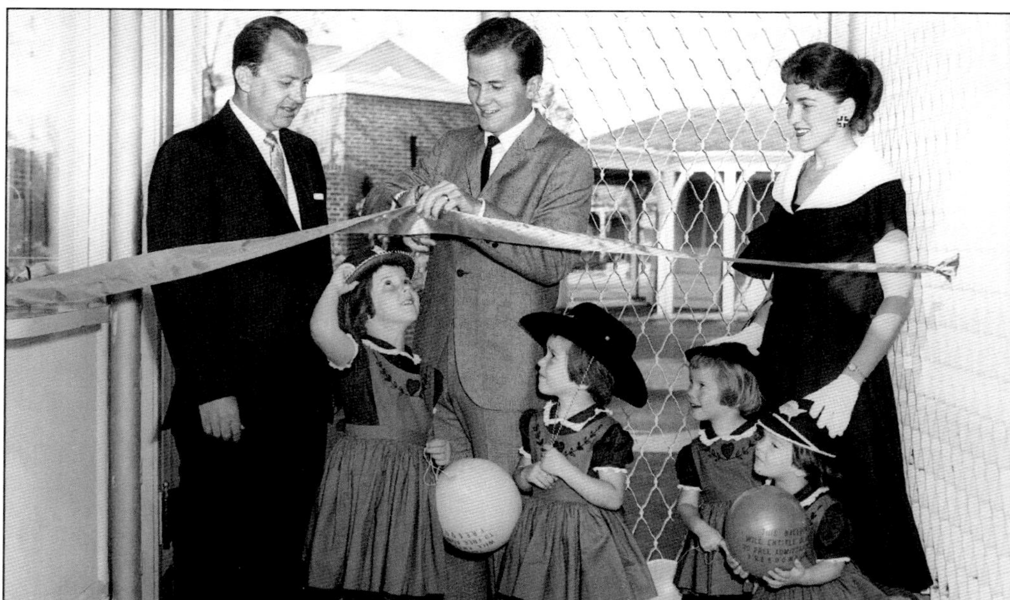

On June 19, 1960, Freedomland opened to an estimated 63,000 visitors. Wood, whose company, Marco Engineering, designed Freedomland, looks on as Pat Boone cuts the opening-day ribbon. Also pictured from left to right are Boone's four daughters, Cherry, Lindy, Debby, and Laury, and his wife, Shirley Foley, daughter of country music great Red Foley. Parking capacity at Freedomland was 7,300 versus Pleasure Island's 3,000-car lot. (Courtesy of Frank Adamo.)

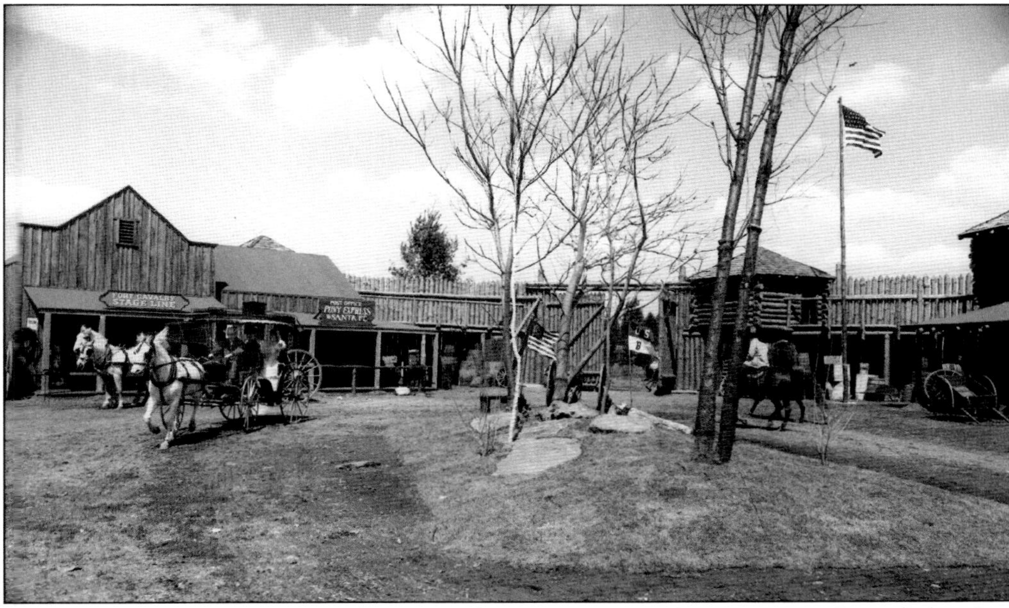

Fort Cavalry, from Freedomland's Great Plains section, no longer exists. Out of the three parks designed by Wood to be modeled after Disneyland, Magic Mountain partially opened for 3 seasons, 1958–1960, Freedomland opened in 1960 and closed at the end of its 1964 season, and Pleasure Island lasted 11 seasons, 1959–1969. (Photograph by Guy Gillette, courtesy of Frank Adamo.)

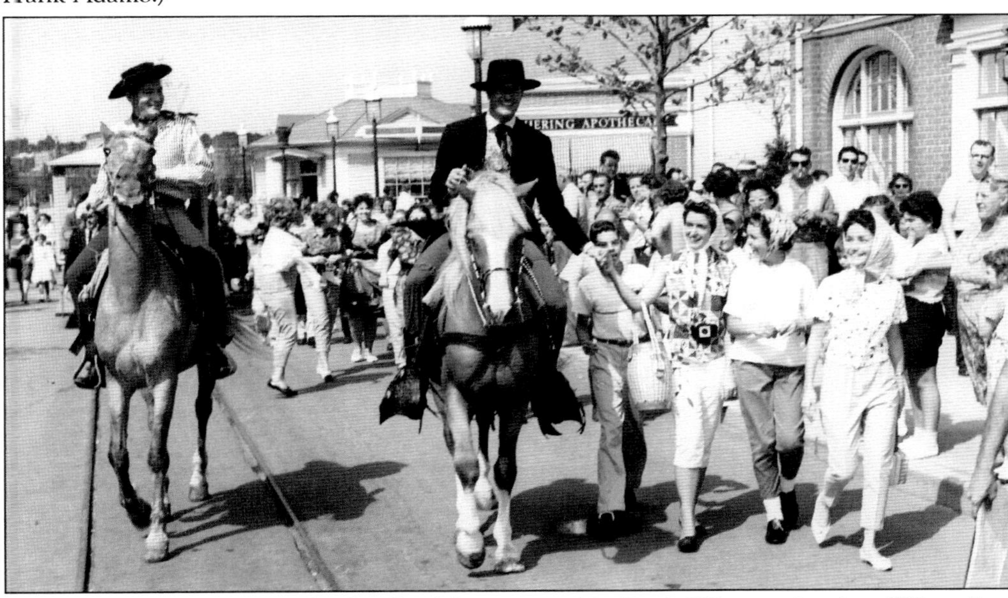

Just like Pleasure Island, Freedomland had the stars too, like Hugh O'Brien, who played Wyatt Earp. This park was built on property owned by prominent real estate developer William Zeckendorf. He was a major investor, and his real estate empire suffered greatly from Freedomland's demise. Pleasure Island's Bill Hawkes, Herbert Lee, and Robert Linnell were on Freedomland's board of directors. Boston's Aberthaw Construction, along with Turner Construction, built Freedomland. (Courtesy of Frank Adamo.)

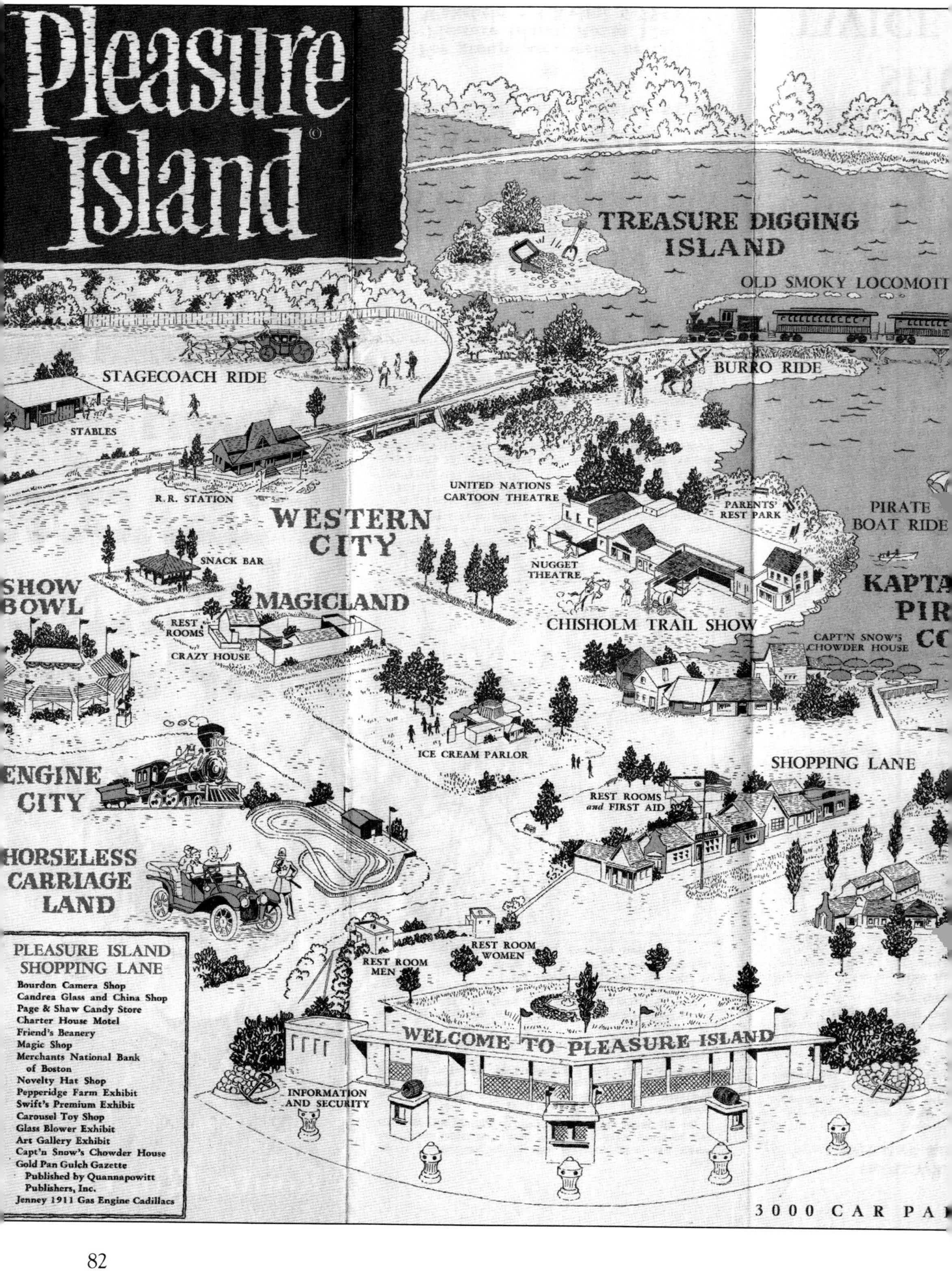
Pleasure Island©
TREASURE DIGGING ISLAND
OLD SMOKY LOCOMOTI
STAGECOACH RIDE
BURRO RIDE
STABLES
R.R. STATION
UNITED NATIONS CARTOON THEATRE
PARENTS' REST PARK
PIRATE BOAT RIDE
WESTERN CITY
SNACK BAR
NUGGET THEATRE
KAPTA
PIR
CC
SHOW BOWL
MAGICLAND
REST ROOMS
CRAZY HOUSE
CHISHOLM TRAIL SHOW
CAPT'N SNOW'S CHOWDER HOUSE
ICE CREAM PARLOR
SHOPPING LANE
ENGINE CITY
REST ROOMS and FIRST AID
HORSELESS CARRIAGE LAND
REST ROOM WOMEN
REST ROOM MEN
WELCOME TO PLEASURE ISLAND
INFORMATION AND SECURITY
PLEASURE ISLAND SHOPPING LANE
Bourdon Camera Shop
Candrea Glass and China Shop
Page & Shaw Candy Store
Charter House Motel
Friend's Beanery
Magic Shop
Merchants National Bank of Boston
Novelty Hat Shop
Pepperidge Farm Exhibit
Swift's Premium Exhibit
Carousel Toy Shop
Glass Blower Exhibit
Art Gallery Exhibit
Capt'n Snow's Chowder House
Gold Pan Gulch Gazette Published by Quannapowitt Publishers, Inc.
Jenney 1911 Gas Engine Cadillacs
3000 CAR PA

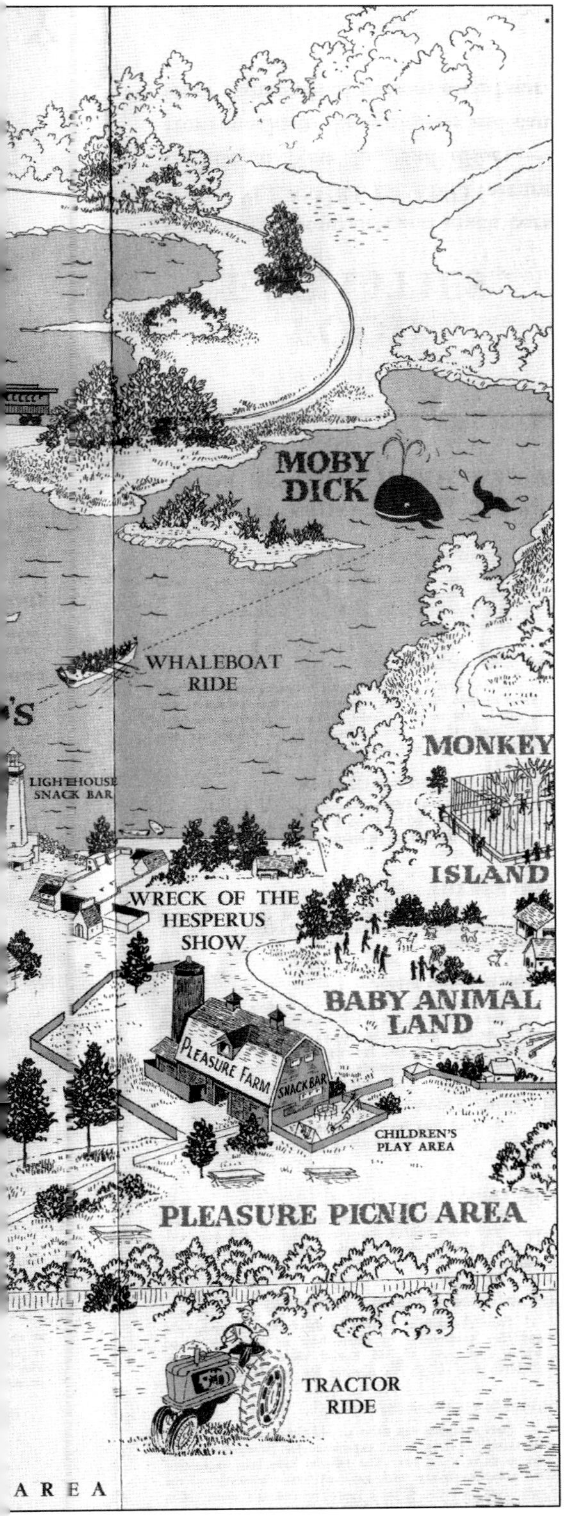

This is a bird's-eye view of the 1960 season at Pleasure Island. The Hood Farm was taken over by the new owners, who added Baby Animal Land and Monkey Island. The Diamond Lil Saloon was renamed Nugget Theatre and ran cartoons. The entertainment shifted to the new Show Bowl next to Engine City, which exited Pleasure Island after the 1961 season. The stagecoach ride also disappeared after the 1960 season. Over the entire 11 seasons, the footprint of the original park never changed, although many of the attractions and vendors operating within the park did. (Courtesy of FOPI archives.)

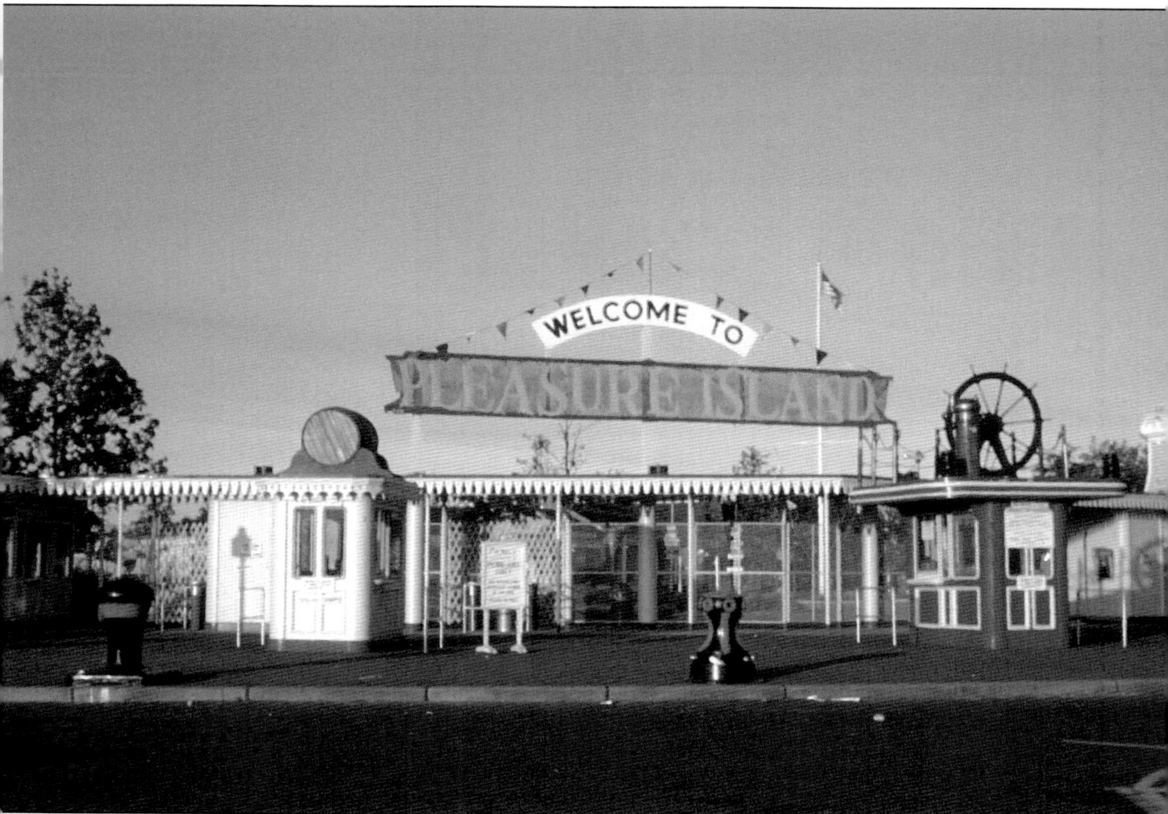

The signature signage at the front gate was changed at least three times during Pleasure Island's 11 seasons in operation. One thing that never changed was the games of chance attraction not being allowed in the park by Wakefield's board of selectmen. The following story came out on June 8, 1960, in the *Wakefield Daily Item*: "The Board of Selectmen last night indicated their solid opposition to any game of skill or chance in Pleasure Island." Also reported in the story, "Mr. Smith [one of the new owners] explained that one goal the park operators are setting is providing more participation by the public in the park." They wanted more revenue to support the park's operation, and the board of selectmen was opposed to what it conceived was a carnival-type operation. Attempts for games of this type were rejected up to and including the last season in 1969. (Courtesy of Patrick Farino.)

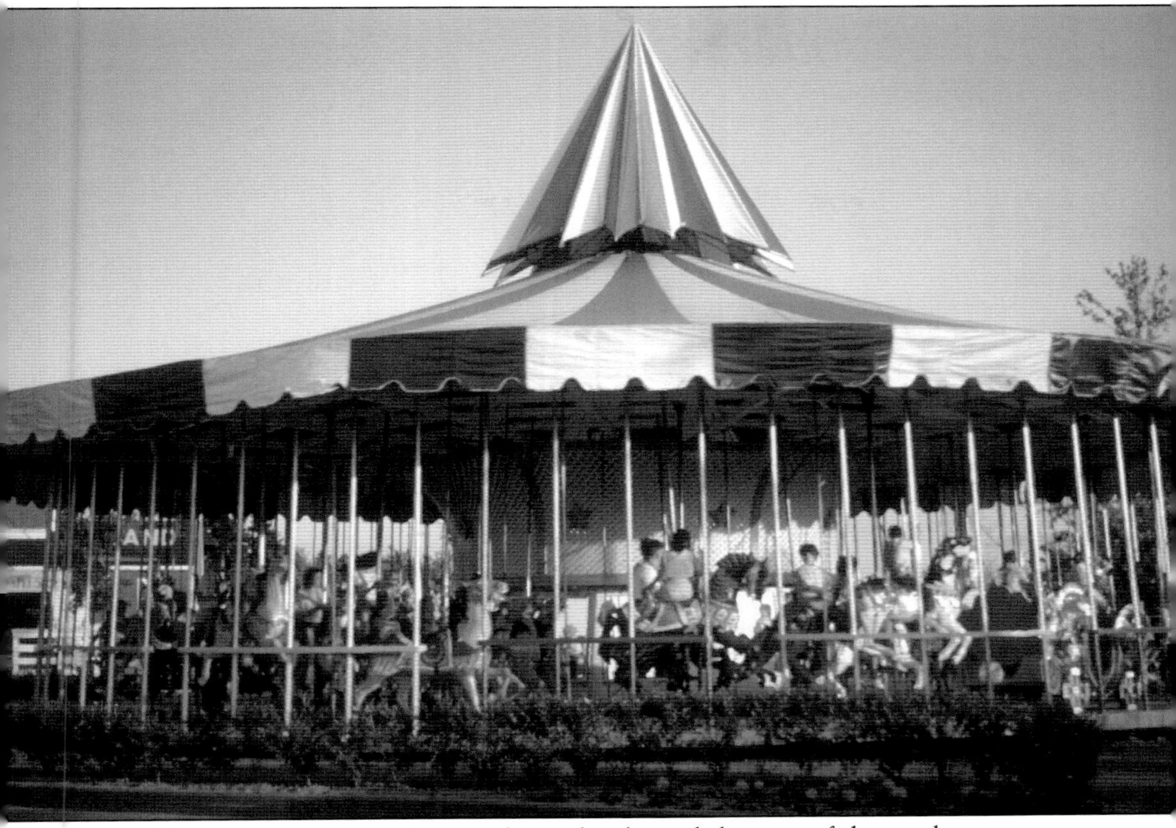

Pleasure Island opened on May 6, 1961, for weekends until the start of the regular season on June 24. The new attractions for the 1961 season included Kart Land (the go-kart attraction just outside the main gate), the Bozo the Clown Skyscraper Slide from the Baby Animal Barn Silo, the Water Buffalo Land and Sea ride that replaced the stagecoach attraction, and, as reported in the *Wakefield Daily Item* on June 20, 1961, "Final touches are now being put on the big Continental Carousel, which will ride 100 adults on the outer perimeter and 75 children on the inside, with hand painted flying horses ready to greet thousands of incoming guests." One could write an entire book on Pleasure Island's carousel. It reportedly came for an old trolley park at Lake Nipmuc Park in Mendon with its carving done by Daniel Muller around 1910. Some scenes from the movie *Charly*, including the one with the carousel, were filmed at Pleasure Island in the fall of 1967. (Courtesy of Patrick Farino.)

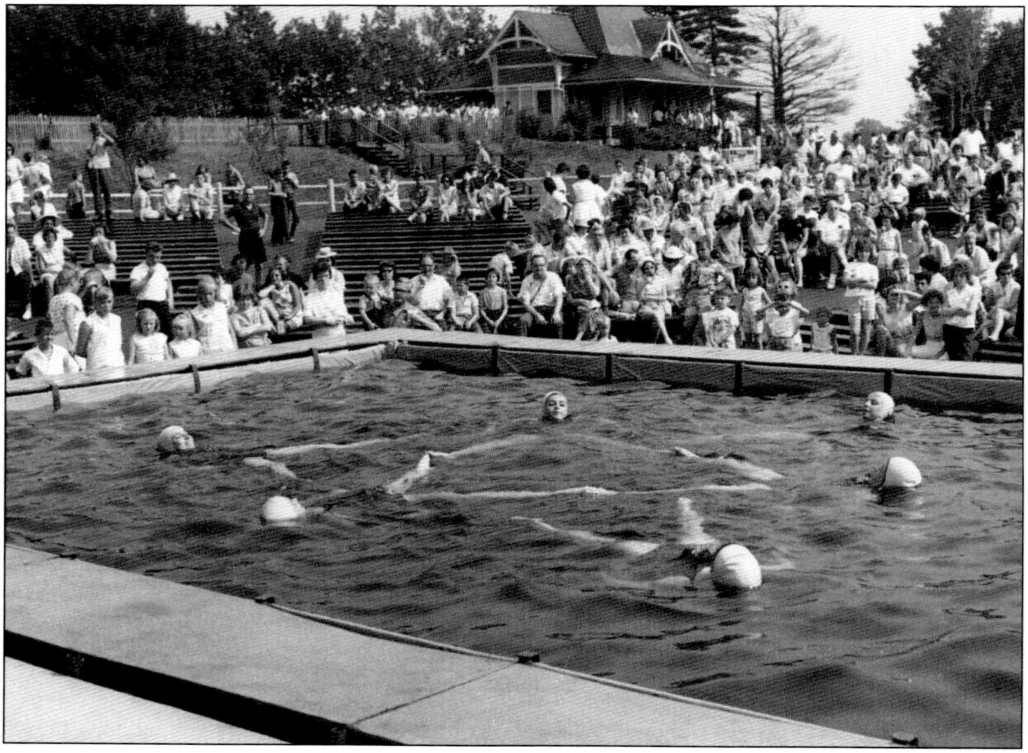

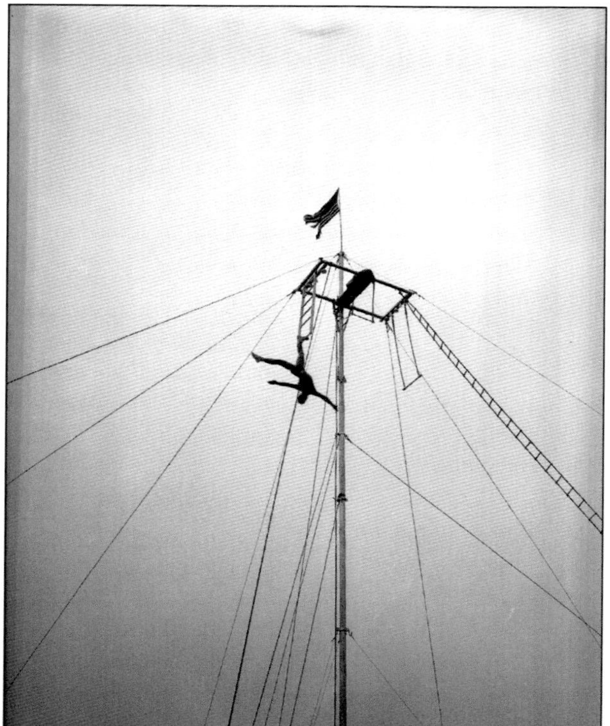

The entertainment at the Show Bowl was one of the major draws to get guests to part with their dollars at the main entrance. In 1960, admission to Pleasure Island was $2 for adults and a $1.50 for children under 12, plus tax, which included all rides and shows. The photograph above has synchronized swimmers performing in a pool set up in front of the Show Bowl stage. The photograph at left is from one of the many circus acts such as the Famous Hannaford Circus, which performed regularly at the Show Bowl. In addition to the top stars of the day, park characters also had a huge influence on its charm. Aspiring local actors and actresses performed either at the Show Bowl, the Nugget Theatre, or around the park, which was the biggest stage of all. (Courtesy of Patrick Farino.)

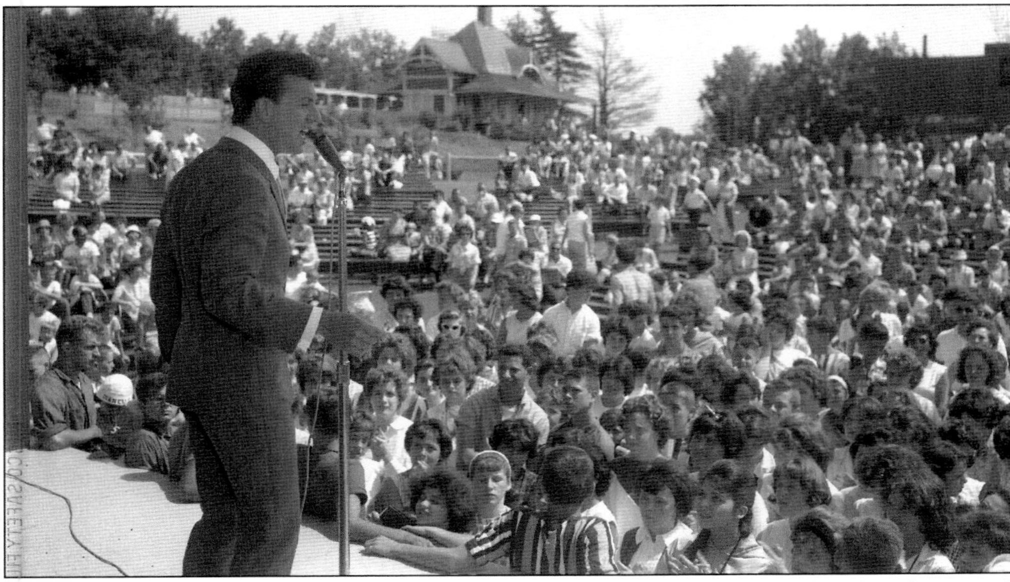

Dion DiMucci, of Dion and the Belmonts, was one of many popular stars who played to crowds at Pleasure Island. With a string of hits in 1958, Dion and the Belmonts won a place on the Winter Dance Party tour with Buddy Holly and Ritchie Valens. After playing in Cedar Lake, Iowa, on February 2, 1959, DiMucci did not take the flight that was leaving for the next show because of its $36 cost. That plane crashed on February 3 shortly after midnight, and the stars on board were killed. (Courtesy of Patrick Farino.)

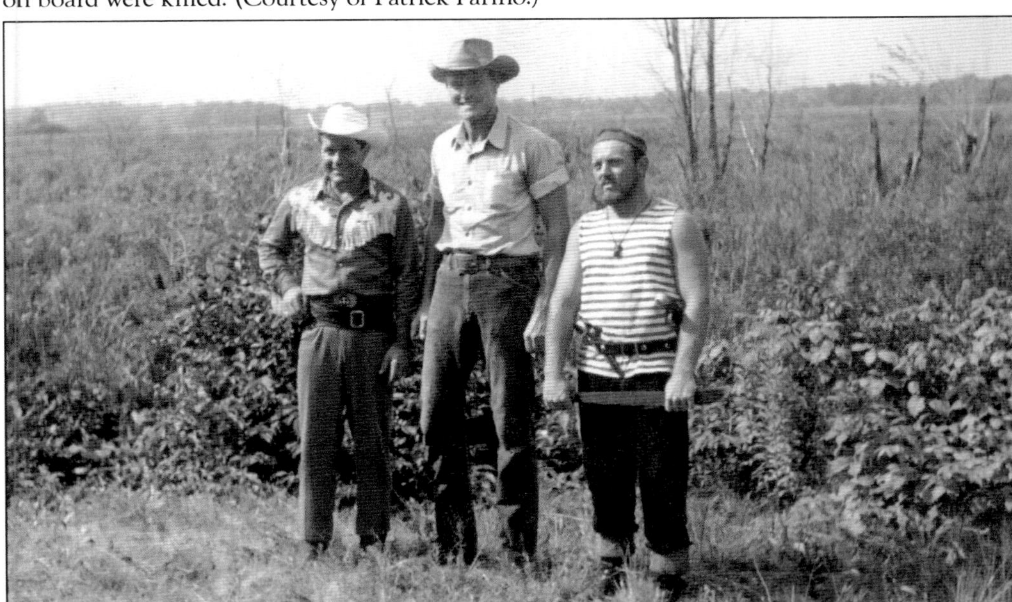

With Pleasure Island's sheriff Sy Milano to the left and character actor Herb Sauve to the right, Chuck Connors (center) is pictured here behind the Show Bowl with the present-day Reedy Meadow in the rear. Connors fit right in with the western theme of Pleasure Island and drew huge crowds at the Show Bowl. On a side note, as an avid horseman, Milano was the former trainer for Rex Trailer's horses. (Courtesy of Herb Sauve.)

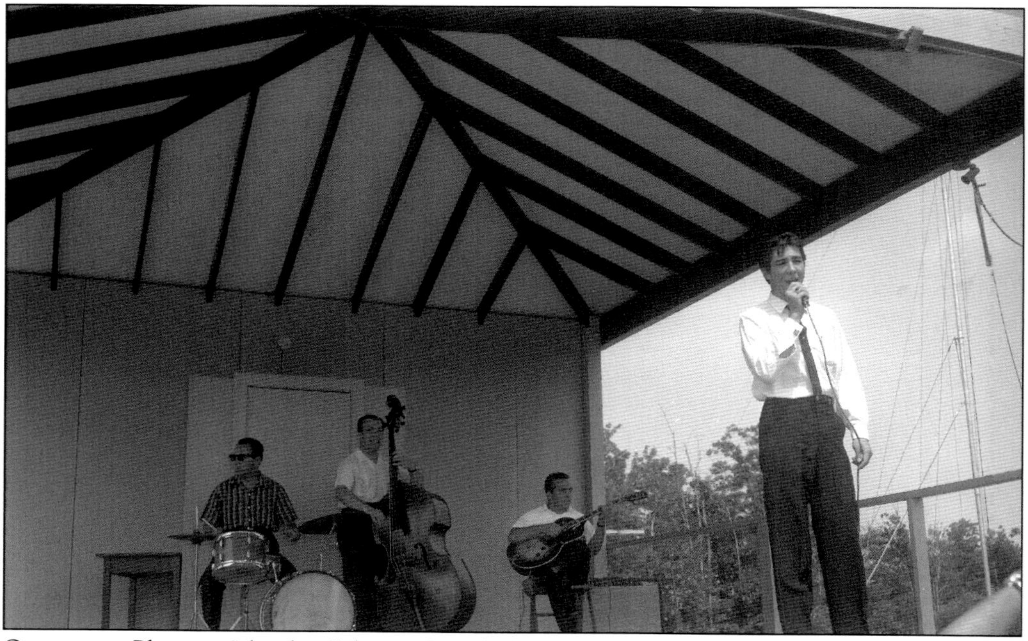

Onstage at Pleasure Island is Johnny Crawford. As an original Disney Mouseketeer in 1955, Crawford also acted onstage, in films, and on television, most notably as Mark McCain of the series *The Rifleman*. Crawford also generated five top-40 hits as a recording artist. (Courtesy of Patrick Farino.)

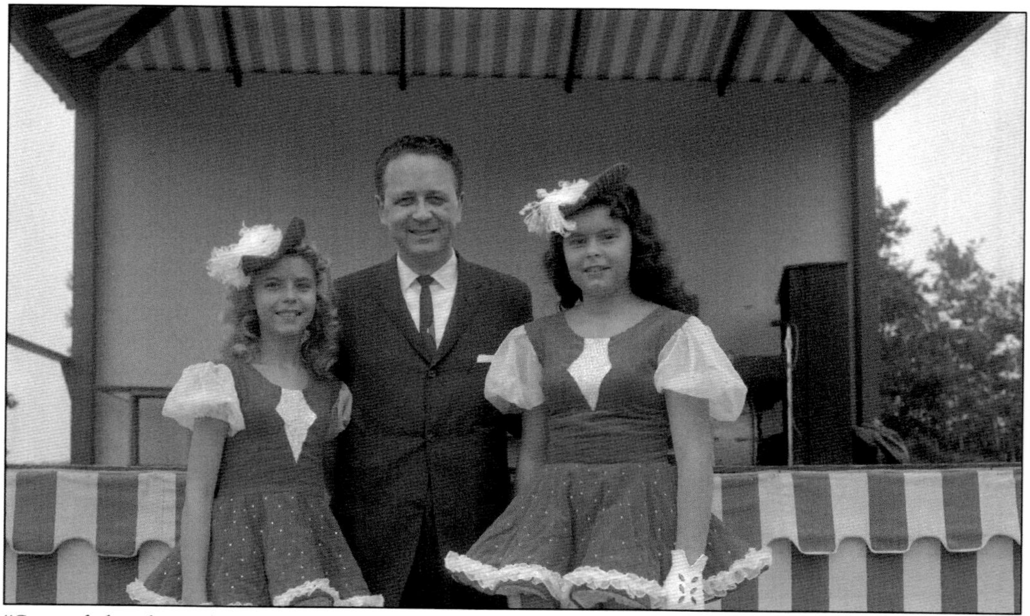

"Star of the day, who will it be?" Many contestants throughout New England applied to be a part of Pleasure Island's weeklong community auditions show. Starting on July 18, 1960, talented youngsters auditioned at each show twice a day throughout the week. On Sunday, July 24, the 12 winners competed for the championship. Show host Gene Jones (center) lived on Pine Street in Wakefield. (Courtesy of Patrick Farino.)

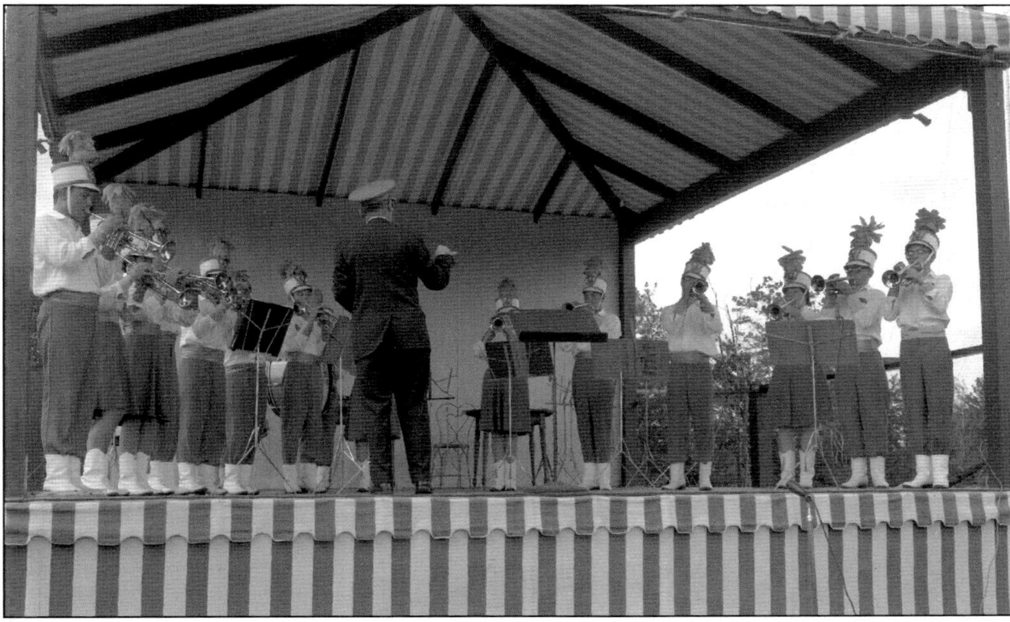

Throughout its 11 seasons, Pleasure Island hosted a number of local personalities like Rex Trailer, Red Auerbach, and Major Mudd. Show Bowl entertainers included popular names such as Duke Ellington and his orchestra, Dinah Washington, Dave Brubeck, Gene Krupa, the Four Freshmen, Flipper (with his own pool), Troy Donahue, Robert Horton of *Wagon Train*, Jimmy Dean, Ricky Nelson, Don Ameche, Joe Ross, Fred Gwynne, Clayton Moore, Lassie, Frank Gorshin, Cesar Romero, Michael Landon, and Jerry Mathers. (Courtesy of Patrick Farino.)

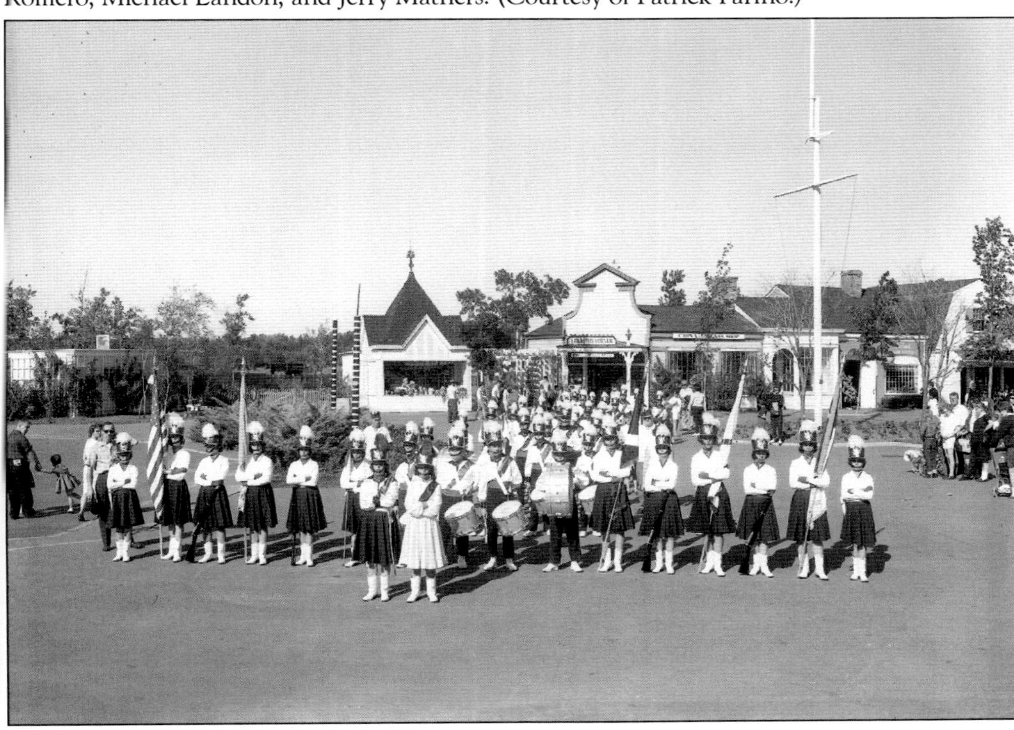

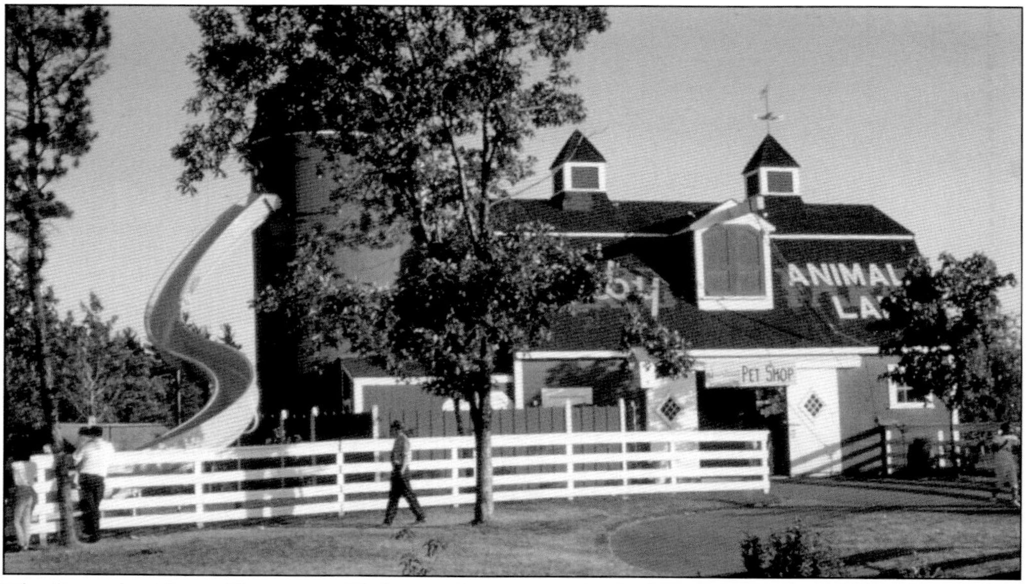

The Bozo the Clown Skyscraper Slide was three stories high. Guests were placed on a burlap sack, and away they went. More than one unhappy camper ended up at the park's nurse's office with burns after they got separated from their magic carpet. Heinz Rube of Germany, who arranged the Franklin Park exhibit, also arranged the Pleasure Island animal farm, which included llamas, deer, sheep, angora goats, pygmy donkeys, giant tortoises, monkeys, bear cubs, flamingos, and more. (Courtesy of Patrick Farino.)

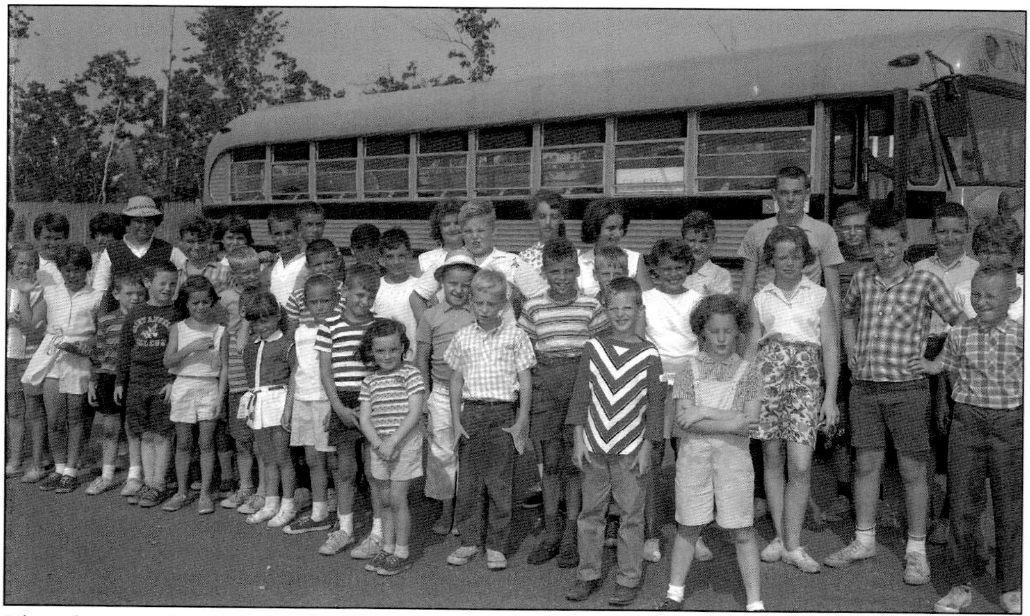

This photograph is dedicated to all the children and their chaperones for their first and maybe only visit to Pleasure Island, this author included. Whether from the YMCA, Boys and Girls Club, city and town recreation departments, or a group of newspaper carriers from Nashua, New Hampshire, thousands of children were introduced to a world unlike any other after stepping off their bus. (Courtesy of Patrick Farino.)

Pleasure Island provided more than attractions and shows. It also offered summer employment for local residents, young and not so young. Mary K. Galvin (at right), age 16, worked at the Hood Barn Snack Bar in 1959. Not including locals employed by the shops and food services (below), the following is a list of Wakefield personnel hired to start the 1963 season: Daniel Calore, Jack Loomis, John Woker, Douglas Reed, Gregory Smith, Barry Spracklin, Peter Puglisi, Douglas Gourley, Margaret Erker, Bernice Kelley, J. Thomas Guttadauro, William McNally, Linda Moran, John Boudreau, Richard Cronin, Henry Stahle Jr., Russell Chapman, Fredrick Beyer, Margaret Sullivan, Marcia Burton, Susan Fiske, Frank Boccelli, Richard Demerie, John DiTonno, Harold MacCaughey, Robert Lally, Douglas Iram, Richard Meuse, Donald Hanson, Richard Silvey, and Henry Rufo Jr. (Right, courtesy of Mary K. Galvin; below, courtesy of Patrick Farino.)

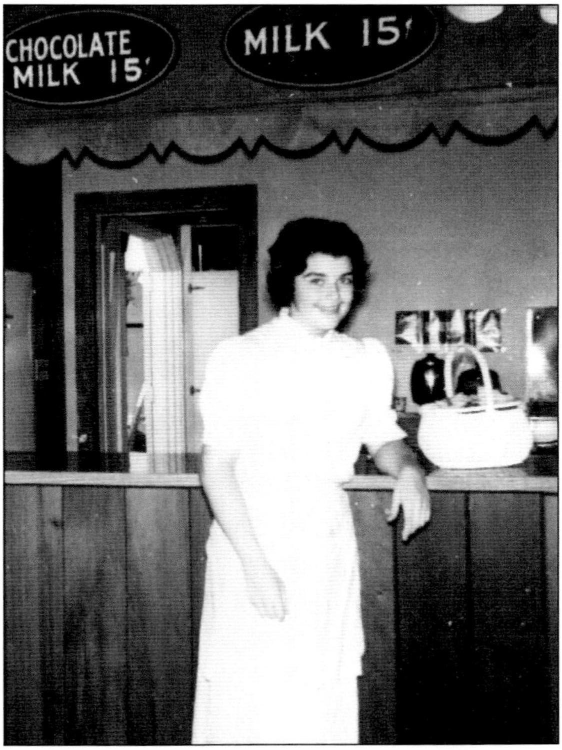

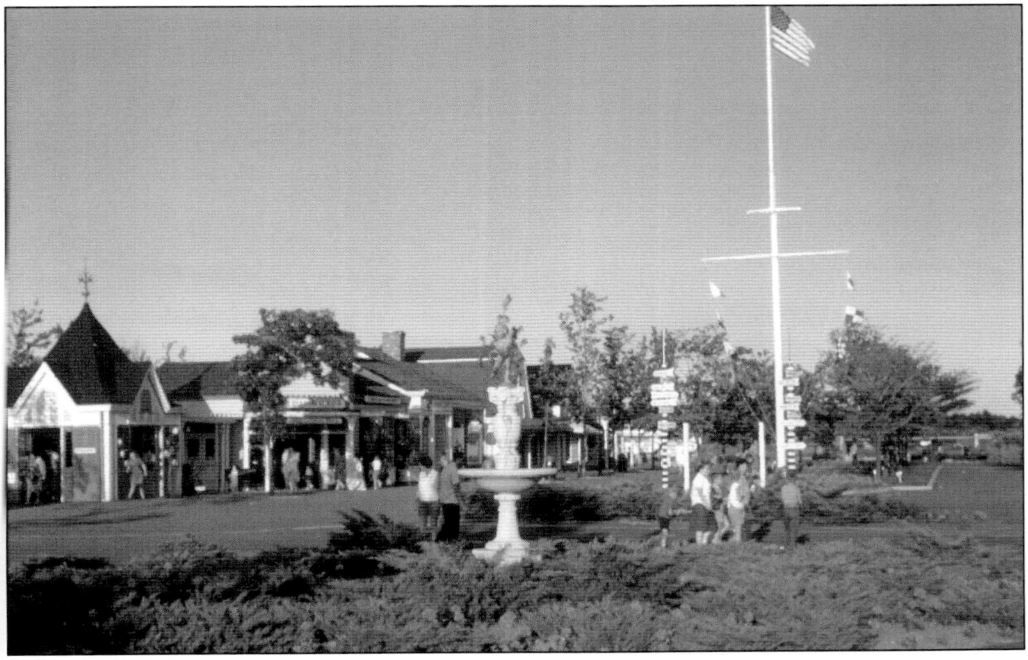

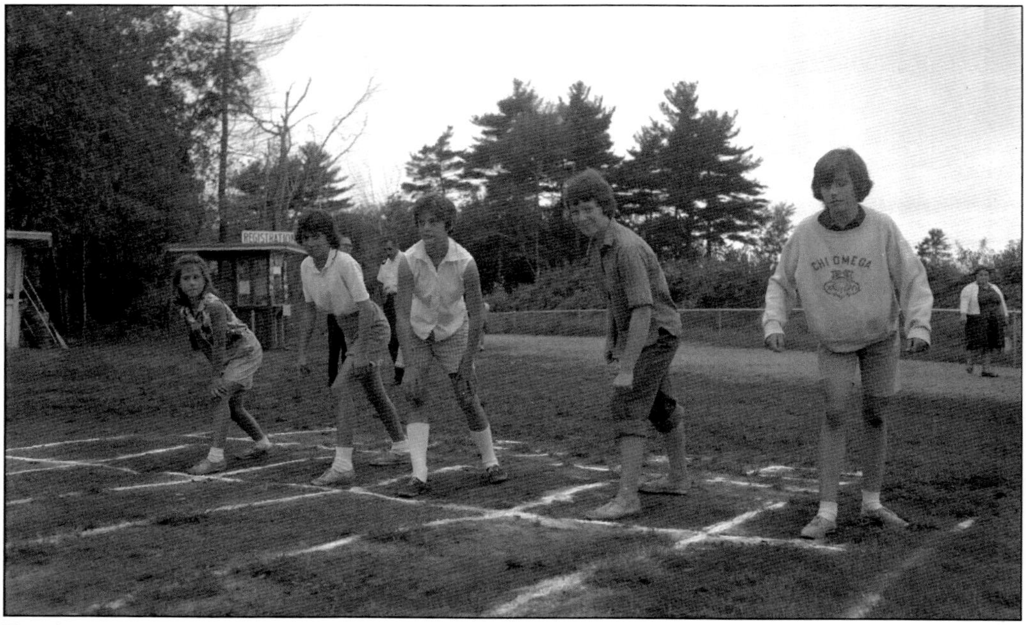

For the 1962 season, Pleasure Island's general manager and partner Walter Smith announced, "In connection with President Kennedy's physical fitness program, there will be a new Olympic center where various physical culture activities will be carried out. The exercises will be directed by trained personnel." The following quotation from Pres. John F. Kennedy is from a *Look* magazine article dated August 13, 1963: "I hope that all parents who share my concern will inquire about the physical fitness programs in their schools. I hope that every active American—particularly if he is a young American—will take part in such a program, for his own good and for his country's good." Boys and girls competed in the high jump, the 100-yard dash, the broad jump, and the football and baseball throw, where a point system determined the winners. (Courtesy of Patrick Farino.)

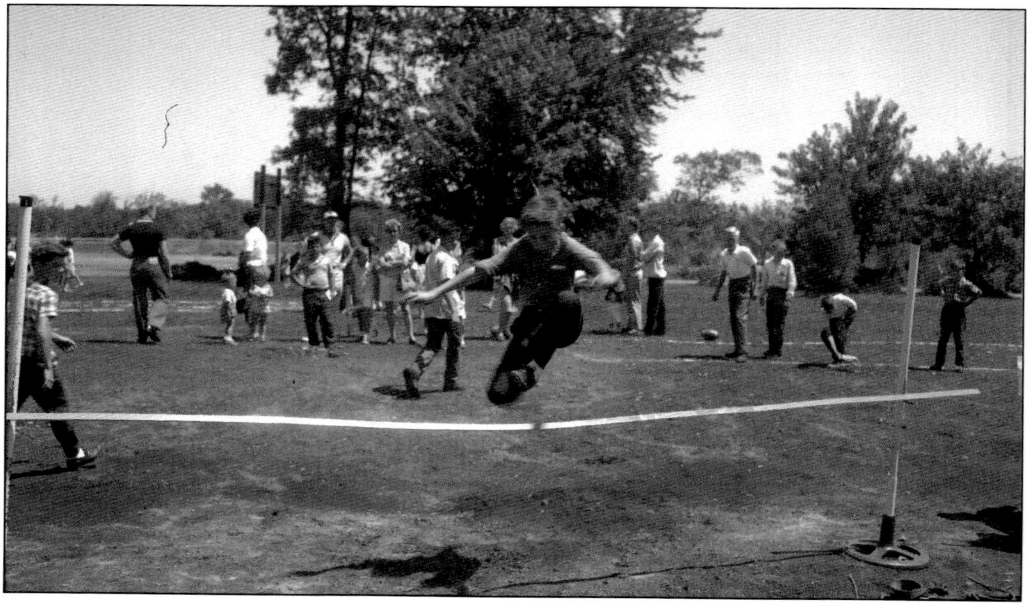

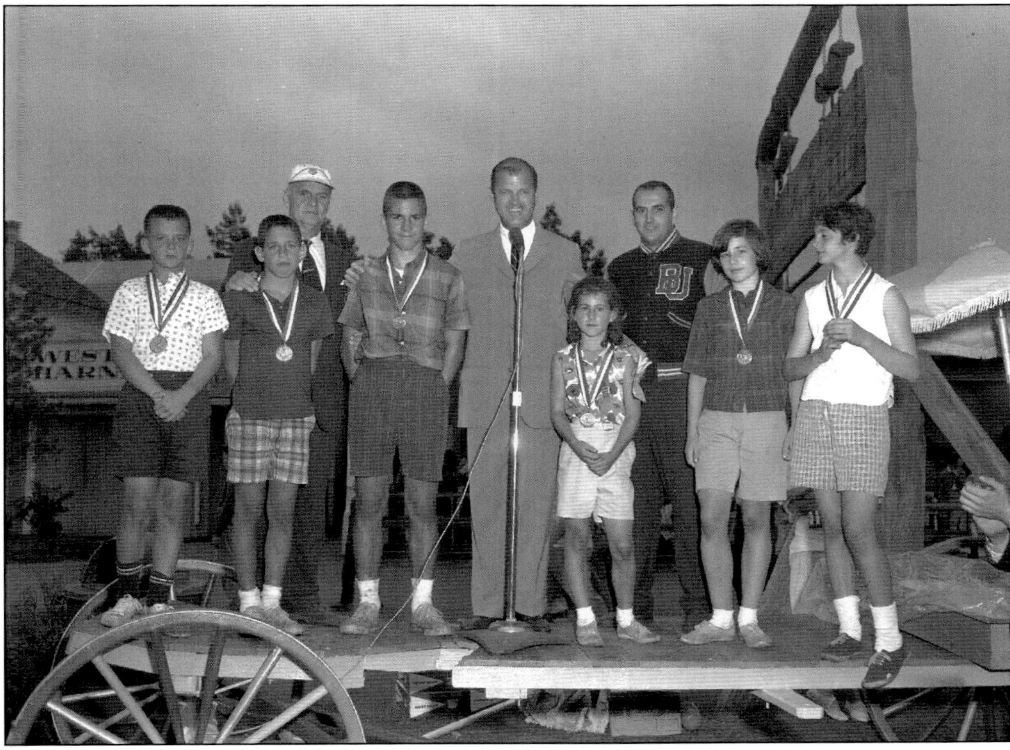

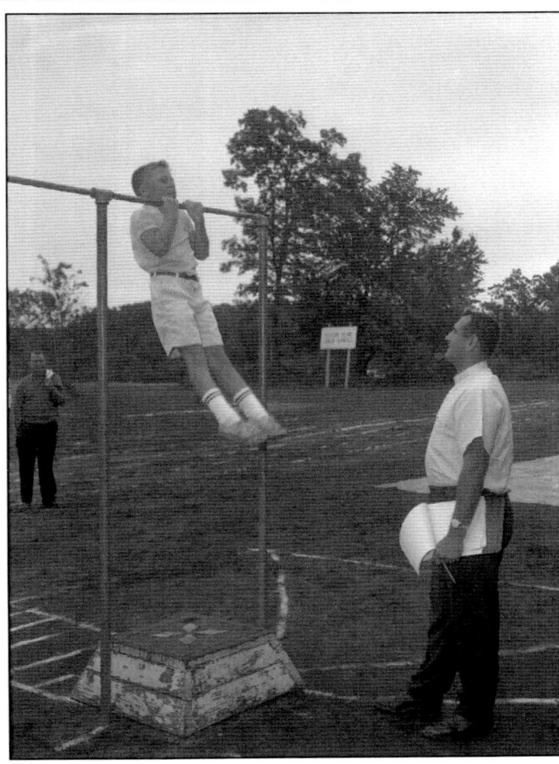

Onstage above in Goldpan Gulch is Smith (center). To the right of him is 10-year-old Leslie Stevenson of Swampscott, winner of the girls' division. To the left of Smith is 14-year-old Paul W. Sweeney of Reading, the boys' division winner. These two Junior Olympic gold medal winners topped more than 7,200 competitors at Pleasure Island, including the runners-up, also onstage. Stevenson and Sweeney flew to Washington, D.C., on January 15, 1963, to visit with Kennedy. Smith and his partners left Pleasure Island after the 1963 season. Smith, Robert Linnell, and ex–Cabot, Cabot and Forbes executive Russell Cox bought the Boston Garden and the Hotel Madison next door. Linnell and Smith also owned an attraction at the 1964 New York World's Fair that was similar to Pleasure Island's Jenney cars. The photograph at right shows what many baby boomers remember doing—pull-ups. (Courtesy of Patrick Farino.)

FREE GAMES, SHOWS & ATTRACTIONS AT THE

1963 TEEN-AGE FAIR

Pleasure Island — Wakefield — Route 128, Exit 32

ENTER THE

LIMBO DANCE CONTEST!

Thomas Limbo Trees invite you to do The Limbo Twist and The Limbo Trix

Limbo Contest continuously at the Thomas Limbo Exhibit — Win Valuable Prizes

Semi-Finals Daily — 3:30 P.M., 6:30 P.M., 9:00 P.M.

SCHEDULE

SATURDAY — JULY 27

- See and meet little Eva, the chanteuse, Roger Williams and the Country Cutups and Adam Wade at our stage spectacular and autograph party! At 2:00 P.M., 5:00 P.M. and 8:00 P.M.
- See the spectacular Rocket Man actually fly with the amazing rocket belt at 1:30, 4:30, 6:00 and 7:30 P.M.
- Watch the Miss Teen USA Semi-Finals at 8:30 P.M.
- Meet Red Auerbach in person at Noon-1:00 P.M.

SUNDAY — JULY 28

- SEE THE SPECTACULAR ROCKET MAN actually fly with the amazing rocket belt at 1:30, 4:30, 6:00, 7:30 P.M.
- See and meet THE TOKENS of "The Lion Sleeps Tonight" fame and other top recording stars as Richie Starr and Janice Hanson at our Stage Spectacular and autograph parties at 3:00 and 6:05 P.M.

MONDAY — JULY 29

- See the climax of the frogmans 80 hour underwater endurance attempt as he emerges from the TAF tank at 8:30 P.M.
  Watch the Teen Age Dance Championship Semi-finals on our stage at 9:00 P.M.

TUESDAY — JULY 30

- Watch or Enter the LIMBO dance festival contest with valuable prizes being awarded at 8:30 P.M.
  HEAR and SEE the craze that's sweeping America, SURFING at our SURF party with color and sound movies and the Surf Sound in Music, all day long.

WEDNESDAY — JULY 31

- DON'T MISS your chance to photograph the semi-finalists in the MISS TEENAGE AMERICA Contest as the contestants pose all day for amateur shutterbugs. Prizes awarded for Best Photos.

THURSDAY — AUGUST 1

- SEE and HEAR the First ANNUAL TEEN FAIR FOLK FESTIVAL with singers and groups competing for beautiful trophies and valuable Recording contracts. Beginning at 8:30 P.M.

FRIDAY — AUGUST 2

- SEE the MISS TEEN USA PAGEANT FINALS with the lucky winner receiving beautiful trophies and an all expense paid trip to HOLLYWOOD, CALIFORNIA to participate in the National Pageant at 8:00 P.M.

SATURDAY — AUGUST 3

- SEE and HEAR the TEEN AGE FAIR "Battle of the Bands" Finals with the winners receiving the New England title TROPHY and a valuable recording contract! Bruce Bradley WBZ Star will MC at 8:00 P.M. Meet and Hear Recording Star Andrea Carroll in person at our Stage and Autograph Parties at 2:00, 5:00 and 8:00 P.M.

SUNDAY — AUGUST 4

- SEE the FINALS in the LIMBO DANCE Festivals with the winners receiving expense paid vacations to FLORIDA.
- Prizes for winners in the continuous contests will be awarded all day.

— ALSO —

Each and Every Day of the Fair

- SEE an amazing exhibition of Sky Diving as parachutists from the Sport Parachute Center at Orange, Massachusetts actually parachute from a plane into the fair at 8:00 P.M.
- SEE and HEAR the "Battle of the Bands" daily playoffs at 12 noon, 4:45 P.M. and 8:30 P.M.
- WATCH DEADLY KARATE and JUDO exhibitions by the Judo Institute of New England at 2:00, 4:00, 7:30, and 9:30 P.M.
- SEE THE SNEAK PREVIEW FALL FASHION SHOW LIVE WITH EVERYTHING FROM LINGERIE TO DRESSUPS at 12:30, 2:30, 5:00 and 8:05 P.M.
- SEE the Custom Car Showing and Customizing Clinic at 12:30, 2:45, 4:45, 6:45 and 9:15 P.M.

[Listen Here!]

WBZ RADIO 103 GROUP W

Pleasure Island presented the fabulous 1963 Teen-Age Fair in its entertainment lineup, for what would be the last season for the second owners of the park. Featured in *Life* magazine, nationally televised, and attended by hundreds of thousands of teens and their families, this event was held at venues throughout the country in the summer of 1963, including Pleasure Island. WBZ Radio was a big part of Pleasure Island with advertising and live broadcasts at the park, starting from the very first season in 1959. (Courtesy of Barbara and Barry Thomas.)

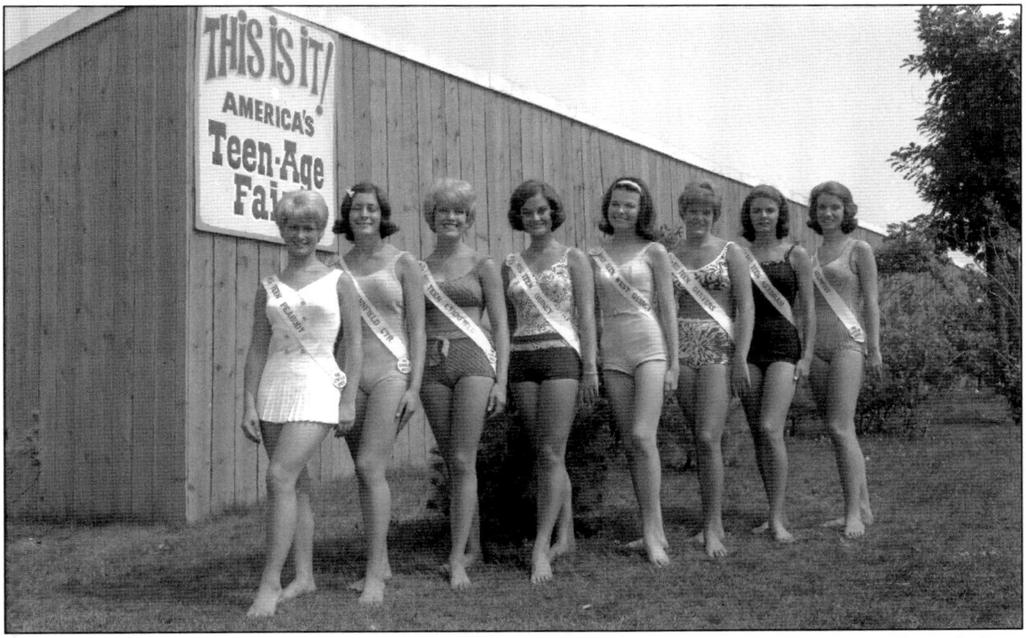

Part of the Teen-Age Fair was the beauty contest. In the photograph above are, from left to right, Miss Teen Peabody, Miss Teen Lynnfield Center, Miss Teen Lynnfield, Miss Teen Quincy, Miss Teen West Quincy, Miss Teen Danvers, Miss Teen Needham, and Miss Teen Belmont. (Courtesy of Patrick Farino.)

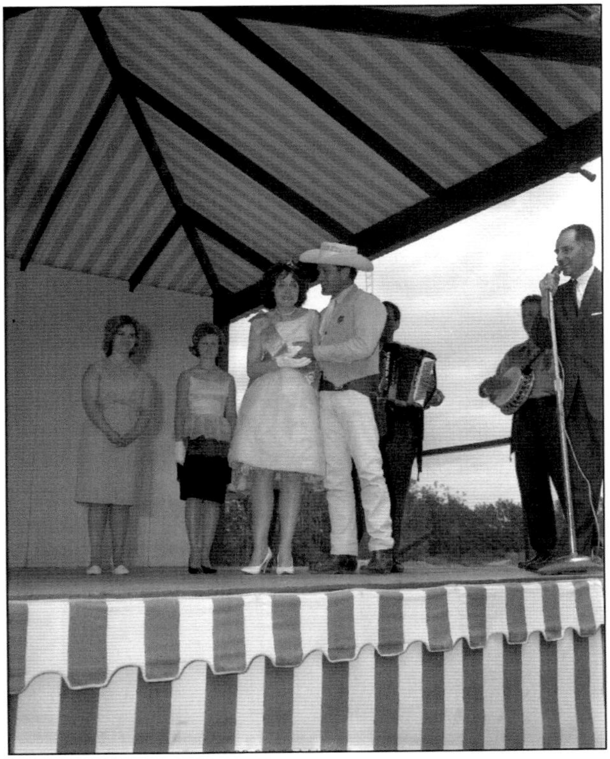

With the sheriff of Pleasure Island Sy Milano presenting the Miss Teen awards, it appears that a very emotional contestant has won one of if not *the* top prize. Milano worked at Pleasure Island starting in 1959 as a character actor. In 1960, he became the official sheriff of the park until the end of the 1963 season. He performed daily with his prize horse, Wildfire. (Courtesy of Patrick Farino.)

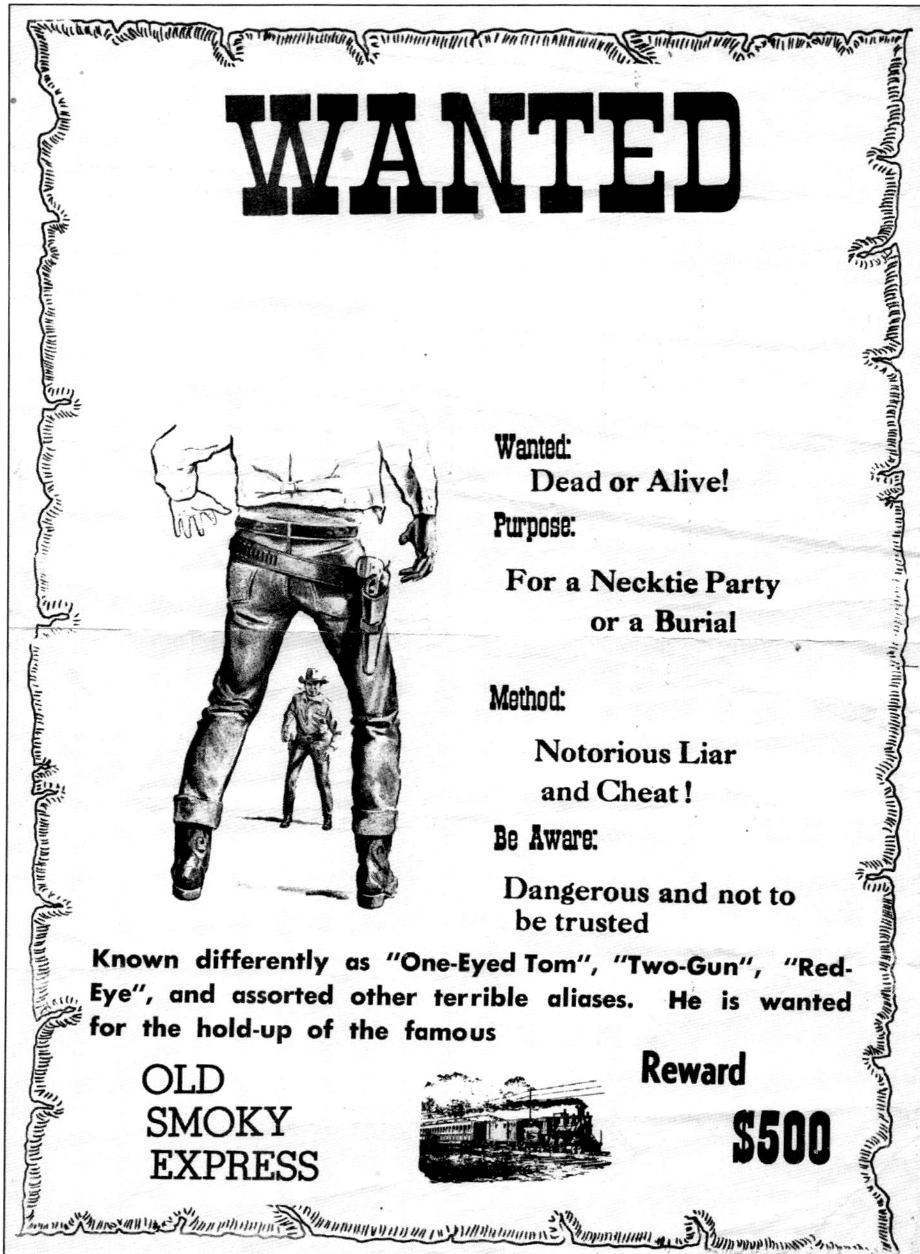

An advertisement in the *Pleasure Island Gazette* from 1966 stated, "You can become a part of the Old West when you step inside the print shop door. For a small fee you can have your own name printed in bold, black lettering on an authentic poster, just like the ones the lawmen used when they were tracking down the James Boys." The printing operation was done on an old hand-operated press, with type set by hand just the way it was in the 1870s. Originally operated by the Quannapowitt Publishers, the *Pleasure Island Gazette*, located in the heart of Goldpan Gulch, was eventually run by Patrick Farino. He operated the shop through the end of Pleasure Island's last season. (Courtesy of FOPI archives.)

Indian Village was set up as an attraction by Pleasure Island's character actors, Herb Sauve and the late Lou Ciarfella, who designed and built the village with authentic tepees, totem poles, and other backdrops. To enhance the experience for the guests, there was a trading post for souvenirs and an archery range. The acting was free of charge. That was the best part. Judi Kramer, Suave, Ciarfella, David Dulong, and many others made the train stop a memorable experience. At right, Ciarfella, as Chief Black Eagle, was a regular on Rex Trailer's *Boomtown*. A local from Wakefield by the name of William O'Brien got a job at Indian Village. He later played Sergeant Billy on *Boomtown*. At Indian Village below are Ciarfella (left), Kramer (center), and Dulong. (Right, courtesy of Herb Sauve; below, courtesy of Judi Kramer.)

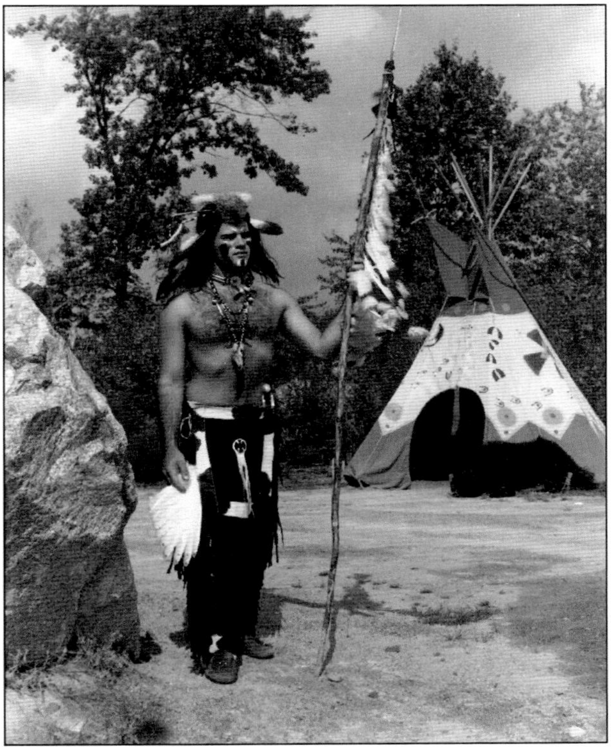

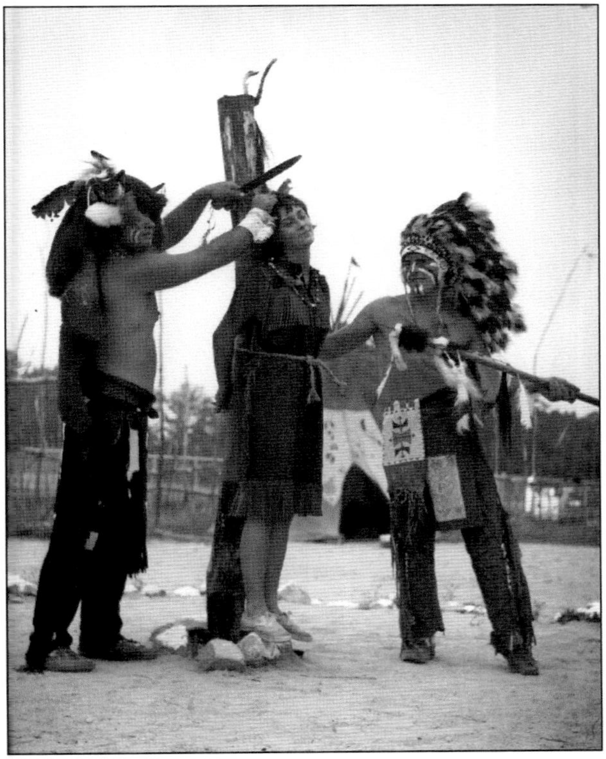

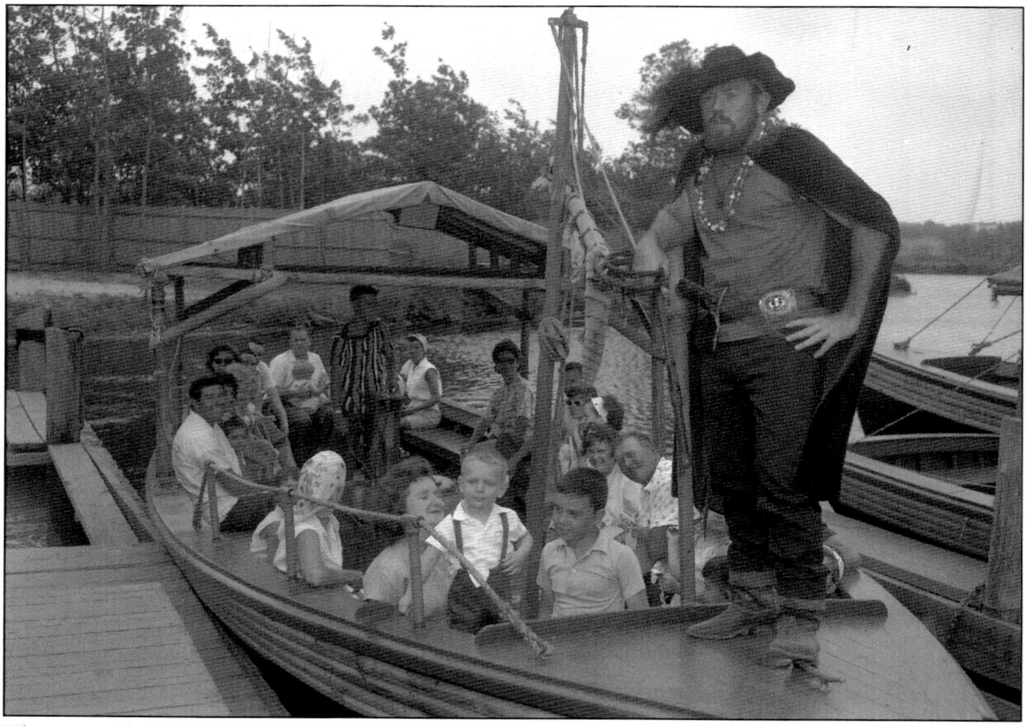

The pirate boats continued to be a popular attraction throughout the life of the park. What child entering Pirate Cove would not believe that they were coming face to face with a real pirate? Herb Sauve (above) was perfect for this part. Sauve was also a regular on *Boomtown*. (Courtesy of Patrick Farino.)

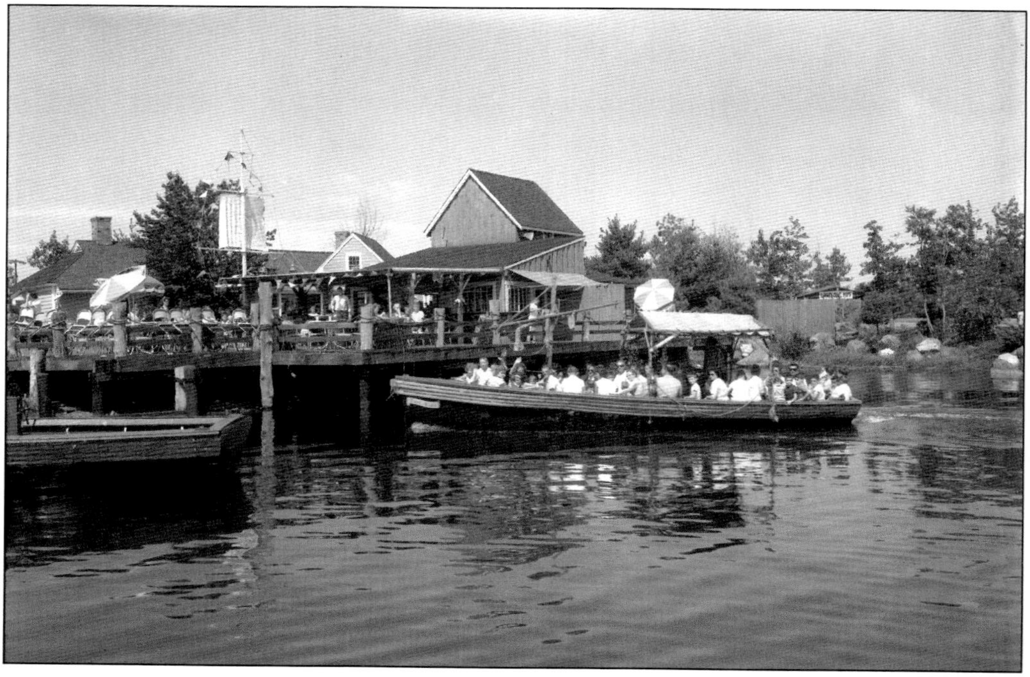

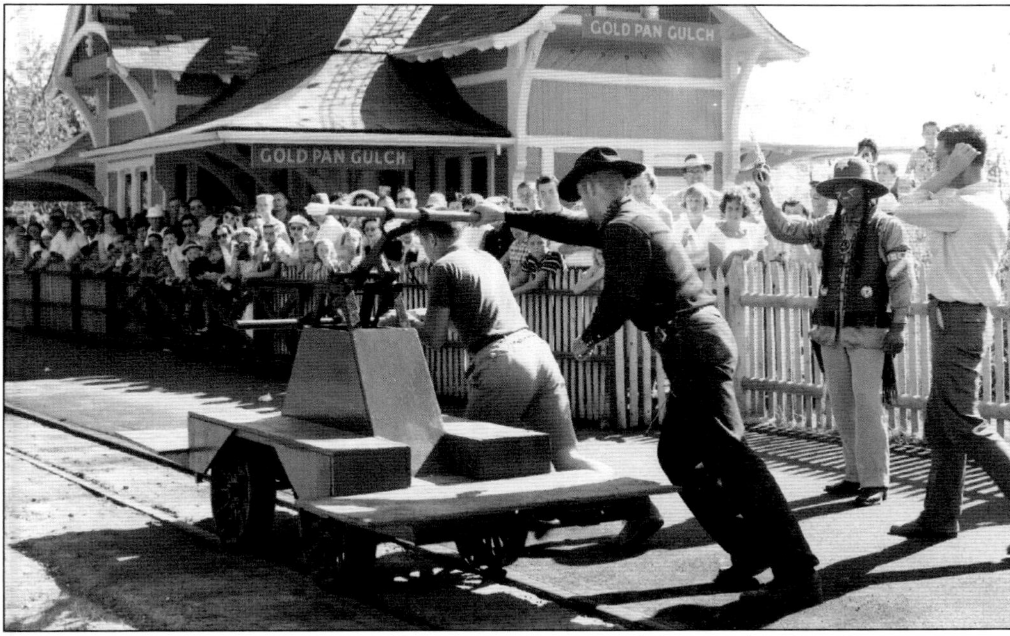

Here is Herb Sauve playing the sheriff, firing a starting pistol during a handcar demonstration at the Goldpan Gulch station. Park announcers, from Ken Saunders in 1959 to Ed Atwater in 1969, directed guests to events throughout the day. The communication shack was in Clipper Cove on the second floor over the Wreck of the Hesperus ride. (Courtesy of Herb Sauve.)

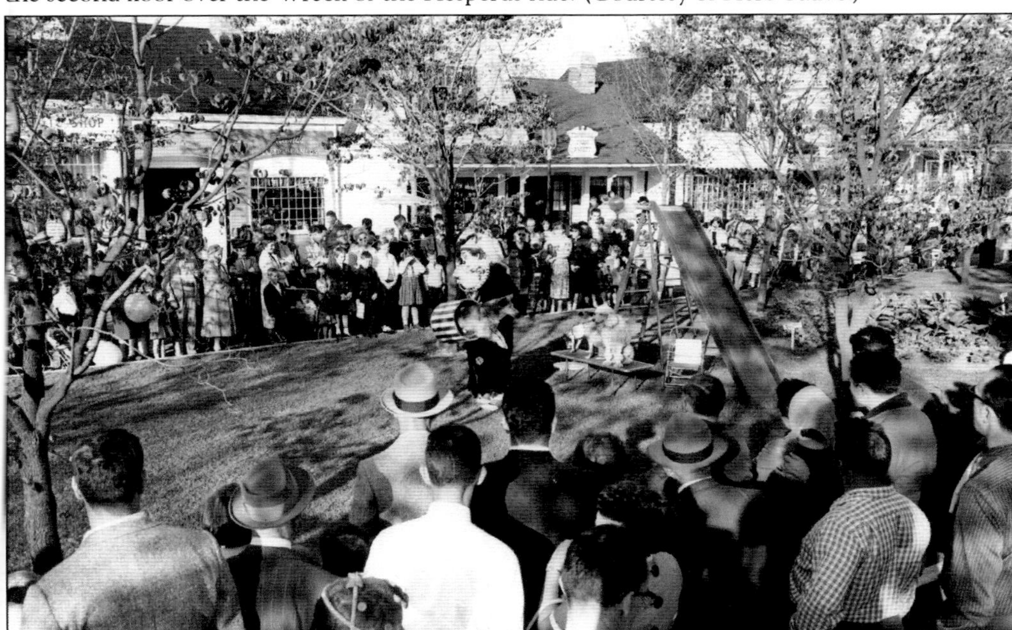

Lined up on Pleasure Island's Main Street for a dog act, the crowd seen in this photograph is from the early years at Pleasure Island. The park spanned an interesting period of American popular culture. The country went from watching *Father Knows Best* to Woodstock during Pleasure Island's 11 seasons. (Courtesy of Russ Adams Productions.)

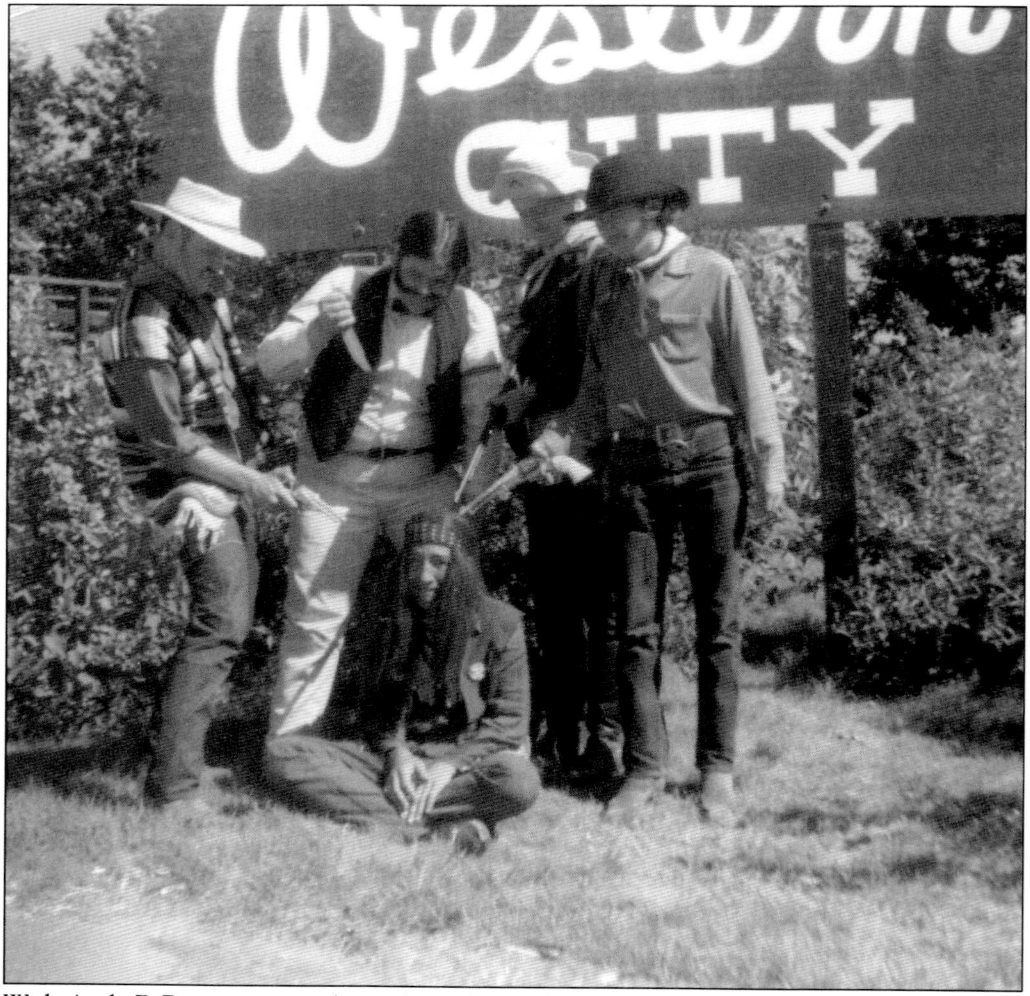

With Andy DiDonato sitting down, four other park characters appear to have him as prisoner. Standing from left to right are Jerry Bly, Sam Donato, Larry Bugden, and Tom Green. Entertainment was always part of Pleasure Island's appeal. Throughout the 11 seasons, the characters within the park changed just as the park's ownership did. In the early years, there were the paid professionals. Eventually acting students from Emerson College started to show up on the payroll, as did local high school students. From supplying their own costumes to writing their skits, the stars of Pleasure Island gave park guests memories that last a lifetime. Among the locals and college students who performed at the park were Ed Atwater, Larry Brehaut, Dave Campanella, Peter Calore, Ronnie Donato, Al "Creach" Krever, and many others. (Courtesy of Priscilla DiDonato Hendrick.)

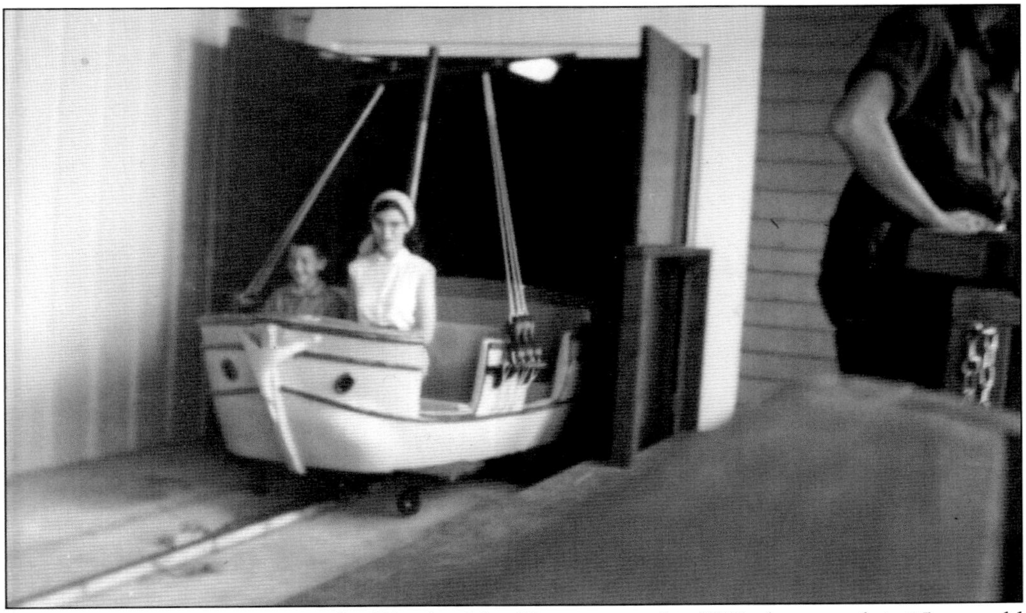

Coming out from a voyage on the Wreck of the Hesperus in this 1959 photograph is 15-year-old Priscilla DiDonato Hendrick and her younger brother Andy. She worked at Pleasure Island from 1960 to 1969 with the exception of one season. Andy DiDonato also worked at the park as an actor and musician. He was part of the Love Thy Neighbor Ragtime Band at the park. The band is still active today. (Courtesy of Priscilla DiDonato Hendrick.)

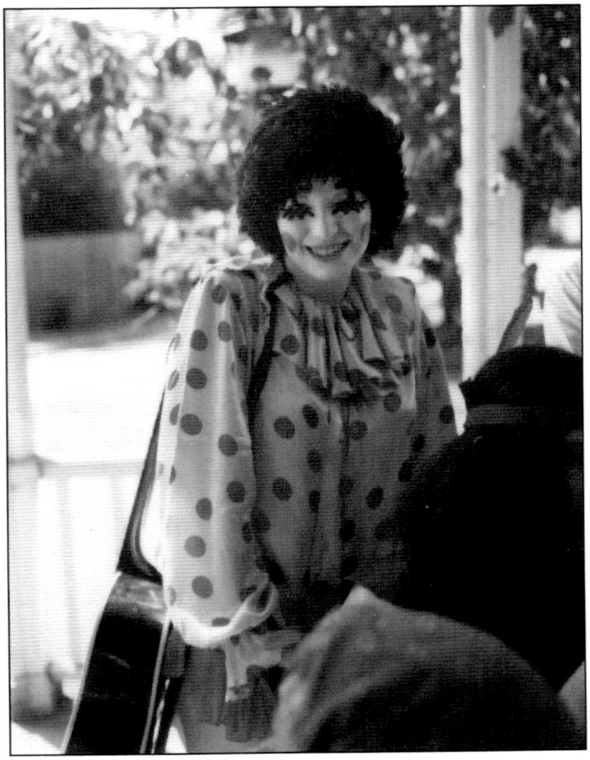

Feathers the Clown was one of the many characters Hendrick played at Pleasure Island. Others included Lady Nell, Gia the Gypsy, and Maggie the Witch. By 1969, in addition to acting, she was also the art director for the last owners of Pleasure Island. The park characters also produced and acted in melodramas in the Golden Nugget Saloon. (Courtesy of Priscilla DiDonato Hendrick.)

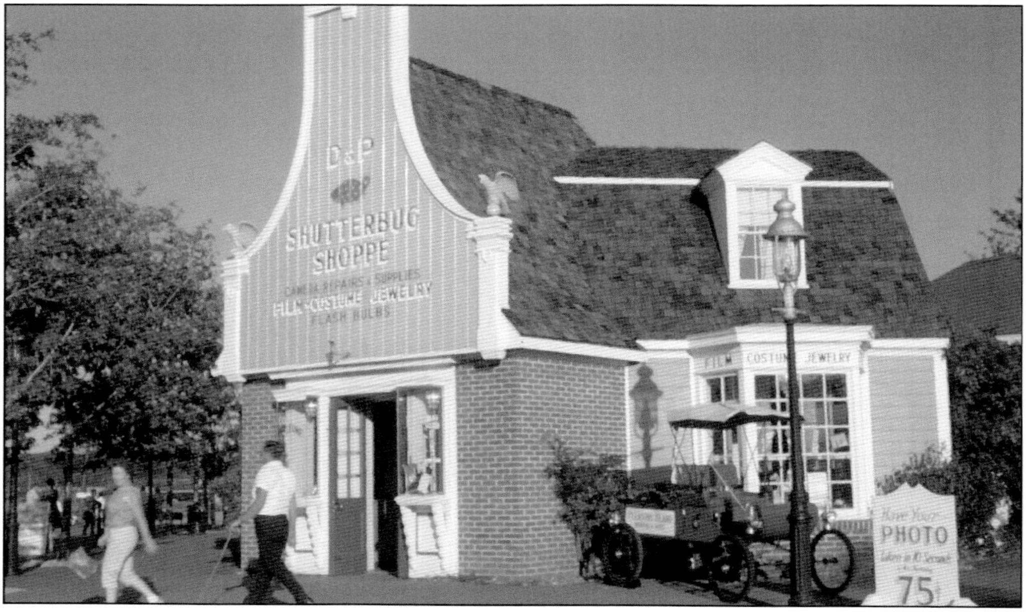

Patrick Farino owned and operated a photograph and jewelry store for many years in Woburn. He expanded his business to Pleasure Island and ended up owning five businesses within the park. One of them was Space Art, where six machines spun while guests sprayed paint on the revolving cardboard. Two others were Shooting Waters and the Gingerbread Shop. Farino eventually took over the print shop. (Courtesy of Patrick Farino.)

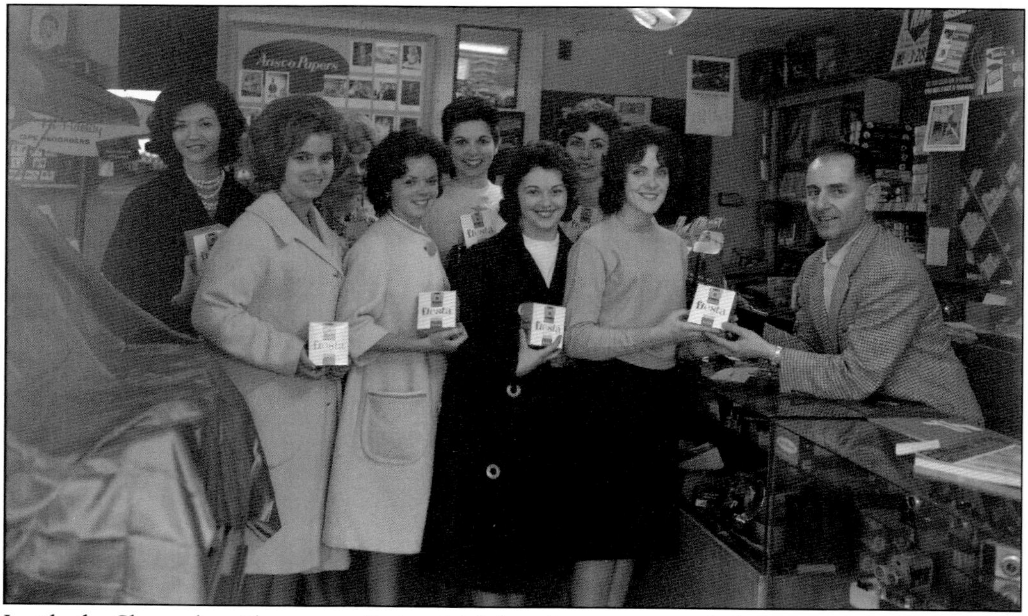

Inside the Shutterbug Shoppe are Farino (right) and contestants of a beauty contest he arranged with the *Woburn Times* newspaper. Miss Fotomate, left of Farino, and the runners-up were all awarded Fiesta cameras. Farino's Shutterbug photographers were stationed throughout the park at the Burro Trail, the Jenney cars, and elsewhere. For $1, they took an instant Polaroid photograph. That price included 25¢ going to his Shutterbugs. (Courtesy of Patrick Farino.)

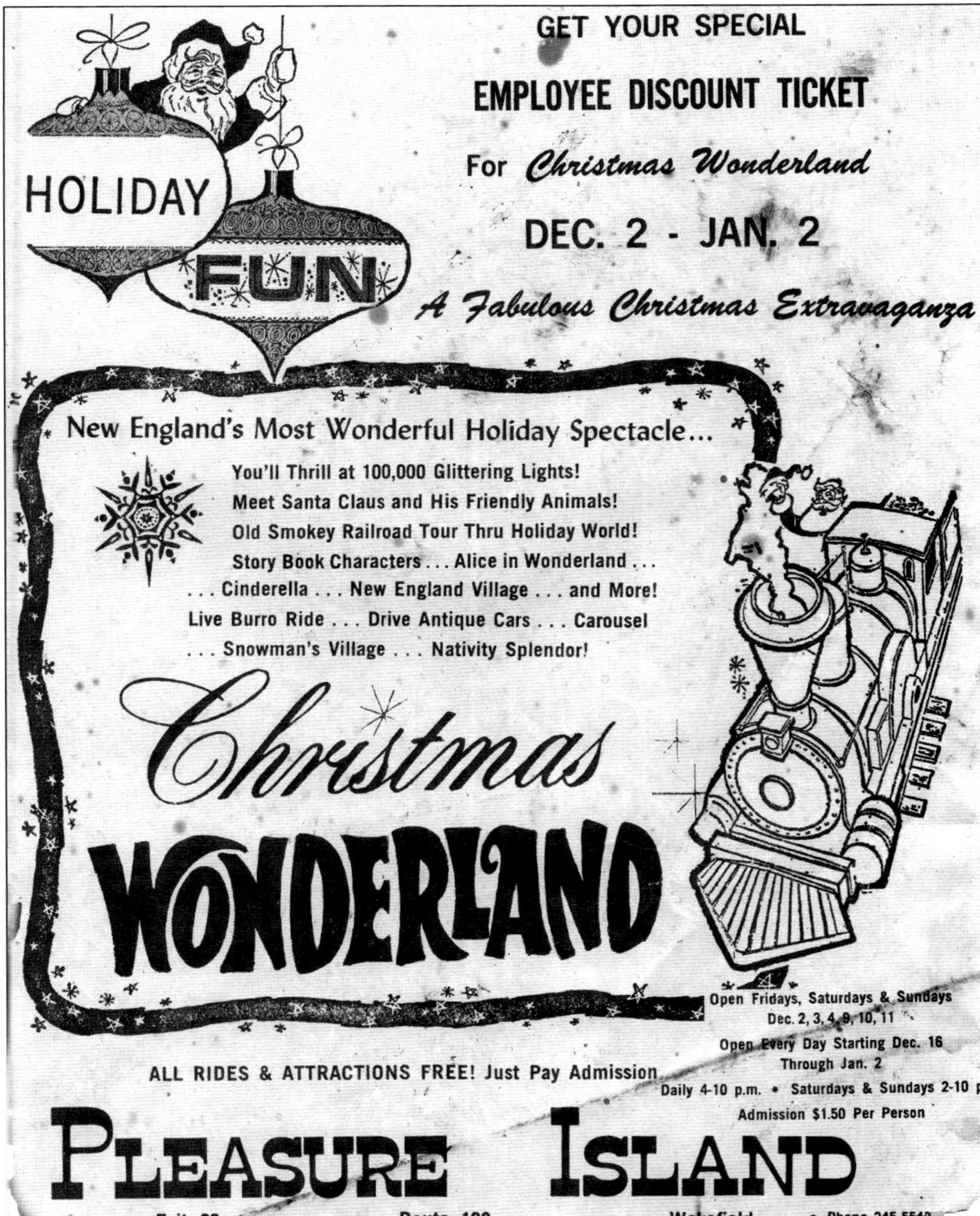

In February 1962, Walter Smith and his partners announced plans to build a $700,000 multipurpose ice arena with seating from 3,000 to 5,000. Because of problems with sewer capacity and needed upgrades, the project was cancelled. Smith was trying to get a 12-month operation instead of the park's 90-day schedule. Boston Ventures opened Pleasure Island for the Christmas seasons in 1965 and 1966. The lighting display attracted the attention of thousands of motorists traveling along Route 128. Unfortunately, not enough of them participated in the winter wonderland. Opening for the Christmas season was a valiant attempt by the new park owners to stretch the operating days, but it was not a success. (Courtesy of FOPI archives.)

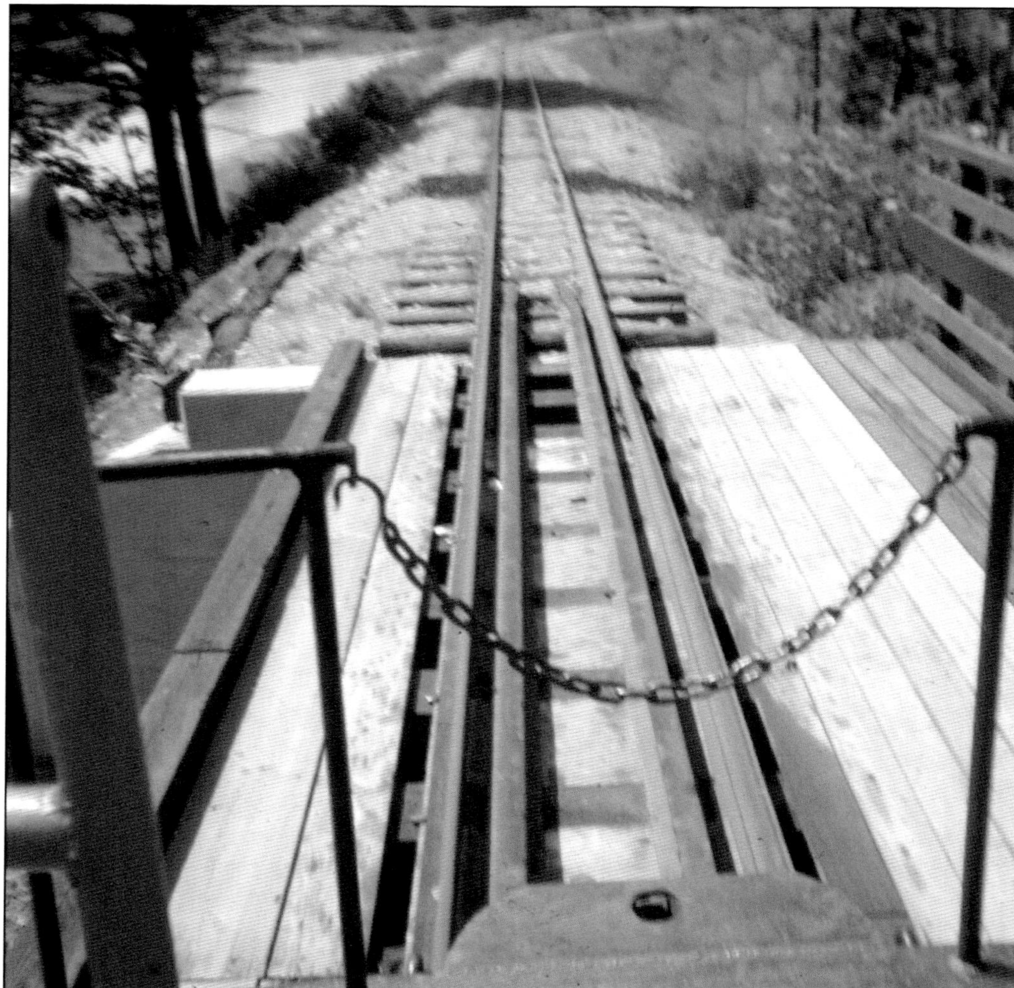

As Old Smoky approaches the Goldpan Gulch station with its tracks behind it, this photograph shows the end of the line for Pleasure Island's last season in 1969. Built on dreams by Bill Hawkes and made a reality by Cabot, Cabot and Forbes, the four owners of Pleasure Island really brought joy and endless memories to thousands of guests. The park's last announcer, Ed Atwater, made this one final announcement on the last day Pleasure Island was open: "Ladies and gentlemen, Pleasure Island will be closing in 15 minutes and this will be the final announcement. Thank you for your patronage over the years. We want to take the opportunity to thank all the people who have worked here, not just now, but throughout the years, that they tried to make life a little happier and you would forget your troubles for just a few hours. Once again on behalf of the staff, management and owners of Pleasure Island, we bid you a fond farewell." (Courtesy of Victor Chin.)

Five

THE END OF PLEASURE ISLAND

In April 1969, Pleasure Island was sold to Fairbanks Amusement Corporation for $1.7 million. It was the fourth and last owner to operate the park. By mid-May, Fairbanks was in front of Wakefield's selectmen requesting "excitement type rides" and an arcade. Licenses were issued for existing attractions with new proposals tabled that evening. With lack of major reinvestments and deferred maintenance, Pleasure Island as a business had been waning even before its last season.

The park closed down after the summer of 1969, reportedly with many of the attractions inoperable. Fairbanks was part of a larger corporation headed by Robert Waldman and his son-in-law David Dick. With the lure of tax benefits to the town, they got a favorable vote at a February 1970 town meeting to rezone Pleasure Island for high-rise apartment buildings. Drawn by a promised 11 percent interest rate, reportedly some $34 million was invested and lost by 4,000 individuals.

Allegedly, Waldman and Dick were commingling money to other companies under their control. Institutional Investors Trust became legal owners after the land and buildings were taken by foreclosure from Fairbanks. Only one of the eight proposed apartment buildings ever was built (present-day Colonial Point). By 1975, Wakefield's town meeting rescinded the high-rise zoning back to industrial zoning. In July 1978, Waldman and Dick surrendered to federal marshals to begin serving prison sentences for fraud. Dick, at 45 years old, received 10 years, and Waldman, at 72 years old, received 5 years.

It was a sad ending for Bill Hawkes's dream. Most of the following photographs in this chapter were taken in the mid-1970s by John "Toz" Toczydlowski. As an adult, he has vivid childhood memories of Pleasure Island. He captured in his images what is impossible to describe in words alone—Pleasure Island dissolving back into the landscape from which it rose.

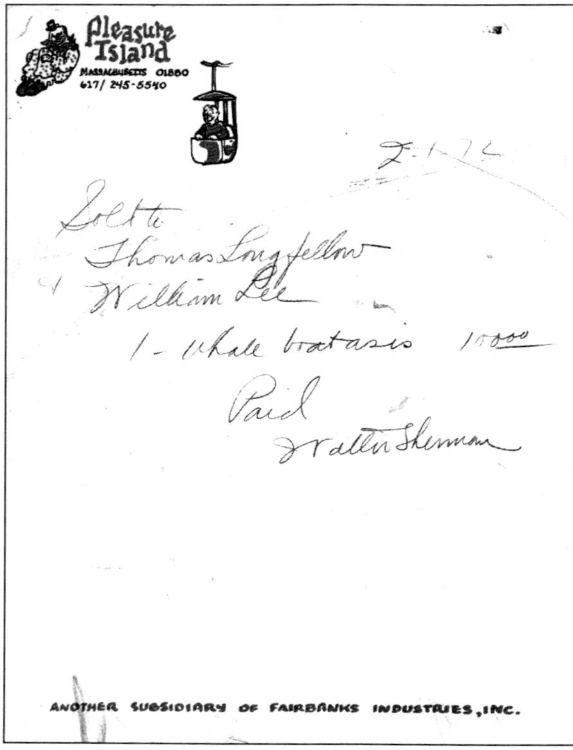

Pleasure Island
MASSACHUSETTS 01880
617/ 245-5540

2-1-72

Sold to
Thomas Longfellow
& William Lee
1- Whale boat as is 100.00
Paid
Walter Sherman

ANOTHER SUBSIDIARY OF FAIRBANKS INDUSTRIES, INC.

Although Pleasure Island's business records from the last three park operators have not surfaced, a small file recently has. Ken and Jim Luciani from Wakefield came across a box of miscellaneous paperwork in an old file cabinet that belonged to longtime park maintenance supervisor Walter Sherman. The bill of sale (left) is a window into the breaking up of Pleasure Island. The dated receipt shows Sherman still selling equipment and buildings some 29 months after closing. What was not sold was carted off by anyone with a crowbar and a pickup truck, burned down by arson, falling down, or, in the end, bulldozed and hauled away. The fleet of whaleboats (below) was taken out for the winter, repainted, and put back in the spring. In addition to the bill of sale at left, Sherman sold at least one other boat for the same price, $100. (Left, courtesy of Ken and Jim Luciani; below, courtesy of Patrick Farino.)

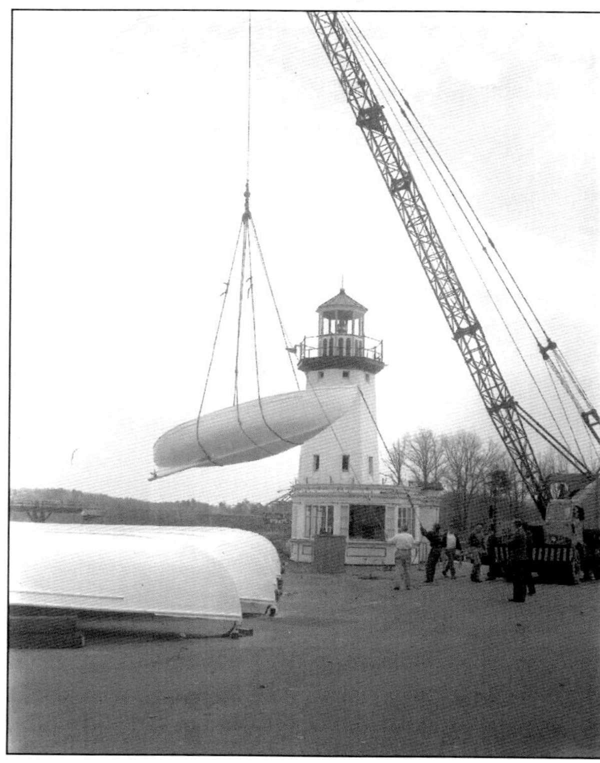

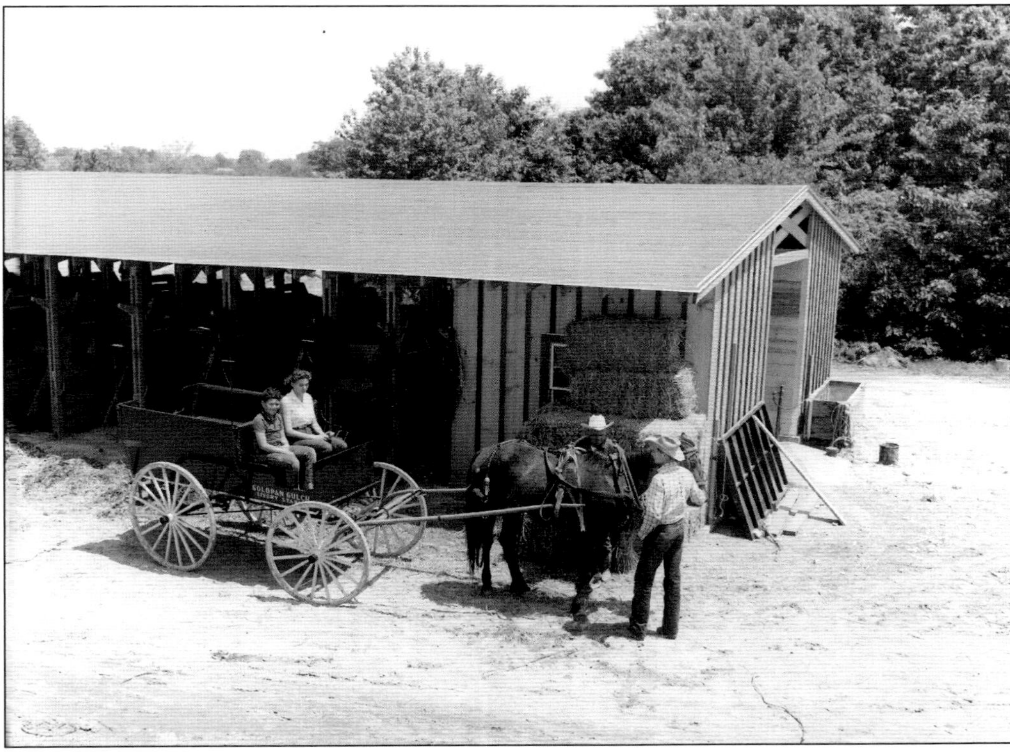

The following is a list of buildings sold in late 1971 and early 1972 by Sherman. From receipts found in his file cabinet, Clark's Trading Post bought the stable (above) for $150; Ray Collamore got the 850-square-foot Whaler's Wharf restaurant for $200; Ralph Key bought four adjoining buildings that housed the Carousel Toy Store totaling 1,166 square feet for $325; Stanley Beers bought the Slanty Shanty for $150; and his friend got the former Slanty Shanty waiting room two days later for $75. Both buildings were turned into camps up north. At right is the bill of sale for the Slanty (or Strange) Shanty. (Above, courtesy of Fay Foto Service; right, courtesy of Ken and Jim Luciani.)

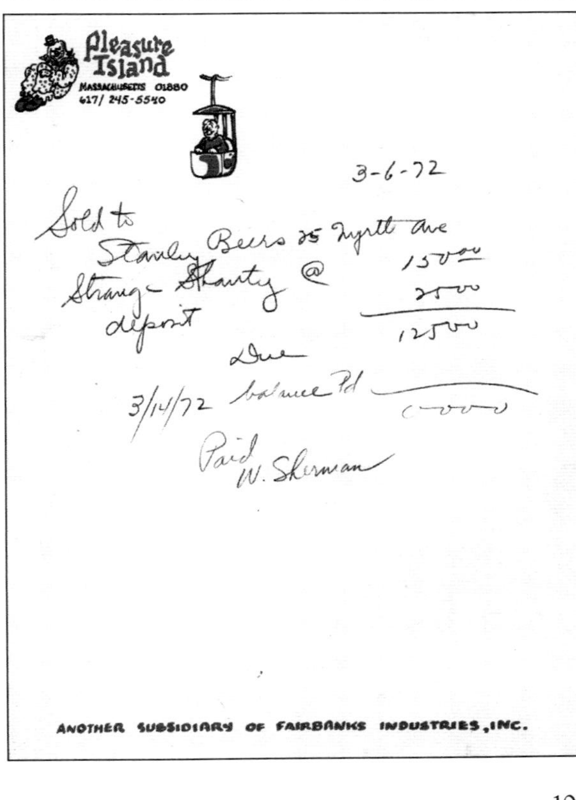

Pleasure Island
MASSACHUSETTS 01880
617/245-5540

3-6-72

Sold to
Stanley Beers 25 Myrtle Ave
Strange Shanty @ 150.00
deposit 25.00
125.00
Due
3/14/72 balance Pd

Paid
W. Sherman

ANOTHER SUBSIDIARY OF FAIRBANKS INDUSTRIES, INC.

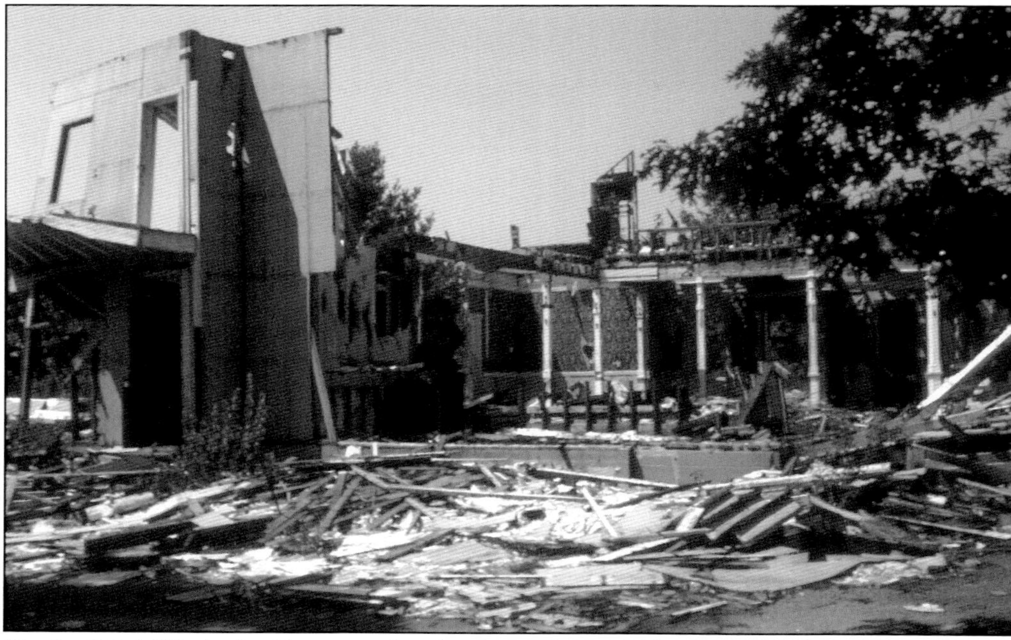

On April 1, 1971, the building complex that housed the Golden Nugget Saloon, the print shop, the Chisholm Trail, and the hotel was set on fire. This photograph is from the former dark ride, looking toward the shell of what had been the Diamond Lil Saloon/Golden Nugget Saloon. It was taken about August 1975. (Courtesy of John Toczydlowski.)

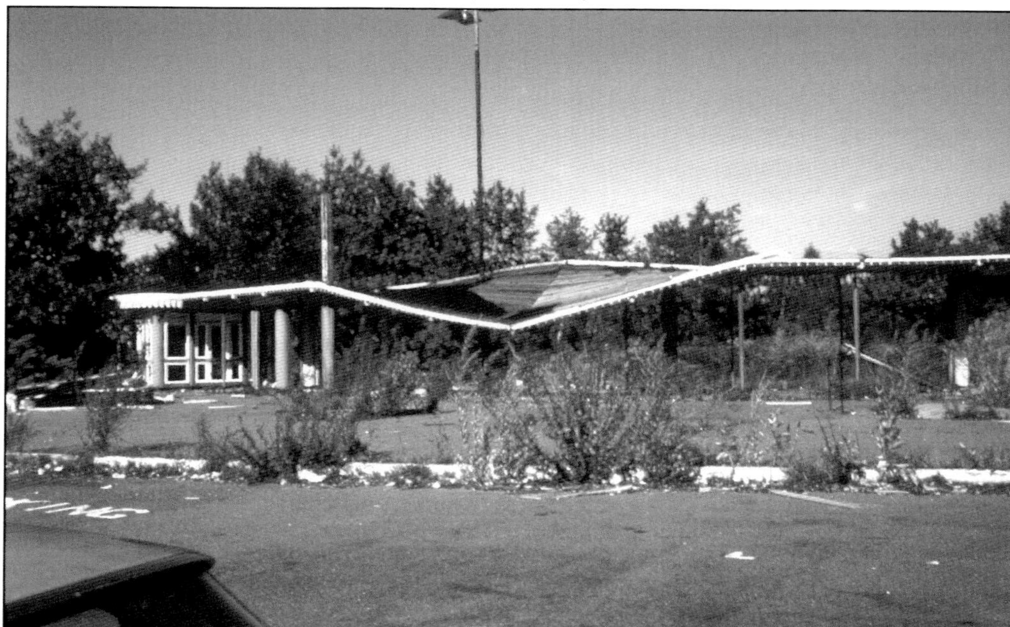

From Pleasure Island's parking lot is the park's signature main entrance. Reportedly over three million guests entered through these turnstiles during the 11 seasons of operation. Pleasure Island was host to numerous outings for employees and their families, such as the Polaroid Corporation. This photograph was taken about September 1975. (Courtesy of John Toczydlowski.)

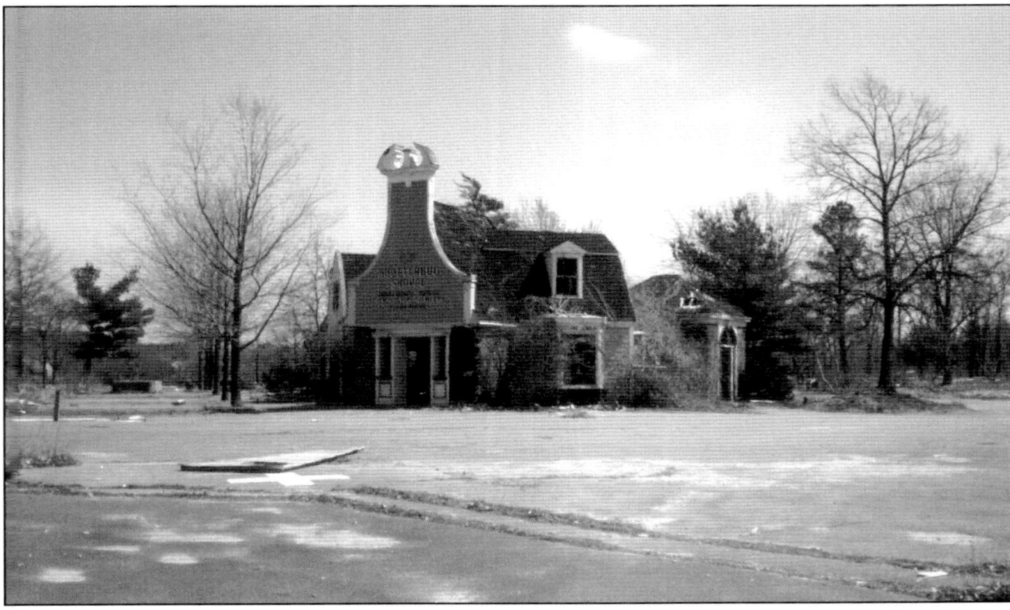

The Shutterbug Shoppe was on the right corner of Main Street looking toward Clipper Cove. The bakery shop was in a small brick building to the right. Found in Walter Sherman's files was a 1964 list of 44 rentable areas for shops and food service vendors throughout the park. Total rental space in Pleasure Island, according to this list, was 20,700 square feet. This photograph was taken about April 1975. (Courtesy of John Toczydlowski.)

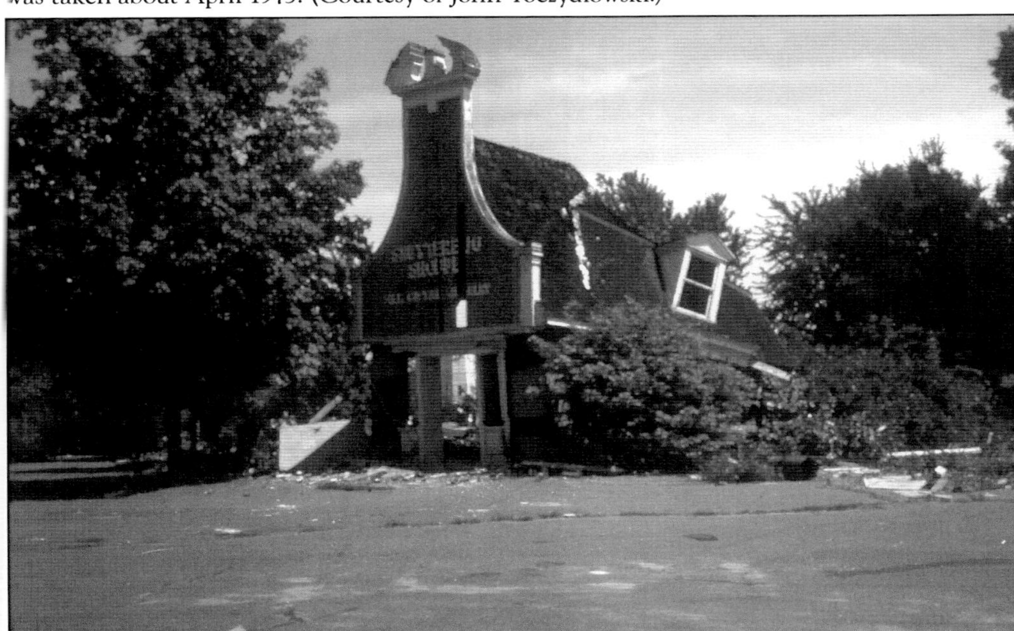

Between April and August 1975, the bakery was torn down. By this point, Pleasure Island had turned into one big attraction—a ghost town. There were three other rental shops in this building, a toy shop in two of the units, and a five-and-dime shop in the end unit. This photograph was taken about August 1975. (Courtesy of John Toczydlowski.)

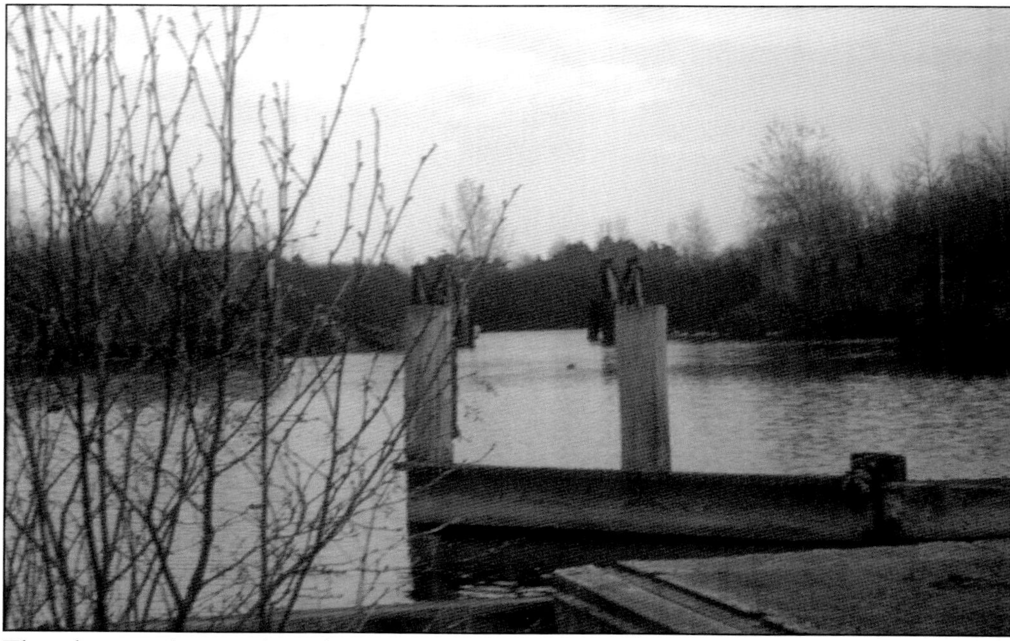

This photograph was taken about April 1975 from the Whaler's Wharf restaurant and pirate boat launch area. Straight ahead are the structures that supported the Old Smoky line trestle bridge, not only built for the Pirate Cove attraction. The Burro Trail also went under the bridge to the left. (Courtesy of John Toczydlowski.)

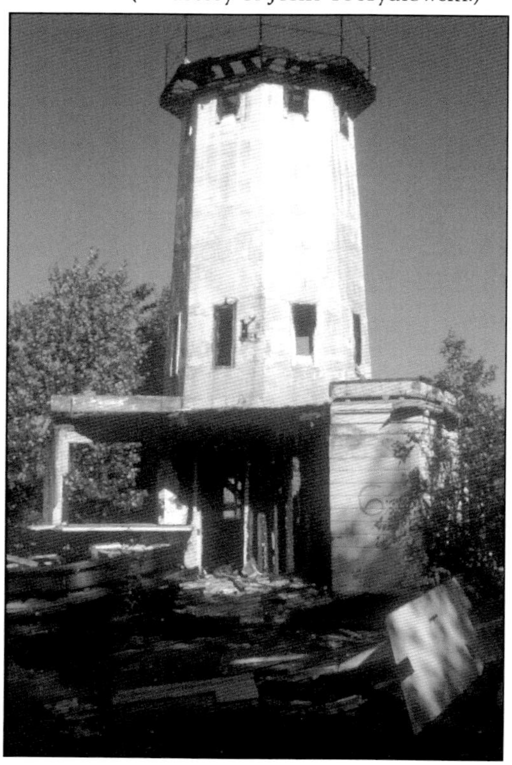

The lighthouse was the icon for Clipper Cove and coincidentally was named Hawkes Point Lighthouse. Numbered for demolition, the building served as one of the many food service facilities throughout the park. Walter Sherman gave a former grade school classmate, Alfred Mellett, the antique light from the top of the lighthouse. Mellett donated it to the Friends of Pleasure Island in 2003. This photograph was taken about September 1975. (Courtesy of John Toczydlowski.)

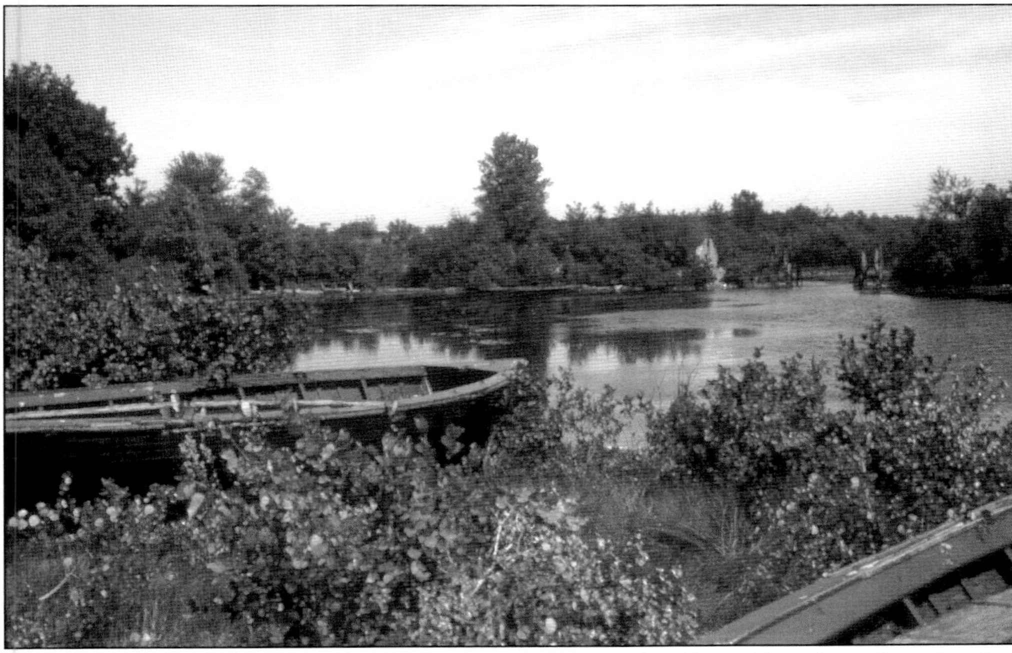

Countless numbers of pirate-seeking guests were transported to Pirate Cove from these beached vessels. They were part of the fleet that serviced the popular attraction. Just like Disneyland, the original plan was a high-capacity, water-related attraction, and it worked well throughout the life of the park. Some of the boat operators were still in high school with braces. Narrating a somewhat-scripted story and operating a boat at the same time was one of the coolest jobs to have at Pleasure Island. Some of these pirate ships were eventually used for planters as part of the landscaping early on in the office park that presently occupies the site of the former theme park. Both photographs were taken about August 1975. (Courtesy of John Toczydlowski.)

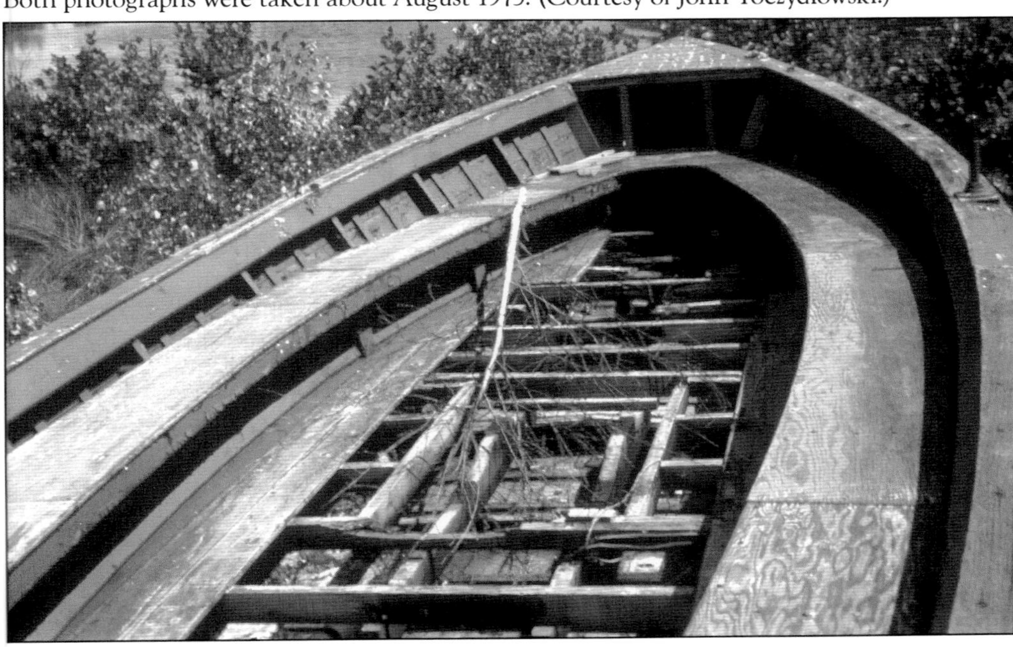

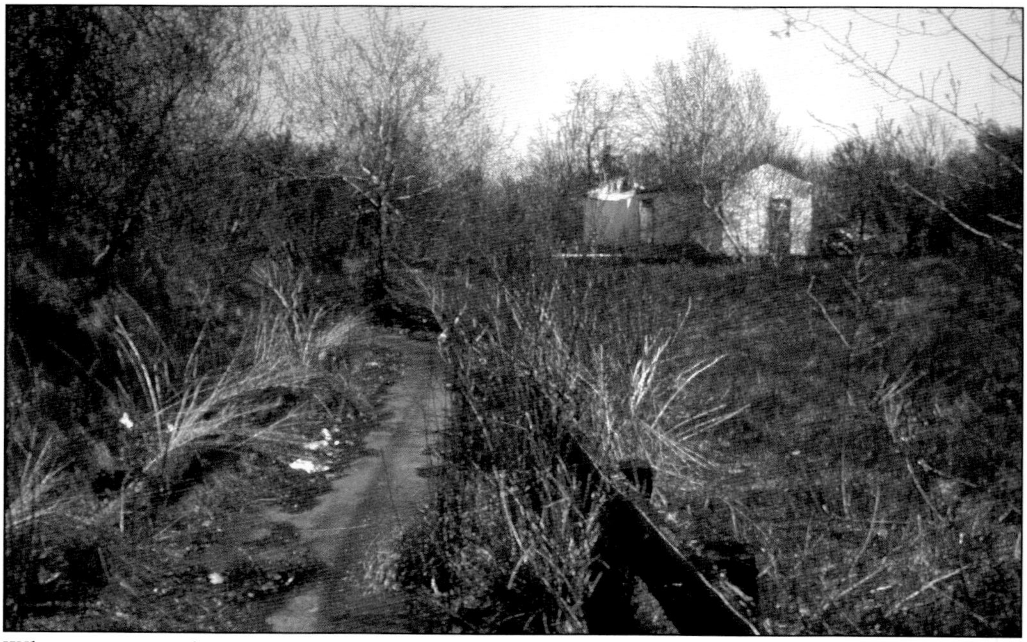

What is seen in this photograph is not exactly how former Jenney car drivers would remember the ride. The building is the replica of the Jenney Oil filling station located at the entrance area for this ride. Building 701 at Edgewater Office Park is located where the Jenney car attraction was. This photograph was taken about August 1975. (Courtesy of John Toczydlowski.)

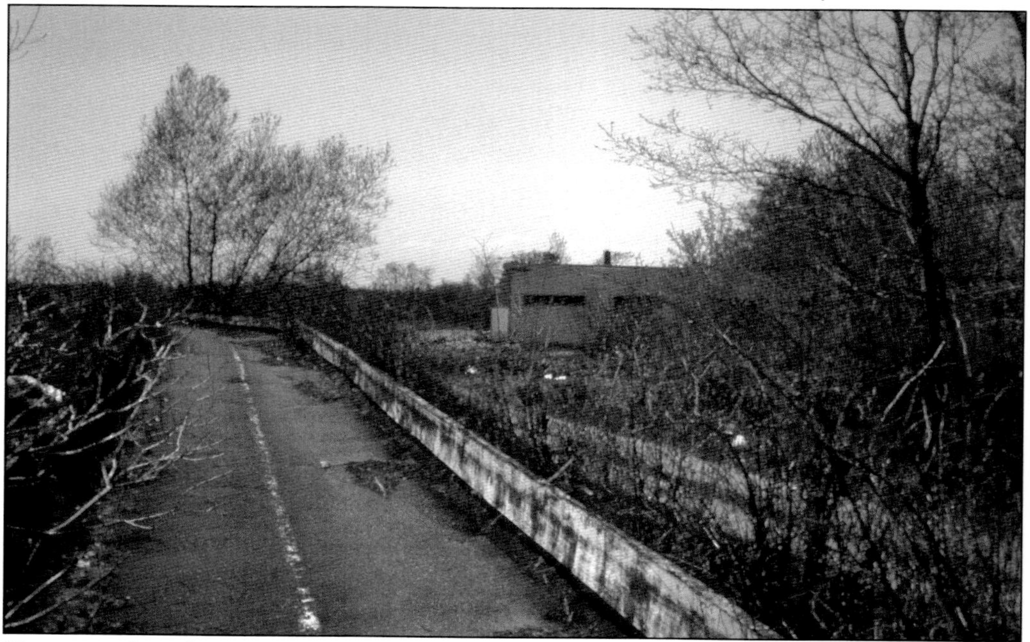

Shown in this photograph is the rear area of the Jenney car track. Off to the right is the maintenance building, and in between the track and the building is where the Engine City Boston and Maine Railroad spur line was located. This area also backs up to present-day Reedy Meadow. This photograph was taken about April 1975. (Courtesy of John Toczydlowski.)

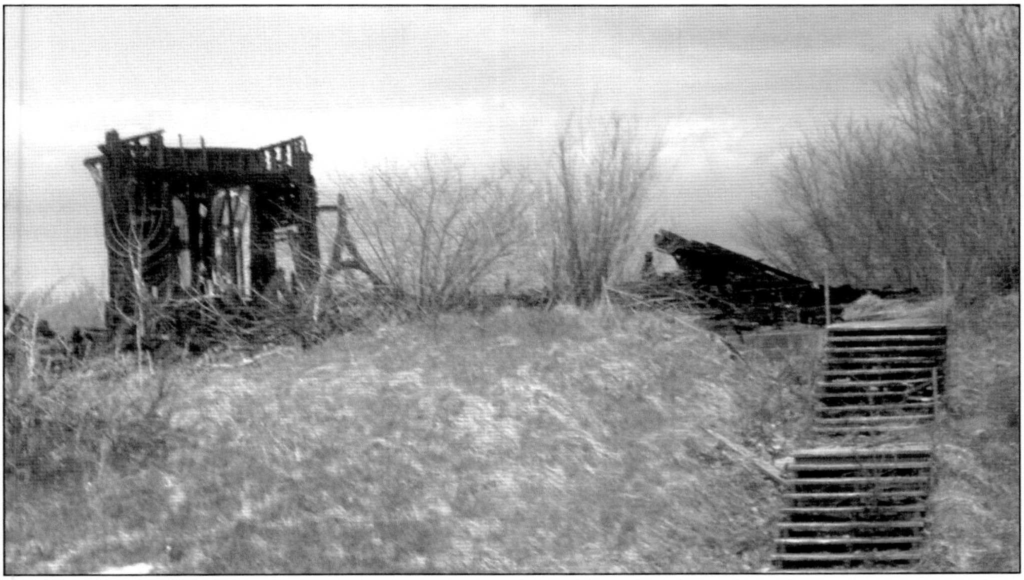

This is what was left of the former Greenwood station after being set afire by an arsonist along with the saloon and attached buildings. Alan Foulds of Reading, who grew up in Lynnfield, recalls seeing the fires from his bedroom window on the evening of April 1, 1971. Between 1971 and 1972, Wakefield had a number of major fires that ended with the arrest of a Wakefield police officer on multiple charges of arson. This photograph was taken about April 1975. (Courtesy of John Toczydlowski.)

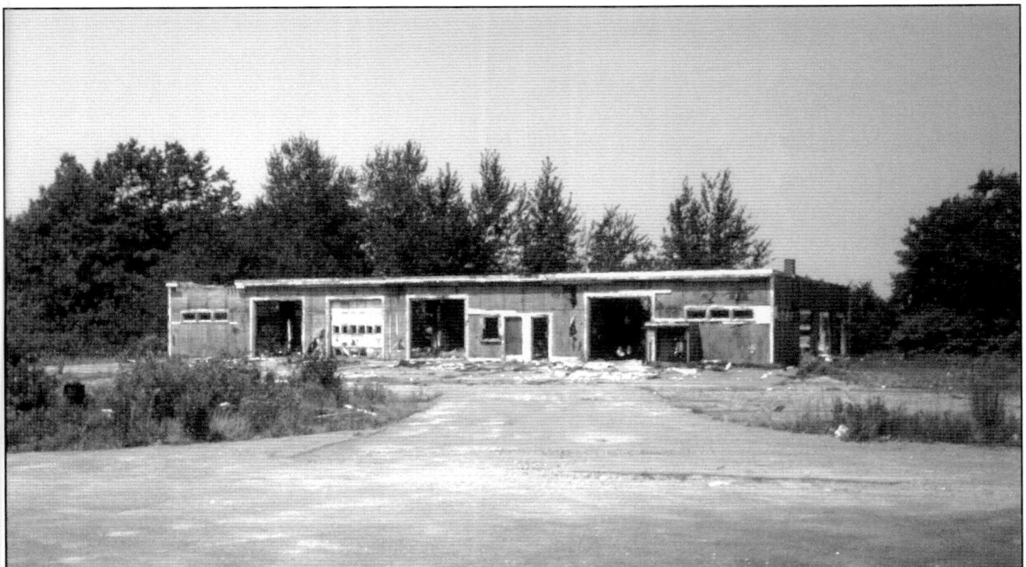

According to former maintenance mechanic Dave Mitchell, the maintenance building was a very busy place. Besides repairing everything from boats to Jenney cars, all of Pleasure Island's offices were here. Looking toward the front center, there were two personnel doors; the one on the left was the cash office. Receipts from the ticket booths and other activities were passed through this window to the cash office attendants. This photograph was taken about August 1975. (Courtesy of John Toczydlowski.)

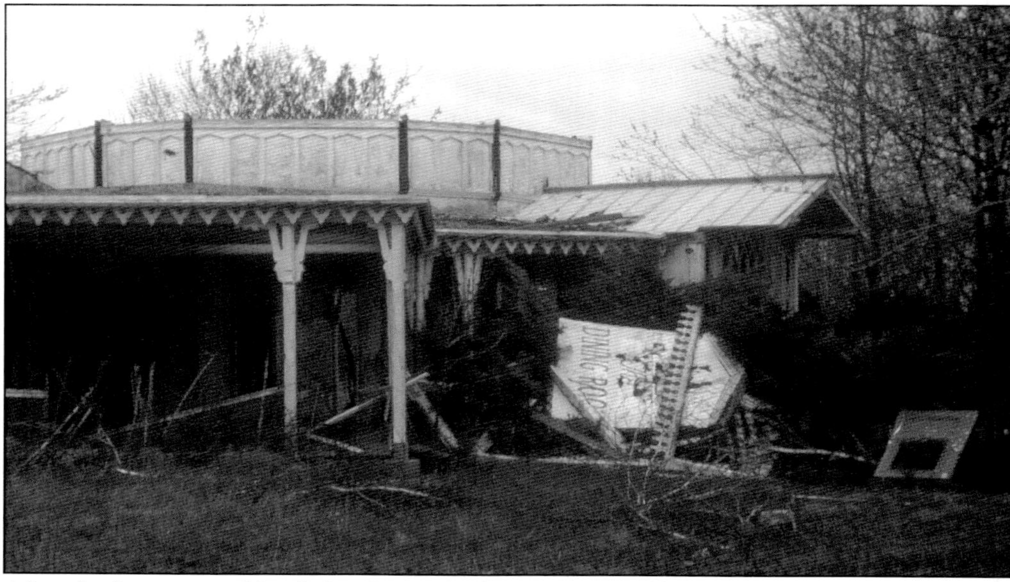

After the first season, Hood's Ice Cream Parlor was operated by the vendor the various owners of Pleasure Island chose for the park's snack stands, food carts, and restaurants. According to Walter Sherman's file, for the 1964 season, Carlton operated the ice-cream parlor (above), the popcorn stand, the barbecue stand, the theater, Whaler's Wharf, the cotton candy stand, the Dairy Twist, the lighthouse, the pizza stand, and the sugarhouse. This photograph was taken about April 1975. (Courtesy of John Toczydlowski.)

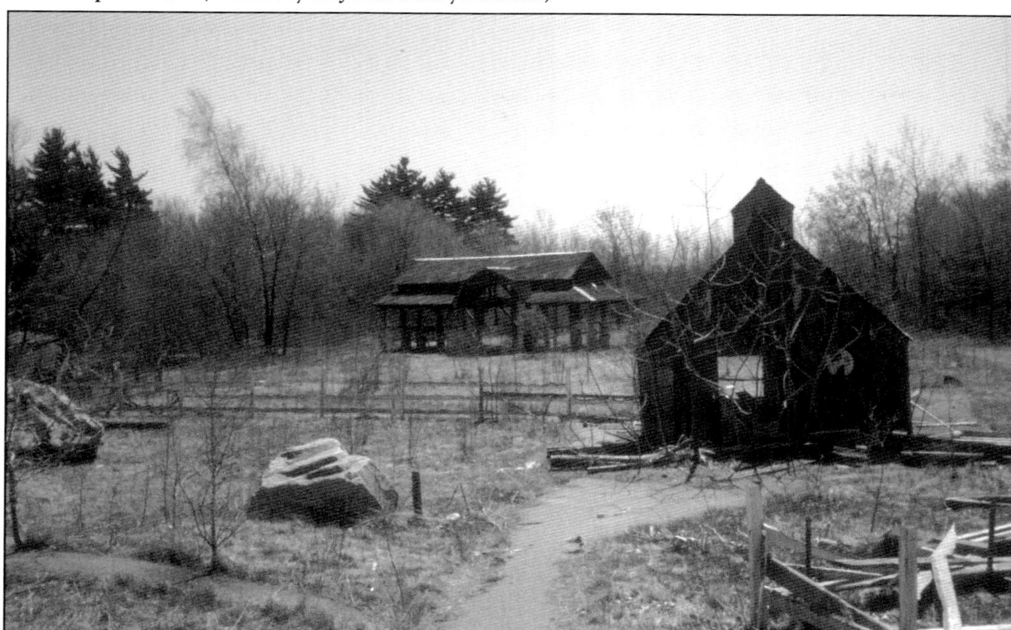

The original 1959 Hood Farm had several buildings besides the barn. There was a sugarhouse, a stable, a blacksmith forge, a windmill, and pig and lamb pens. The farm train ride had a tunnel made out of hay. Above are two of the buildings plus some of the fencing. This photograph was taken about April 1975. (Courtesy of John Toczydlowski.)

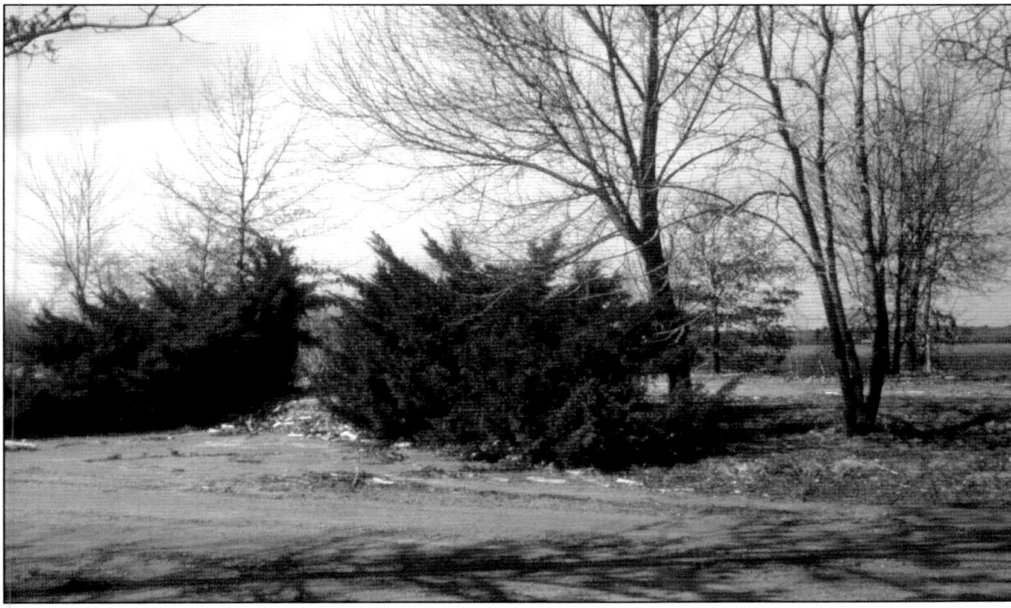

Building removal was completed by the fall of 1975. It was just about 17 years from construction to destruction of the park. After the building removal was completed, what remained until the area was redeveloped were the trees and plantings from the park's construction, some of which are still there today. The concrete slabs, underground infrastructure, and paving were removed as Edgewater Office Park was constructed over the former park's footprint. The photographs show the entrance area to the ice-cream parlor (above) and Clipper Cove looking out on the inner and outer harbors (below). Both photographs were taken in the fall of 1975. (Courtesy of John Toczydlowski.)

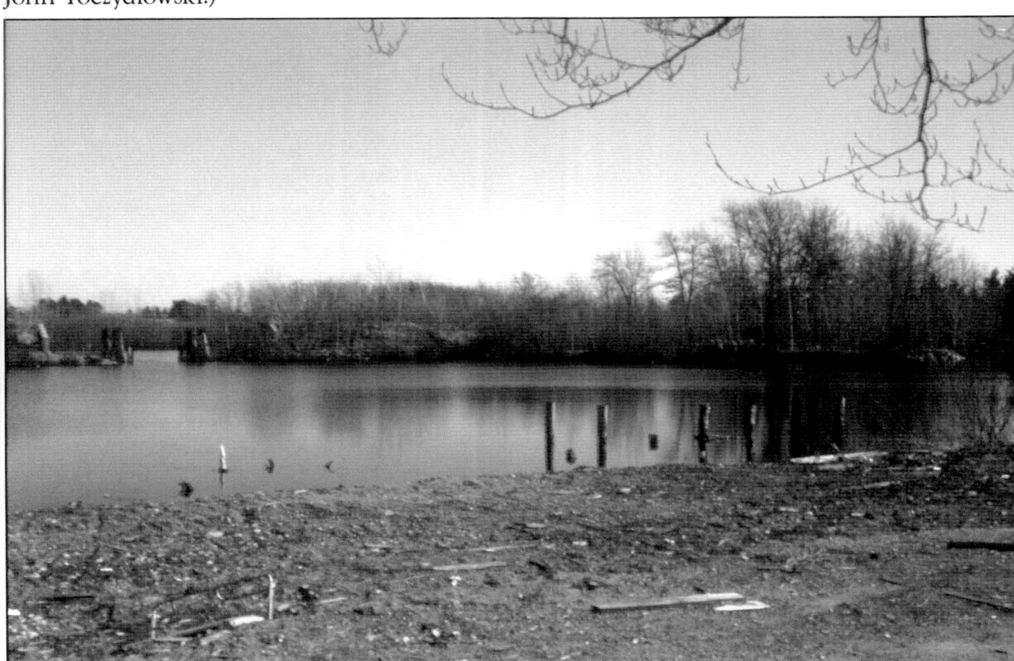

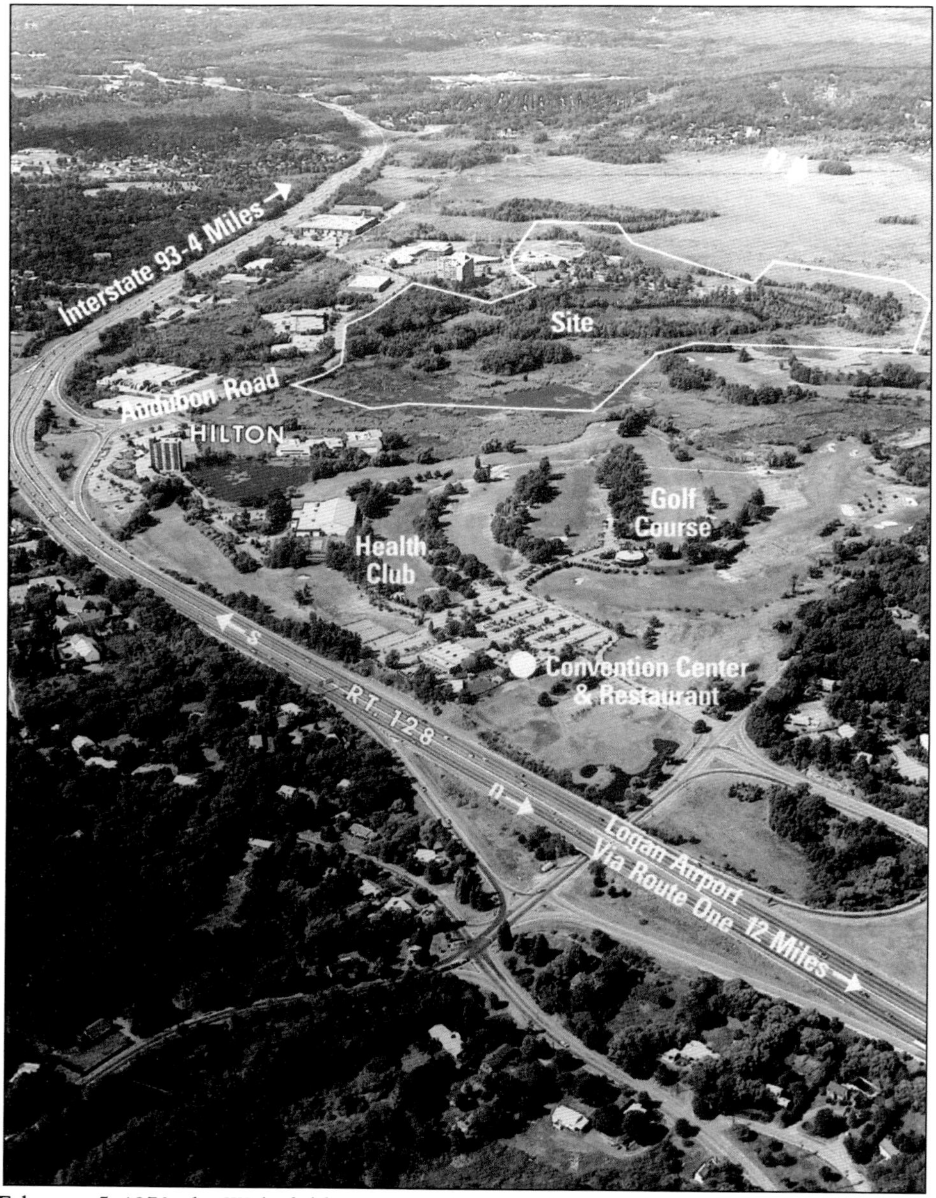

On February 5, 1970, the Wakefield town meeting passed an article changing the Pleasure Island site from an industrial district to a high-rise apartment district. On March 17, 1975, the town meeting passed an article changing the 144-acre site back to an industrial district. According to a story in the *Boston Globe* on February 9, 1986, "Texas developer, Edward Callan hired a research firm in 1982 to canvass some of the markets on the east coast. His first entry into the Boston market was the 2.7 million dollar purchase of a 132 acre site in Wakefield." The photograph above, taken in the early 1980s, shows the former Pleasure Island site and home of the future Edgewater Office Park. Development started in 1985 and ended with the park's seventh office building in 2003. Metcalf and Eddy moved into brand-new building 701 on Labor Day weekend 2003. Edgewater's buildings are beautifully designed, well maintained, and offer spectacular views of the ponds and adjoining marshland. (Courtesy of FOPI archives.)

Six

PLEASURE ISLAND REVISITED

On March 24, 2000, this author purchased nine Pleasure Island postcards at the annual antique show at Wakefield's First Congregational Church. Local resident Kory Hellmer enlarged the postcard images, and Hellmer and this author posted them on the town's information stations around Lake Quannapowitt. That was the start of the ongoing outreach for information about Pleasure Island, much of which is included in this book. During the summer, Hellmer developed the Pleasure Island Web site while this author went through microfilm from the local newspaper to gather information, particularly time line dates throughout the life of the park. Also during the summer of 2000, land-clearing operations started up for the last two office buildings at Edgewater Office Park. This author photographed and videotaped the newly exposed foundations and pathways, which looked just as they did when the park was leveled in the mid-1970s. During the fall of 2000 with the Web site up and running, many of the park's past employees were located, including Jean and Bill Hawkes, the man who created Pleasure Island. Former *Boston Herald* feature writer Christopher Cox wrote a story about Moby Dick still being in the water, which former 1959 park announcer Ken Saunders read. Saunders contacted this author and donated a copy of his 1959 park announcements and background music to the Friends of Pleasure Island. WCVB–TV's *Chronicle* show aired a segment about Pleasure Island by producer Tony Hill in January 2001 and again in July. The Friends of Pleasure Island became a 501(c)(3) nonprofit organization in April 2001. By the end of 2001, Hawkes donated his collection of photographs (many appear in this book), artist renderings, park business records from 1959, and several boxes of research material. In November 2002, the Friends of Pleasure Island hosted a reunion starring Rex Trailer and Sergeant Billy (played by William O'Brien) for former park employees, guests, and anyone and everyone interested in Pleasure Island's unique history.

The goal of the Friends of Pleasure Island is to document Pleasure Island's history and share it with current and future generations.

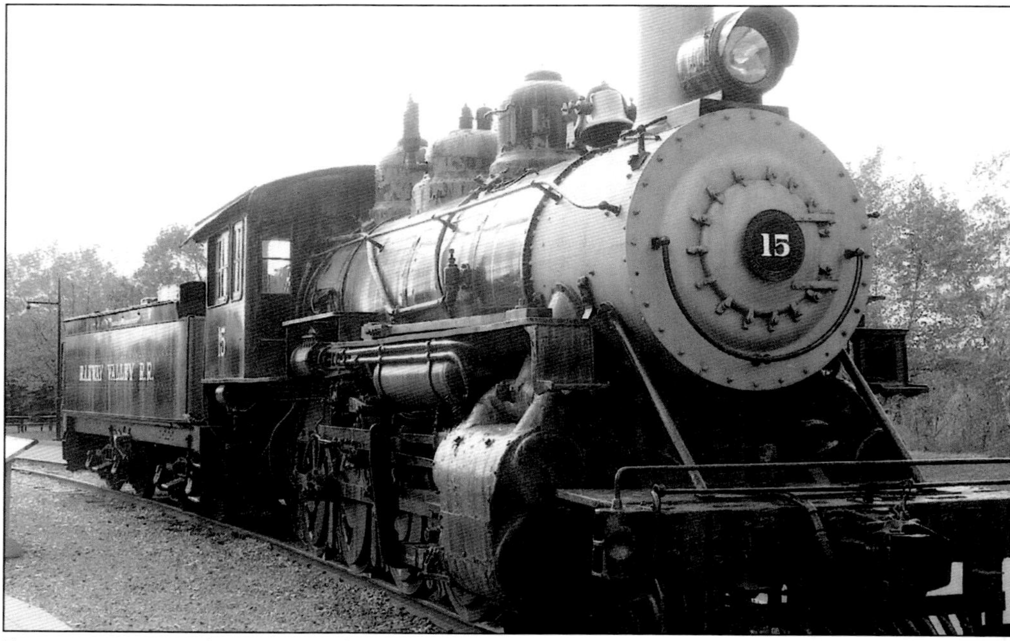

Former visitors to Pleasure Island's Engine City during the park's first three seasons will be pleased to know that some of the big toys they got to play on presently reside in Scranton, Pennsylvania, at Steamtown National Historic Site. When entering the access road toward the parking area, the very first vintage locomotive on display is the Rahway Valley Railroad No. 15 (above). In the yard is the Canadian Pacific Railway No. 2929 with its tender (below). In the shop (opposite page) is the Boston and Maine Railroad No. 3713. In addition to seeing a bit of Pleasure Island's past from Engine City, Steamtown National Historic Site offers visitors an interpretive history of the steam locomotive era at the former Scranton Railroad Yard. (Author's collection.)

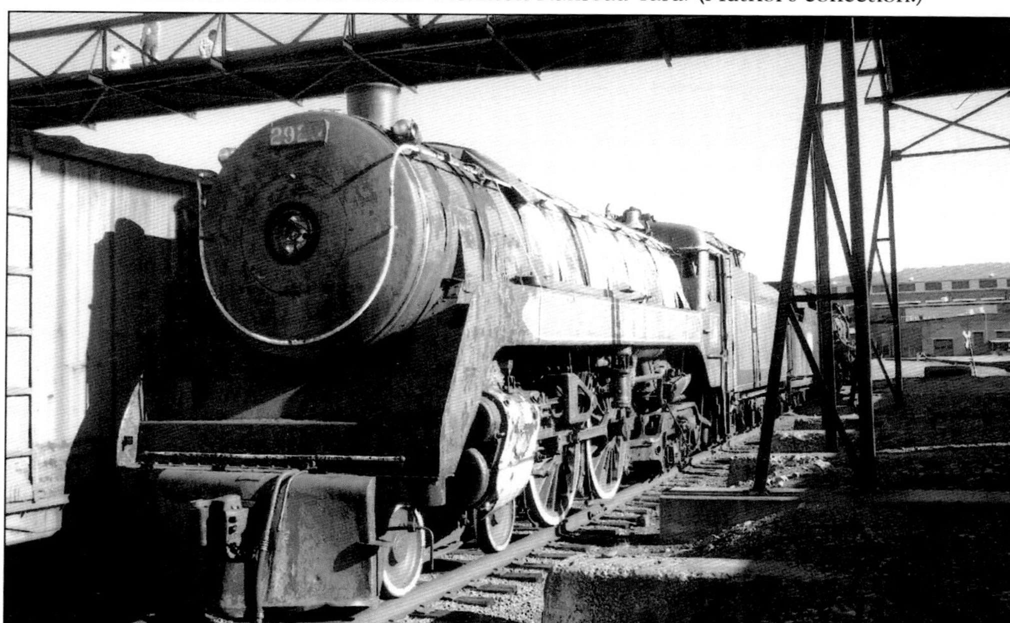

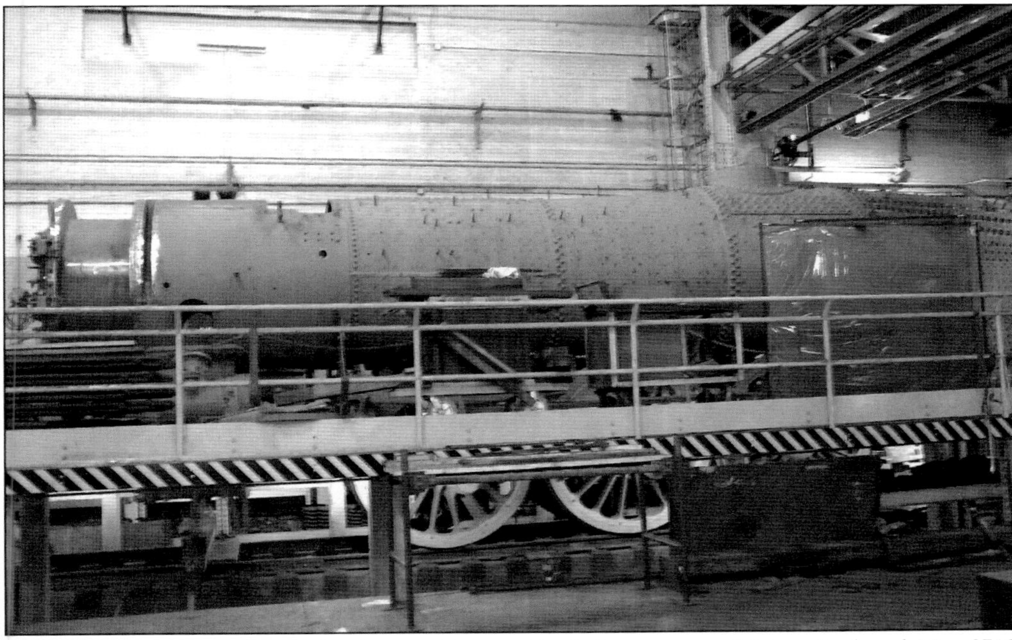

These photographs feature the former Engine City's Boston and Maine Railroad No. 3713. Restoration at Steamtown National Historic Site shops has been ongoing for several years. By the mid-1990s, Steamtown National Historic Site and Lackawanna and Wyoming Valley Railway Historical Society formed a partnership to complete the restoration of No. 3713 at the old Delaware, Lackawanna and Western Railroad shops. When completed, No. 3713 will go in service for the Steamtown National Historic Site excursion service. (Author's collection.)

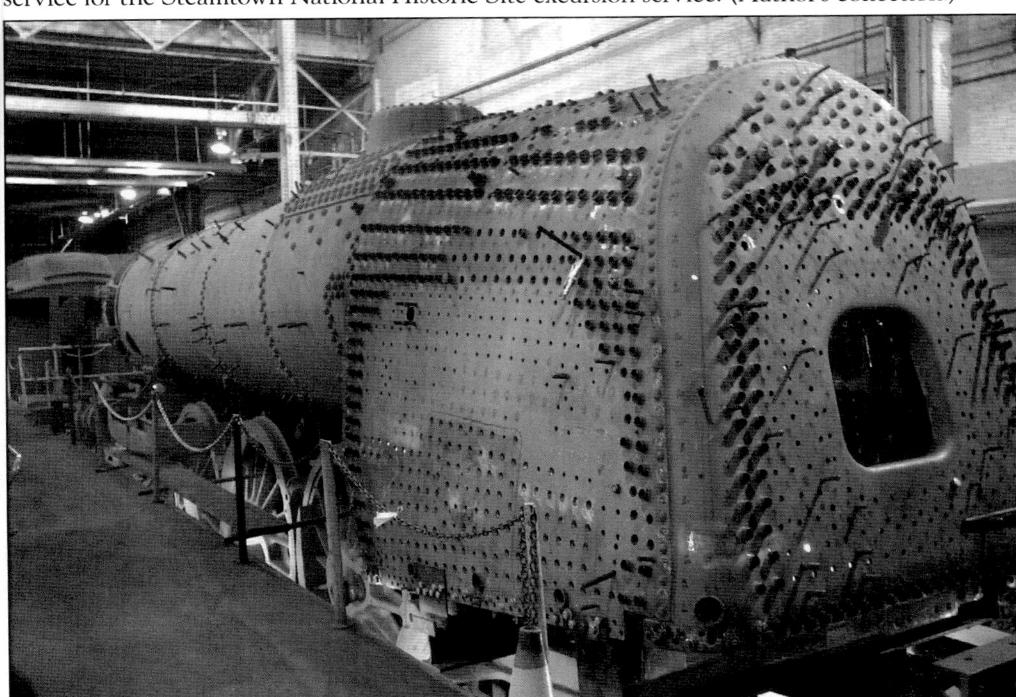

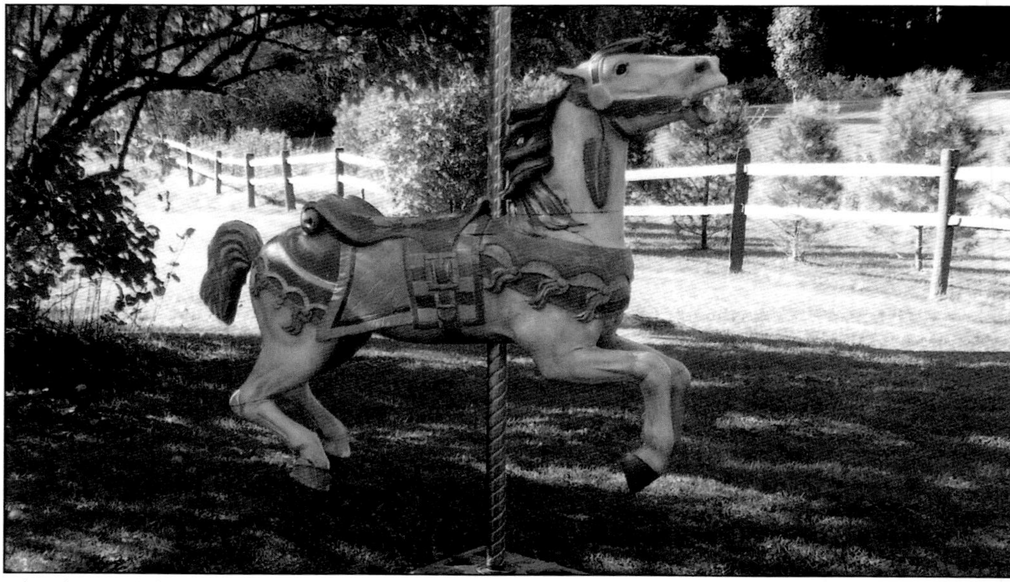

This beautiful carousel horse is from a private collection belonging to Michelle Carpenter from Connecticut. Master carver David Muller created this and the other carvings, including the chariot seats, for the carousel that came to Pleasure Island. In 2006, longtime park maintenance mechanic Gil Arrington's nephew Richard A. Miller donated two carved panels from the chariot seats and other artifacts of his late uncle's to the Friends of Pleasure Island. (Author's collection.)

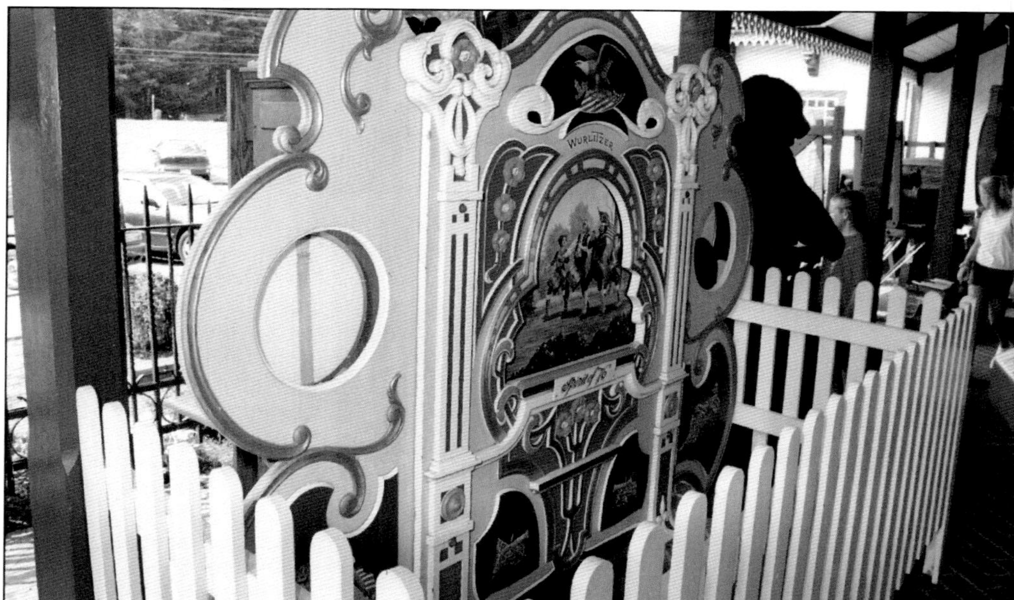

Anyone who rode on Pleasure Island's prized carousel can once again enjoy its music. Pleasure Island's Wurlitzer band organ went to Clark's Trading Post in Lincoln, New Hampshire. It is located near the main entrance, which is a replica of a Victorian train station. The station came board by board from another C. V. Wood–designed theme park, Freedomland. (Courtesy of Raymond DiPirro.)

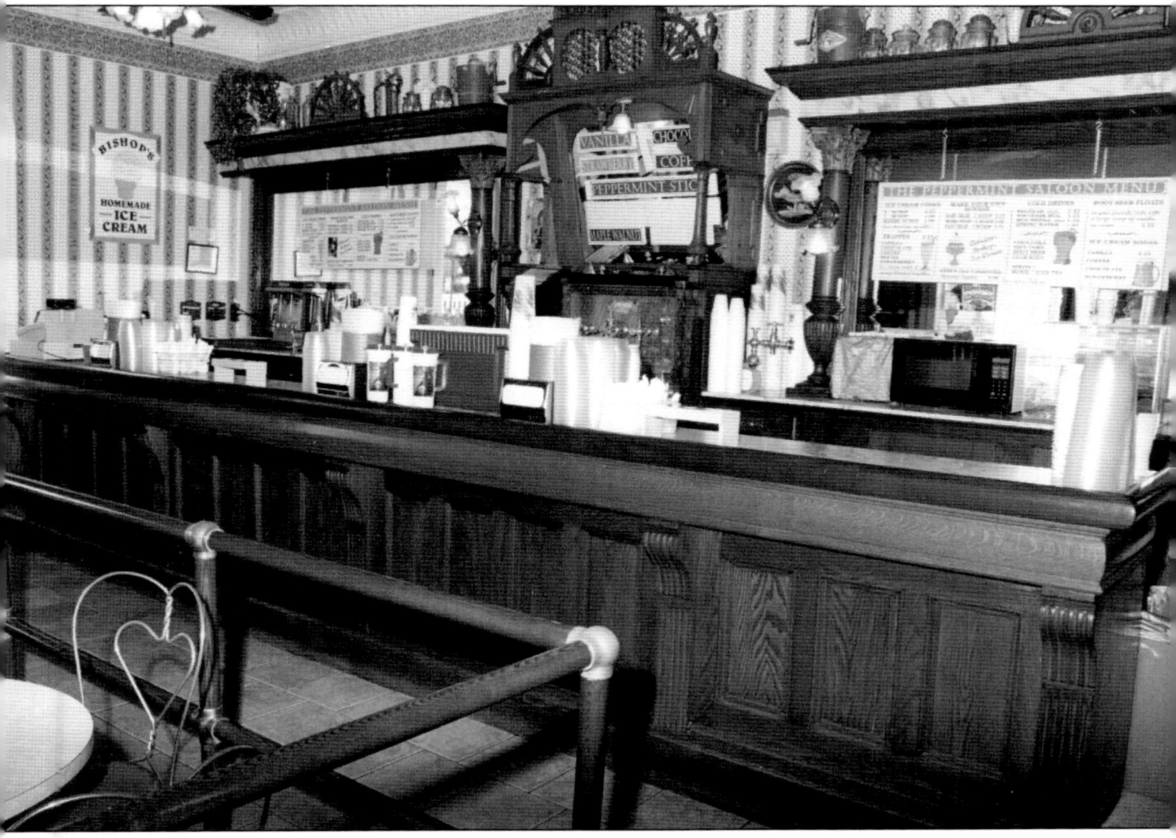

According to information while researching Freedomland, Clark's Trading Post purchased not only a train station but also all the antique (electrified) gas post lights that are spread throughout its facility. Does anyone want to visit the Slanty Shanty again? One can, at Clark's. Marco Engineering's blueprints of Freedomland's Casa Loca, which shared a similar design with Pleasure Island's Slanty Shanty, were used to construct the Tuttle's Rustic House at Clark's. Part of the Diamond Lil Bar (above) is now used to serve ice cream at the Peppermint Saloon. Inside the saloon, there is a plaque that describes the history of the bar from Pleasure Island. Just as Edgewater Office Park was built within Pleasure Island's footprint, the former Freedomland site is now home to Co-op City, with over 15,000 apartments. (Courtesy of Raymond DiPirro.)

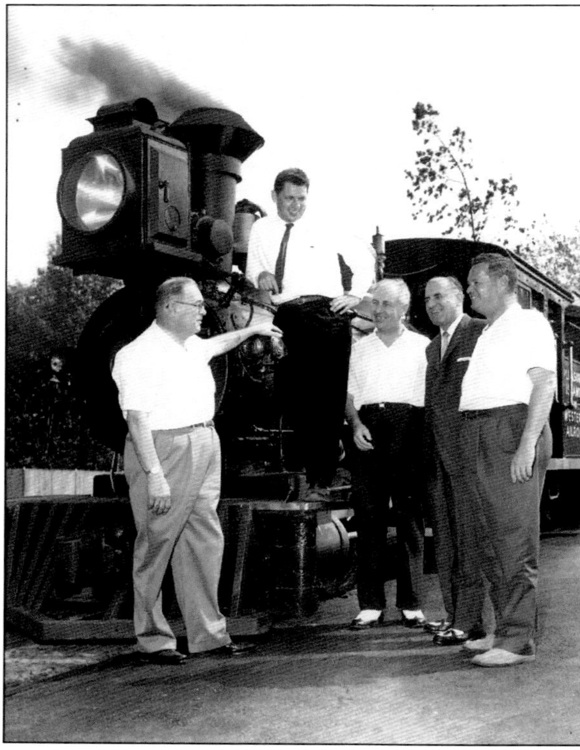

In this 1959 photograph, Bill Hawkes is standing on the Edaville Railroad's No. 3 engine. To the far right is Pleasure Island's publicity director Joseph Doyle, who took over Marco Engineering's Lloyd D. Settle's position at Pleasure Island. The train whistle from Old Smoky could be heard miles away. (Courtesy of Russ Adams Productions.)

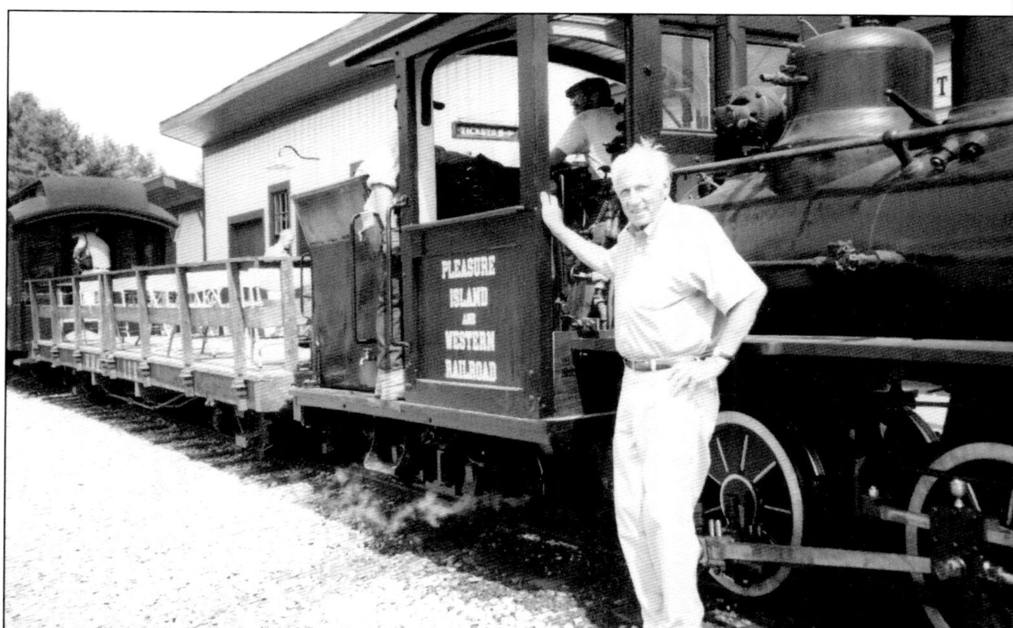

On July 31, 2004, Hawkes (in front) and this author went to the WW&F Railway Museum in Alna, Maine. That summer, Pleasure Island's No. 5 (renumbered by the WW&F as No. 10) was celebrating the completion of a year-and-a-half renovation. For that summer season, No. 10 carried the name Pleasure Island and Western Railroad. (Author's collection.)

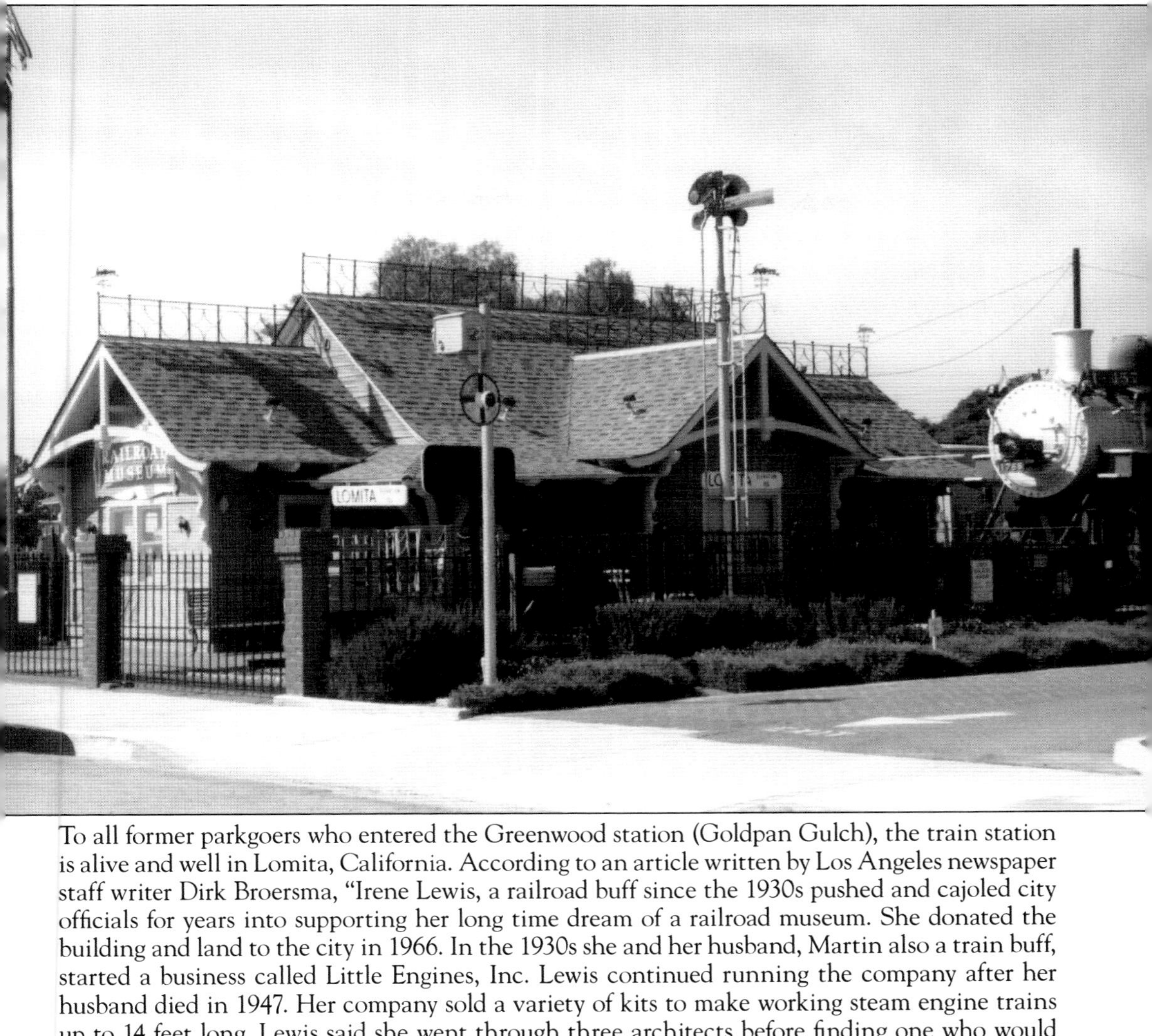

To all former parkgoers who entered the Greenwood station (Goldpan Gulch), the train station is alive and well in Lomita, California. According to an article written by Los Angeles newspaper staff writer Dirk Broersma, "Irene Lewis, a railroad buff since the 1930s pushed and cajoled city officials for years into supporting her long time dream of a railroad museum. She donated the building and land to the city in 1966. In the 1930s she and her husband, Martin also a train buff, started a business called Little Engines, Inc. Lewis continued running the company after her husband died in 1947. Her company sold a variety of kits to make working steam engine trains up to 14 feet long. Lewis said she went through three architects before finding one who would tackle the task of duplicating the Quaint Massachusetts Depot." Coincidentally, Walt Disney was a customer. The Lomita station is a close copy of the Greenwood station. Next to the station is the No. 1765 mogul built by Baldwin Locomotive Works in 1902. (Author's collection.)

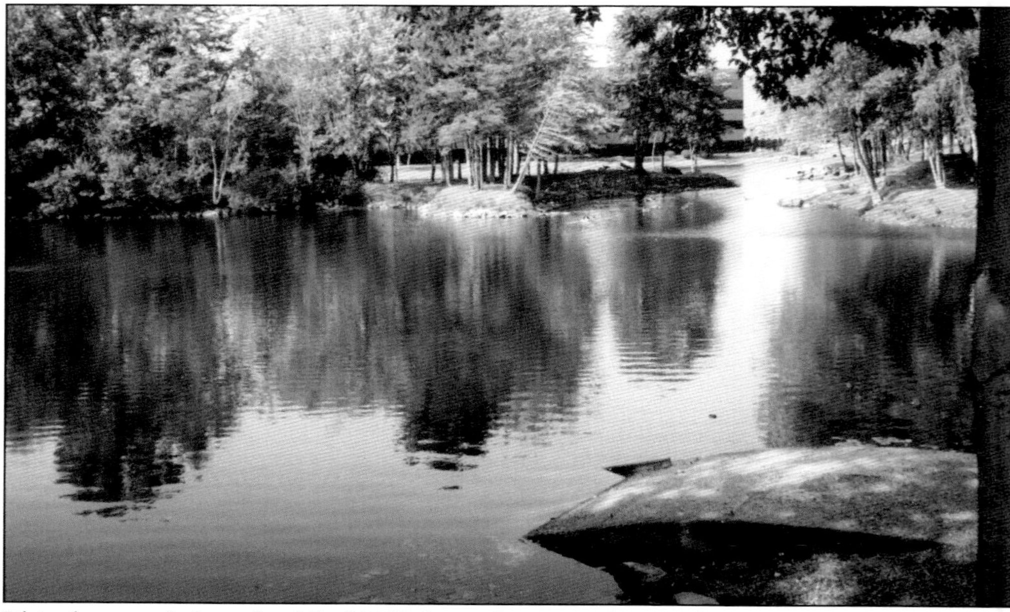

This photograph from the fall of 2002 shows the ramp where Moby Dick was launched into his lagoon. The ramp was also used to take the fiberglass whale out in between operating seasons or for maintenance. The beginning of the 120-foot under track can be seen just above the waterline. Straight ahead is the channel the powered whaleboat entered on the search for the great white whale. (Author's collection.)

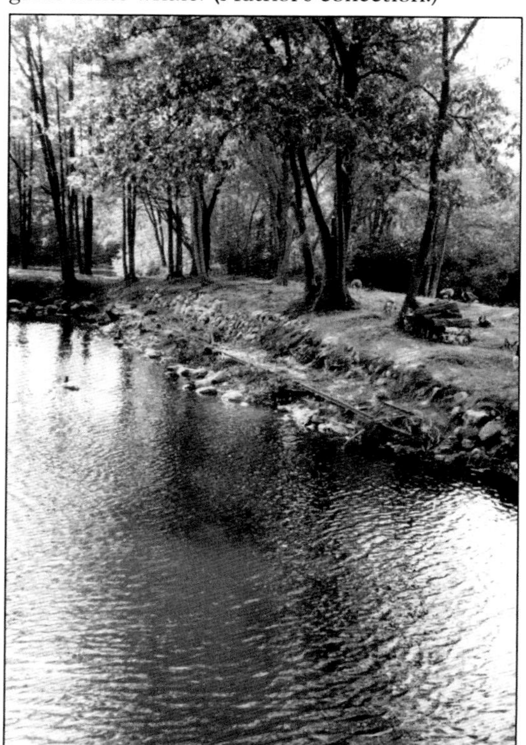

Just after Pleasure Island opened, Paul Benzaquin of the *Boston Globe* interviewed special effects designer Glen Robinson. "Just as the boat eased past the point of land nearest the inlet, there was a tremendous roar from the right and a full sized rhinoceros came charging down towards shore. The rhino stopped his violent charge just as he reached the water's edge." Part of the 40-foot rhinoceros track can be seen above the waterline. This photograph was taken in the fall of 2002. (Author's collection.)

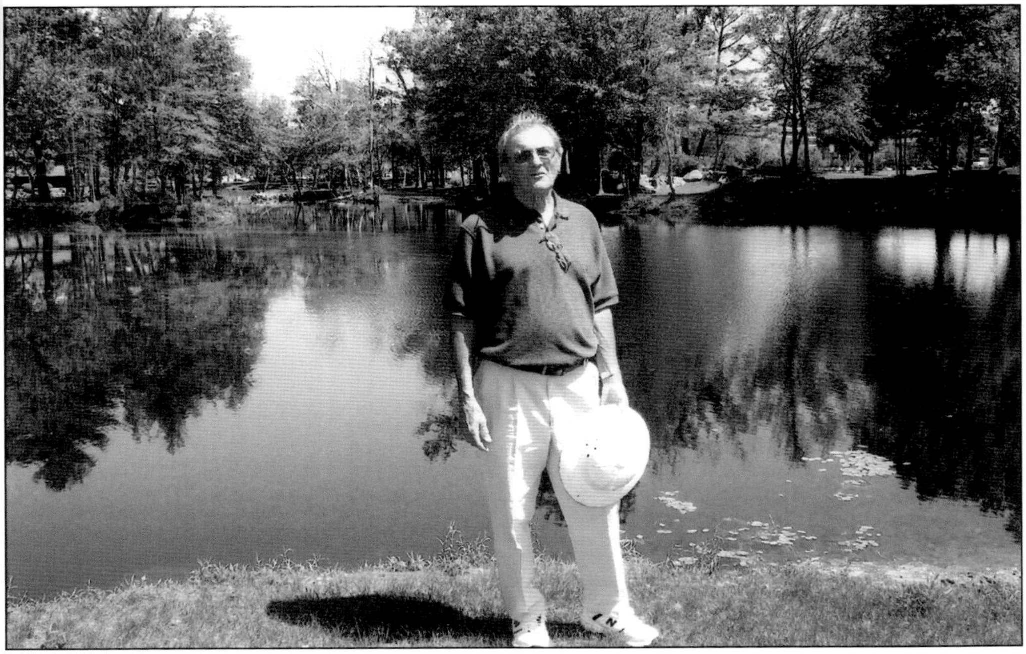

Standing onshore on June 13, 2008, is Bill McGrath. Behind him is the site of the Moby Dick Hunt attraction. Local electrician Pat Nigro and McGrath from International Brotherhood of Electrical Workers Local 103 were the first two electricians to work at the Pleasure Island construction site and were both foremen. They got the task of wiring the special effects for the Moby Dick Hunt. (Author's collection.)

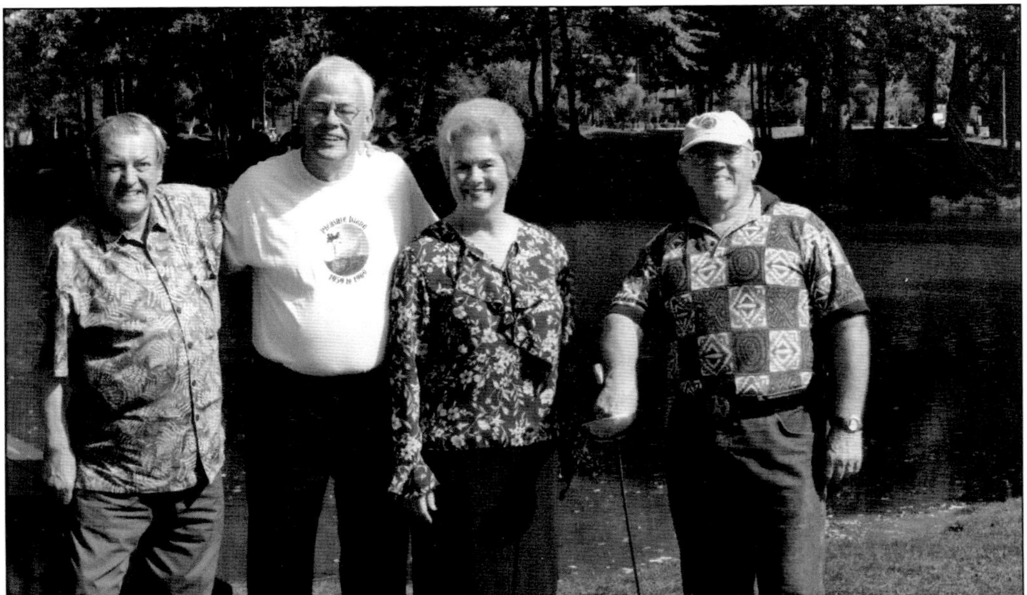

At a walking tour of the former park site on September 21, 2003, are four former Pleasure Island employees from the first season. From left to right are Bob Harmon, Ken Saunders, Patricia (Nordling) Rowe Douglass, and Herb Sauve. (Courtesy of Mark Sardella.)

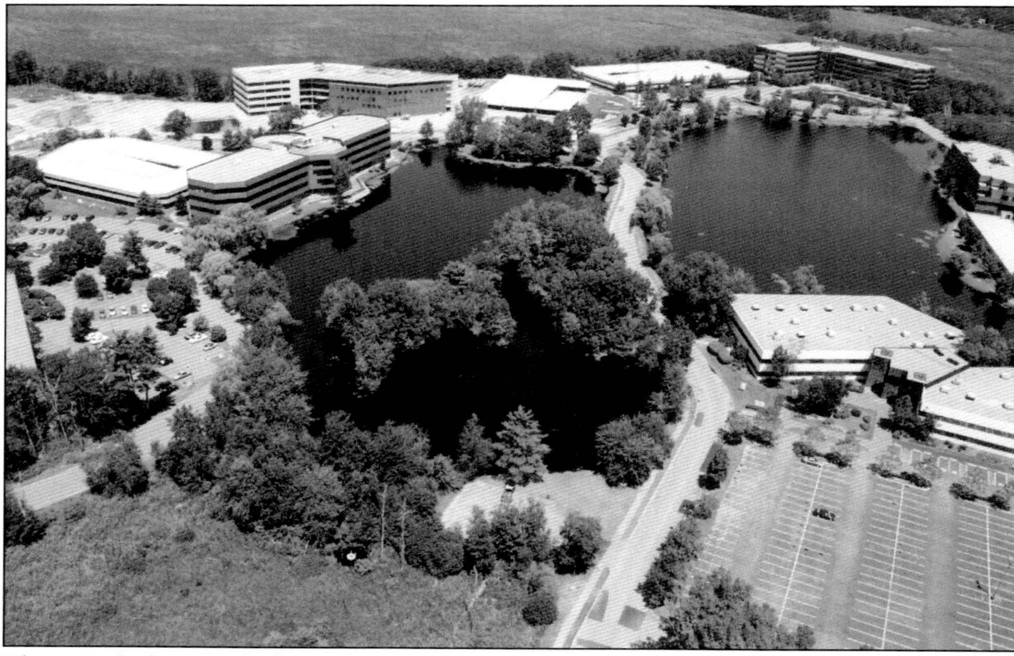

This aerial photograph from the summer of 2001 was taken by Raymond DiPirro. Part of Edgewater Drive follows the route of the Old Smoky line between the inner and outer harbors. The Moby Dick Hunt was located in the lower left pond. (Courtesy of Raymond DiPirro.)

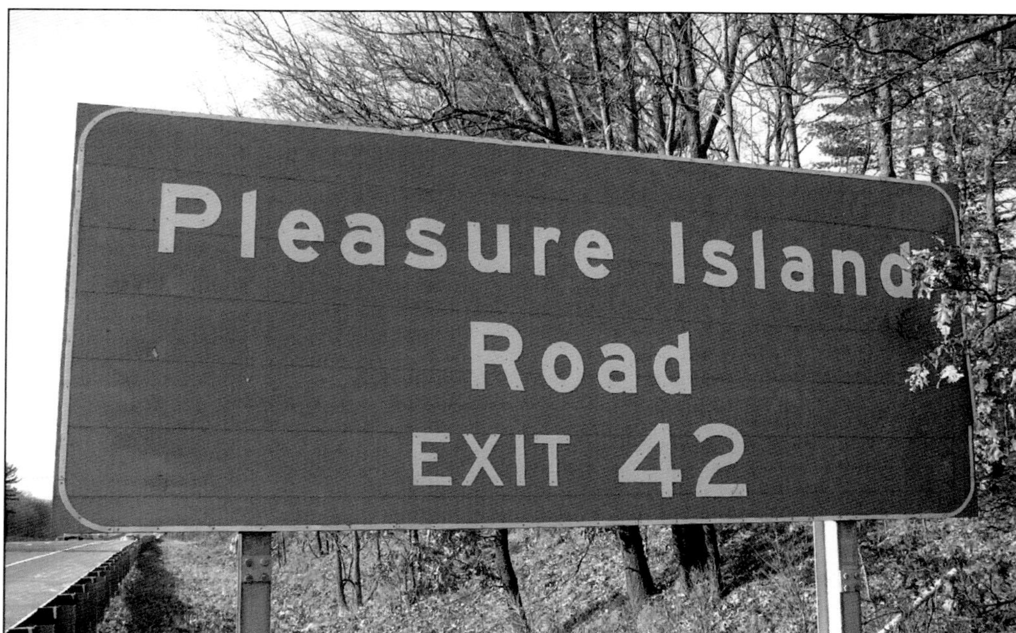

This sign on Route 128 south is an icon. Not only does it remind one about Pleasure Island, it also inspired local folk group City of Roses to write, record, and produce a song titled "Pleasure Island Road." In 2004, a DVD was released with home movies supplied by the Friends of Pleasure Island. It can be seen on YouTube. (Author's collection.)